AUTOBIOGRAPHY of a
DEMOCRATIC NATION
at RISK

A Book Series of
Curriculum Studies

William F. Pinar
General Editor

Vol. 26

PETER LANG
New York • Washington, D.C./Baltimore • Bern
Frankfurt am Main • Berlin • Brussels • Vienna • Oxford

JoVictoria Nicholson-Goodman

AUTOBIOGRAPHY of a DEMOCRATIC NATION at RISK

The *Currere* of Culture and Citizenship in the Post-9/11 American Wilderness

PETER LANG
New York • Washington, D.C./Baltimore • Bern
Frankfurt am Main • Berlin • Brussels • Vienna • Oxford

Library of Congress Cataloging-in-Publication Data
Nicholson-Goodman, JoVictoria.
Autobiography of a democratic nation at risk: the *currere* of culture and
citizenship in the post-9/11 American wilderness /
JoVictoria Nicholson-Goodman.
p. cm. — (Complicated conversation; v. 26)
Includes bibliographical references and index.
1. Citizenship—Study and teaching—United States. 2. Democracy—
United States. 3. Culture—Study and teaching—United States.
4. Multiculturalism—United States. I. Title.
LC1091.N53 370.11'5–dc22 2008049554
ISBN 978-1-4331-0144-1
ISSN 1534-2816

Bibliographic information published by **Die Deutsche Bibliothek**.
Die Deutsche Bibliothek lists this publication in the "Deutsche
Nationalbibliografie"; detailed bibliographic data is available
on the Internet at http://dnb.ddb.de/.

The paper in this book meets the guidelines for permanence and durability
of the Committee on Production Guidelines for Book Longevity
of the Council of Library Resources.

© 2009 Peter Lang Publishing, Inc., New York
29 Broadway, 18th floor, New York, NY 10006
www.peterlang.com

All rights reserved.
Reprint or reproduction, even partially, in all forms such as microfilm,
xerography, microfiche, microcard, and offset strictly prohibited.

Printed in the United States of America

This book is dedicated, first, to my parents, Brenda Alice Nicholson and Willard Powell Goodman, who raised me to free thinking and to the quest, and who inspired in me the genuine love of learning, of the arts, and of life; and second, to my Russian husband, Viktor, artist and fellow-wanderer, who always shows me another way to see. Third, I dedicate this to my children, Johanna, Nathaniel, and Andrew Custer, who follow their own lights in this new American wilderness and who enhance my understandings with their critiques of our shared world. Finally, I dedicate this book to Noreen Garman, who introduced me to curriculum studies and its deeply thoughtful paths of inquiry and to Maria Piantanida and all of my wonderful and extraordinary colleagues in the Study Group in Pittsburgh, who shared their insights and ponderings with me and made my thinking so much clearer over the years.

Table of Contents

Acknowledgments	ix
1 Prologue: The New American Wilderness	1

Part One: Theoretical Dimensions of the Study

2 Autobiography of Post-9/11 America: The Framework	25
3 Social Cartography: A 'Line of Flight' for Curriculum Inquiry	55
4 'Nation-ness,' Nationalism, and Post-National Space	77

Part Two: Autobiography and Civic-Cultural Struggle

Introduction: Autobiography as Currere	103
5 A Post-9/11 American Autobiography: Part I	109
6 A Post-9/11 American Autobiography: Part II	131
7 Mapping Autobiographic Terrain: Cultures of Citizenship	151

Part Three: Ongoing Fragmented Dialogues

8 The Public Sphere: Risk, Uncertainty, and Techno-Culture	181
9 Contours of a Curriculum for the New American Wilderness	205
10 Epilogue	229
Notes	235
References	237
Index	249

Acknowledgments

I would like to gratefully acknowledge those whose help made this work possible. First, my heartfelt thanks to *Curriculum as Complicated Conversation* Series Editor Bill Pinar, whose work on autobiography as *currere* inspired this book. His generosity in lending guidance and support has been immeasurable. Second, I offer my enduring appreciation to Noreen Garman, Professor of Education and Coordinator of the Social and Comparative Analysis of Education program at the University of Pittsburgh, who is mentor, friend, colleague, and sage to me. She has tirelessly assisted in advancing my thinking and promoting my work and has supported me in every possible way over the years. Third, I offer belated thanks to Rolland G. Paulston, Professor Emeritus of Comparative Education at the University of Pittsburgh, now deceased, for his energy and instruction, his willingness to open space for dialogue, and for his artful approach to mapping emerging trends in sites of educational and social change. He lent a playful post-modern eye to my own repertoire of ways of seeing and of being-in-the-world. Additionally, to the associations of scholars that make this kind of scholarship possible and keep voice alive, my deep gratitude: the American Association for the Advancement of Curriculum Studies, Bergamo, the Curriculum and Pedagogy Group, and the Study Group facilitated and led by Noreen Garman and Maria Piantanida. Finally, I offer my gratitude to Chris Myers, Rebecca Shapiro, and Sophie Appel at Peter Lang for their patient direction, assistance, and support.

...consistent lying, metaphorically speaking, pulls the ground from under our feet and provides no other ground on which to stand. ...The experience of a trembling wobbling motion of everything we rely on for our sense of direction and reality is among the most common and most vivid experiences of men under totalitarian rule.
   —Hannah Arendt (2006/1977), *Between Past and Future*, 253

The ties which hold men together in action are numerous, tough and subtle. But they are invisible and intangible. We have the physical tools of communication as never before. The thoughts and aspirations congruous with them are not communicated, and hence are not common. Without such communication the public will remain shadowy and formless, seeking spasmodically for itself, but seizing and holding its shadow rather than its substance. Till the Great Society is converted into a Great Community, the Public will remain in eclipse. Communication can alone create a great community. Our Babel is not one of tongues but of the signs and symbols without which shared experience is impossible.
   —John Dewey (1991/1927), *The Public and Its Problems*, 142

1
Prologue

THE NEW AMERICAN WILDERNESS

> Disorder... is continually breaking in; meaninglessness is recurrently overcoming landscapes which once were demarcated, meaningful. It is at moments like these that the individual reaches out to reconstitute meaning, to close the gaps, to make sense once again. It is at moments like these that he will be moved to pore over maps, to disclose or generate structures of knowledge which may provide him unifying perspectives and thus enable him to restore order once again. His learning... is a mode of orientation—or reorientation in a place suddenly become unfamiliar. (Greene, 1971, cited in Flinders and Thornton, 2004, 141)

This narrative of the place and times in which we dwell is the story of *America*[1] become wild again, but not as in former nostalgic renditions, in tales of encounters with pristine wilderness and wide open spaces romanticized through the passing of time to exclude other stories, counter-stories (Lopez, 2002) of human struggles within and over these spaces. No, this *new* American wilderness feels more like the familiar, however flawed, having become unfamiliar, like being lost in unrecognizable space, like disorder having broken into our national reverie of being and becoming (Greene, 1971, 1988, 1995). This feeling is accompanied, furthermore, by a dreadful anxiety, the fear that nothing will ever make sense again.

In such darkness, one may take comfort in the refrain (Deleuze and Guattari, 1987), and America has a variety of refrains that comfort by providing illusions of (and allusions to) utopias where darkness is, in the end, overcome. As a child of the Second World War, I am skeptical about utopias. Wary of ideologies as well and operating on the basis of *remembrance*, I write from an autobiographic center grounded in the past and keen on understanding the present, yet also as one who thirsts for brighter possibilities than are currently on offer for the future. This, then, is a tale that is told from multiple narrative layers, written from an autobiographical-intellectual space that can perhaps best be described as the *within-beyond*.

This narrative is a uniquely American autobiography that integrates past and present and projects both as *possibility* into future. Although America has fallen short of her own ideals in new, unforeseen ways in these times, purportedly entering a new *dark age* (Berman, 2007), the refrain admittedly threaded throughout these pages sings America potentially standing upright and whole, and thus sings hope for education as well—in its fullest, finest sense, as knowledge, experience, and understanding of self and world, past and present, leading to wisdom to face the future (this, it must be acknowledged, may itself be considered utopic space in our times). Education, in this refrain, is yet a primary source of hope for the bettering of ourselves, of the state of things now and of things to come, and of the world at large.

Such hope, however, is diffuse, transgressing against limits as it disperses across the convoluted space of 'through education' in search of the *possible* (Greene, 1971), a space nevertheless capable of yielding up "what Bourdieu calls realist utopias" (Giroux, 2004, 133). What shape this space takes depends significantly and in multiple ways on the dynamics of the social context within which 'through education' is conceived and in which it is embedded, as well as how educationist actors use that space. 'Through education' is mired in civic-cultural striving—e.g., in hegemonic domination and resistance to that control, in structural artifice for enforcing change or, alternatively, for maintaining the status quo—and in numerous ways finds itself squeezed between vortices competing for influence and power, the toll paid in young human lives wasted, destroyed, lost, their potential contributions to a better nation and world snuffed out.

Optimism is a signifier of the American spirit, and so I write *for* hope and with hopefulness, elusive companions of this American dreamer/explorer. I cannot fight feelings of loss and disorientation, however, without naming and acknowledging the 'wall' that stands between us and the dreams we might yet dream (Hughes, 1968, cited in Greene, 1988, 6). I cannot relinquish the desire for a turn yet to come, a turn that could repair the wrongs, heal the wounds, and, in some future end—or rather, in some new beginning—restore our faith in all that is sound in what humans have been trying to work out through eons of civic and cultural struggle as we reach for something better, something beyond what *is*. Striving is the key, and in striving, we reach past the '*es muss sein*,'[2] the 'given' (Greene, 1988, 10).

We find what vision may be found in our connections with the 'in-between' (Reynolds and Webber, 2004, 30), the 'unexplored and unnamed territories' between imploded binaries (Marshall, Sears, and Schubert, 2000, 225), for instance, that are empowered by the life of the imagination. The life of the imagination is intimately connected to developing the ability to 'fight with hope,' and without that hope, there can be no authentic dialogue (Freire, 1970, 80). Authentic dialogue, moreover, is essential for a moral fabric sorely needed (Greene, 2008) in a deliberative democracy where moral disagreement is a constant (Gutmann and Thompson, 1996). What follows, then, is a uniquely American narrative of the new wilderness within which we wander. It is, ultimately, a narrative of both fear *and* hope, both loss *and* possibility. It is a tale of the momentary demise of imagination and of the forced eclipse of moral disagreement at a specific, troubled moment in our beleaguered autobiographic project as a nation. Yet it is also a tale of the potential of this 'project' for being revived by small acts of civic courage, acts conceived and enacted despite the 'impoverished landscape' of education (Garman, 2006), 'the nightmare that is the present' (Pinar, 2004, 5).

This narrative unfolds as a curriculum of our times, the troubled tale of America on the precipice, the abyss below, hope beckoning from the offing, (always) just around the corner. It is, in short, an autobiography of a nation potentially imagined together in better ways than what we have seen manifest so far (an America yet to emerge)—or, alternatively, an America we fear may have already emerged, an America moving backwards through time to old antagonisms and primordial reactions to challenges and complexities. In such times, *who we say we are* as a nation becomes central to thinking about how we educate ourselves and our children. May America yet fulfill her aspirations for a democratic way of being-in-the-world grounded in faith for (and faithfulness to) democracy as it has been dreamed by so many (West, 2004). May Americans yet apprehend our 'human and communal responsibility' (Gough, 1993, 11) to 'sing' this dream into being (Gough, 1993, 13).

The New American Wilderness (In Musical/Song Form)

First Piece: The Within, *a Polonaise*[3]

Since September 11th, 2001, the American public has been blindsided by a convergence of internal and external forces complicating both domestic and international domains. Our situation has become increasingly complex and dangerous, due in part to a psycho-social slippage that occurred in that social moment, presaged by a blatant public exercise of ideological power manifesting in socio-cultural, political, technological, and economic terms. This psycho-social slide, of tremendous significance in its own right, was augmented by an official public use of manipulative rhetoric designed to cloak *radical change* behind a normalized triumphal-nationalist narrative of the nation.

This radicalization, it turned out, would amplify inequities negatively impacting public well-being for every segment of our society, with the exception of the extremely well-to-do, who received both public assistance and a heightening of their privilege(s) in this moment and who continue to be the sole beneficiaries of change(s) in present context. In fact, the manipulation of official public rhetoric both for camouflaging domestic re-ordering and for advancing foreign policies that are revolutionary in their aggression and scope introduced a kind of *doublespeak* into this context surreally reminiscent of all-too-familiar science fiction scenarios.[4] The narrative of this new American wilderness, then, may resemble science fiction, but is, tragically, the state of things as they are now, exposed as it finally may all be in the rebirth of *writing* (Barthes, 1989) in our times. This condition circumscribed the terrain within which American educators struggled to make sense of their responsibilities to present and future generations as democracy came under threat, a scenario that persists, but *may* be challenged in 2009 (hope speaks forth its promise).

The struggle for power between political parties in 2000 had itself been publicly acrimonious, as evidenced by: media reduction of the election to public spectacle; Machiavellian maneuvering at the polls to eliminate opposition party voters and votes in Florida; astonishing legal battles over the outcome; and a final, but contentious and partisan Supreme Court *pronuncio* determining the winner (Lewis, 2007). This election-become-spectacle produced a national tremor of disbelief among many concerned citizens, the first of what might be seen as a series of *shock waves* rolling over us in the months and years to follow. (It was also duly noted in foreign press as a tumultuous and remarkable event in American politics.)

Further, the outcome seemed to put the finishing touches on publicly rending the nation in two along a supposed cultural fault line, with Red State rule winning out over Blue State publics in every conceivable way. As we watched representation of those *not* on the so-called 'Right' dissolve into vapors before our eyes, some held that this ascent to power was the result of an election that had in fact been 'stolen,' the first of many suspect events ultimately contributing to public distrust. Despite initial protests calling for further investigation, the matter was finally settled when, in a gentlemanly manner, former Vice President Al Gore reassured the country that all would be well and asserted that Americans would get behind their new leader, George W. Bush. That remained to be seen, since we had already become a '50-50 nation' (Micklethwait and Wooldridge, 2004), and the divide had become an open, raw wound. The message coming from the Right quickly became, as Lynne Cheney used to say when signing off on her radio talk show, "Get Right or Get Left Behind." There was a new strangeness in the nation, a sense that something extraordinary had happened, but there had been no visible movement, not much had changed. No one outside the circle of power, in fact, could have foreseen what loomed ahead, not even the most diligent and concerned American citizens.

The September 11th terrorizing attacks on the World Trade Center and the Pentagon, along with the frustrated, but tragic attempt to use the now-famous Flight 93 to attack a then-undetermined target in Washington, D.C., presented the nation's citizens with a *second* shock wave. This shock wave, of enormous proportions in its own right, was further intensified by the mysterious anthrax incidents, which resulted in a number of deaths and contributed to growing public hysteria. Crisis management became the rhetorical order of the day, but no genuine crisis management took place. (In fact, the 'answer' just recently provided in August, 2008, about the source of the anthrax has come under scrutiny by a wary public, trust having been destroyed over the past seven years.) The public naming by our authorities in 2001 of Osama bin Laden's Al Qaeda as the culprits killing thousands when the planes they flew into the World Trade Center ended in a total meltdown of those twin towers, the culprits who blasted a hole in the Pentagon, killing hundreds more, did not ease public fears, in fact, but further exacerbated them as American citizens naively wondered how we could be so hated and simultaneously worried about the *next* round of attacks.

This *second* shock wave would be cunningly exploited to manipulate an unwitting public as heightened and continuous use of triumphal-nationalist rhetoric—designed to justify all that followed—ensured that the effects of these very real events, augmented by particular bits of *disinformation*, would have the intended political outcome. That outcome was, in fact, largely formulated (for its domestic audience) in terms of a *unity-as-defense* posturing. To some extent, it must be acknowledged, a rise in nationalistic fervor was to to be expected as a natural response to an extraordinary attack on home soil. However, it slowly became evident that this triumphal-nationalist rhetoric was being positioned by those in power as the new mediator of 'Truth' for the nation, as they publicly announced our new *Unity*, then sought to enforce it by working both behind the scenes and in full public view as well to curb and demonize dissent, even as they mouthed approval of civic debate and espoused cultural harmony.

In fact, certain state-centric media venues—via their 'talking heads'—quickly came out to ensure that any utterance differing from or contesting this rhetorical Oneness was measured against a standard set by this new brand of Right(ness), emboldened now by its totalized leadership positioning and gloating over its social, political, and techno-economic power. This rhetoric was seamlessly interwoven with the radical neo-liberal/neo-conservative global agenda of our presumed leaders, who sought to lay claim to the entire discursive space of the nation as a prerequisite for laying claim to the entire discursive space of a new world (dis-)order. Those in power would position their ideology as the progenitor of a new 'identity' for the nation, one that would come to be lamented even amongst our allies and friends around the world, and eventually by citizens here at home as well. Resistance to this new narrative for the nation on our shores would swell only slowly, over time, as multiple revelations of abuses of power emerged. The initial result was an accelerated production of aggravated public anxiety. This created a 'new and revised' America, a *post-9/11 America*, the new American wilderness. In this book, the autobiography of this post-9/11 America circumscribes the space of 'through education.'

For more and more concerned citizens, what ever-so-slowly (and even more painfully) came into full view amounted to a political-cultural-economic *coup* serving the exclusive interests of those in power. This unveiling formed the *third* shock wave—one that rolled out incrementally over time, assaulting our (democratic) sensibilities in waves of recognition as it emerged into daylight. Their agenda appeared to include the following: *first*, to cement power in the Executive branch of government so as to weaken the power of Congress either to conduct oversight or to legislate public policy when it parted from Executive will; *second*, to disenfranchise and disempower anyone *not* included in their 'base' (neo-liberal/neo-conservative elites) while publicly pandering to social conservatives and actively working to enflame their passions against any and all opposition, real or imagined—which Arendt (1968) refers to as the 'temporary alliance between the mob and the elite' (326); and, *third*, to employ militarization and unilateralism for the purpose of global domination (Project for the New American Century, 1997).

The Bush-Cheney administration, in short, seems to have had its way with the whole of the structure of governance and, for a time, with public opinion as well, even as the nation was turned in unprecedented and radical directions. What has occurred is a social re-ordering beyond the scope of our ability to imagine it, and so we wait to know and to see what will become of us, even as we live with the unmistakable effects of this radical revolution, evidenced in almost every facet of daily life. Part of what I work towards here is a fuller *seeing* of this transformation of America. I have space to consider just a few instances of public fraud and failure on the part of our government as signposts indicating the intent of the regime in power whose actions (and non-actions) helped to forge the parameters of this new American wilderness.

First, it was belatedly revealed that this administration had dismissed realistic concerns and cautions of agencies charged with our protection *because* those agencies were advising against a course of action that had already been predetermined by the administration for its own purposes (see, e.g., Berman, 2007; Dean, 2005; Hersh, 2005).[5] Such revelations emerged piecemeal over time in what MSNBC's *Hardball* host Chris Matthews (2001) referred to as 'rolling disclosure,' a process by which we are told what politicians want us to be told, when it seems convenient *for them* for us to know—in other words, as a way of holding back vital information. Other weapons included in the White House arsenal for maintaining secrecy and exploiting obfuscation include such diversionary strategies as: stonewalling, sidetracking the public conversation, using a continuous logic of 'spin' to evade critique, exercising their power not only to rewrite history, but also to withhold or destroy the *materiel* needed to reconstruct it for posterity, and 'leaking' selectively to control the shape and impact of stories about to emerge. Such strategies turned out to be useful for getting the public acclimated to radical change by ensuring that insight into the workings of this authoritarian regime while it was under construction would only be afforded incrementally. It would take reporting on (writing about) an extraordinary series of events for the public to see that these events added up, in the end, to a startling revolution in the socio-political, cultural, military, and techno-economic condition (and position) of the nation. In the interim, the administration was free to aggressively pursue its agenda, untrammeled by any resisting force capable of slowing, diverting, or stopping its course.

For those of us who are children of world war and operate on the basis of *remembrance*, parallels between the behaviors of this administration and those of totalitarian regimes—regimes Americans fought against more than half a century ago—shrieked to be noticed, but discourse about this was neither public enough nor loud enough. That would require more revelation via writing than Americans had access to in that moment, yet some of us could intuitively *feel* that a new incarnation of a nightmarish past might be re-emerging, only this time on home soil. As Dewey (Boydston, 1988) argued in *Freedom and Culture*, the emergence of totalitarianism *could* happen here, since the strength of democracy is dependent upon its retention in culture.[6] This emergence, moreover, may have already occurred in our times, since its signifiers are omnipresent in administrative and communicative tendencies, as noted here. In this post-9/11 moment, the public sphere failed, and failed completely. The space of 'through education' has yet to cope sufficiently with this event.

The neo-conservative foreign policy worldview would be abetted by a terrorizing "neoliberal domestic restructuring" at home (Giroux, 2004, xv). The coupling of this neo-liberal domestic agenda with what some call the new neoconservative imperialism of the Bush-Cheney administration (e.g., Harvey, 2005; McLaren and Farahmandpur, 2005; West, 2004)—which Habermas (2006) calls America's 'revolutionary' turn towards hegemonic unilateralism (xvi)—would prove to be devastating for our already-weakened democracy. Our new vulnerability as a 'free' nation became increasingly apparent as our right to dissent was stifled in the name of national security (Chang, 2002; Giroux, 2002; Lapham, 2004); an amorphous (and initially hidden) surveillance project intruded itself into American private life and, once exposed, into public consciousness; constitutional rights and guarantees of freedom were suspended; and public opinion was dismissed as irrelevant to Executive policy.

Meanwhile, America's (global) elites continued to enhance their status and privilege both at home and around the world, as was partially demonstrated by: repeated tax cuts and more corporate welfare for the already-wealthy (in the face of a costly war and in spite of the build-up of a national debt of historic proportions); a transition to non-mandatory (voluntary, or self-imposed) 'regulation' for corporate giants to enhance their profitability while ignoring public interests; war-profiteering via sweetheart (no-bid) contracts for billions of dollars to politically-connected (e.g., to Vice President Cheney's and friends') companies; and the quiet formation of large privatized global security forces ('mercenary armies') loosely connected to the State Department and silently spread around the world (Scahill, 2007). It should be noted that all of this transpired without even the slightest veneer of accountability (although a reckoning of some sort *may* begin in 2009). These revelations about the new American wilderness would not be quickly unveiled, and the full extent of the strategies used by our new global corporate elites to enhance their privilege(s) has neither been thoroughly investigated nor fully reported at the time of this writing. We have much yet to learn, and one must read constantly and widely to know what is going on—what is happening to and in post-9/11 America.

As noted, a startling neglect of now increasingly disenfranchised (largely, but not exclusively, minority and poor) American citizens trickled down through various official capillaries of judicial and administrative response (or, more properly, non-response) as 'disaster capitalists' devised means to use the *shock* resulting from catastrophic events to satisfy their own privatization agendas both at home and around the world (Klein, 2007). This was demonstrated, on the one hand, in the total failure of leadership during the devastation of New Orleans as a result of Hurricane Katrina in 2005—and, on the other, in the privatization and profiteering that has led to excruciatingly slow progress in restoring the poorer parts of the city in the years since and to prioritizing instead upscale private development and a greater profit margin (e.g., two-fold increases in the price of rental units) (Klein, 2007). The tremendous displacement of impoverished, traumatized people across this country has yet to be sufficiently addressed at this time, and this displacement impacts the space of 'through education.'

The idea that government has a legitimate function to play in helping the disadvantaged has been dismissed under this reign of unregulated, global capitalist power (see, e.g., Books, 2003, 2007; Giroux, 2004, 2005), this 'wild capitalism' (Barber, 2001, xxiii). The appalling Katrina debacle demonstrated this not only to Americans who would scrutinize that situation, but also to a world that watched in horror and stunned disbelief as the American government failed its own citizens, much as we had watched the twin towers plummet on September 11th. What was truly tragic, in addition to the tremendous loss and suffering of the victims of the disaster, was that indifference was mistaken for ineptitude by both the American media and the American public. The issue of the administration's competence-in-crisis became the new cause for concern, rather than intent playing out through inaction in the face of disaster, and this deception, no less, occurred in an aggravated high-risk, high-anxiety environment.

Abuse of power was also evidenced, although with a different trajectory, by the revelation in 2007 that U.S. attorneys who failed or refused to pursue political prosecutions were fired and replaced with more ideologically-attuned personnel who would wage legal and public media offensives against Democrats, regardless of the merits of a case. Further, some disclosure of discrimination on ideological grounds in the hiring process itself for Jusice Department personnel emerged as Congress held hearings on this matter (U.S. Department of Justice, 2008). The purpose here appears to have been to politicize the U.S. Justice Department as part of an effort to establish a permanent one-party state with absolute power in matters of (what would now be passed off as) 'justice.' The effect of this effort was to create a defacto police state controlled by one party and operating exclusively in its interests and on its behalf. What was left behind in this scenario was the principle that the Justice Department serves the nation, not a particular political ideology or party. At present, this situation continues and has also not been fully reported on by public press, let alone sufficiently addressed in legislative terms.

The realization that the Bush-Cheney agenda reflected a foreign policy radical in its aggression and revolutionary in its scope; indifference to the plight of the disadvantaged; and powerful, partisan retribution against any and all opposition to their will dawned very slowly. This was partly because those who were seriously watching could not *believe* their eyes and ears; partly because mainstream media networks were effective in legitimizing policies and in convincing their audiences that there were good reasons for whatever the White House did; and partly because too many Americans were not watching *at all*. In fact, the blame for present circumstances cannot fully be laid at the feet of this administration, despite their culpability; it was, after all, the public itself—and the public sphere that serves it—that were to blame for letting their agenda 'slide' so far and for so long. Public awareness of the broader dimensions of the problem(s), however, required yet another rolling-disclosure discovery that took years to fully unfold—that the administration had employed a public disinformation campaign in their efforts to engender support for a 'preemptive war' against Iraq.

This became clear only after the press began to uncover details, on a piecemeal basis, of another scandal—the White House 'outing' of a covert CIA operative (Valerie Plame Wilson), an outing that apparently occurred as retribution for her husband's anti-disinformation whistleblower activity. Former ambassador Joe Wilson's public exposure (in an Op-Ed in *The New York Times*) of a falsehood in President Bush's pre-invasion speech—the now-famous 'sixteen words'—turned into yet another public spectacle. It also demonstrated the willingness of those in power to blatantly use propaganda to achieve their desired ends. Vice President Cheney's chief of staff 'Scooter' Libby was, at the end of a lengthy process, convicted of obstructing justice for lying to a Grand Jury during the course of an investigation into the outing that focused on its potential origins. Libby's obstruction of justice prevented the truth from being discovered, thus effectively derailing the investigation.

President Bush responded to Libby's conviction by granting a partial commutation of his sentence, an action that pundits said demonstrated the premium placed on loyalty by this administration. While I would frame it differently (given that this 'outing' was an act of treason), the result was that it ultimately became obvious to the public—by then suffering prolonged shock and a fresh sense of digust and distrust from the many deceptions, disasters, and scandals during the Bush-Cheney years—how ruthlessly and recklessly this administration wielded power, but there was nothing to be done, short of impeachment, and that was rejected as an option since we were (are) at war. That card, in any case, was not to be played—not even in 2006, when leaders of the Democratic Party, newly elected to a tight majority position in Congress, slid that card to the bottom of the deck. Some of us began to wonder whether America turned upside down could ever find an upright position, and what it would take to cause such movement. The answers are unclear even now, in spite of the massive (and increasingly obvious) damage that has been done. We await change in 2009 with great hope and yearning, but the prospects for deep and lasting change yet remain to be seen.

While many Iraqis had suffered intensely under the brutal dictatorship of Saddam Hussein, Americans had *not* initially been urged to support war as a means of alleviating their suffering, but rather as a means of fending off further—both imminent and quite possibly nuclear, we were told—attacks on the homeland. The invocation of 'the mushroom cloud' threat in multiple and repeated public statements by various members of the White House cast of players (President Bush, Vice-President Cheney, and Secretaries of Defense and State, among others) drew supportive response from most Americans, as was anticipated. The rhetoric of this imminent threat—and accompanying disinformation—worked well for those using it to induce fear and compliance (see, e.g., Barber, 2004), and we find ourselves still embroiled in a conflict that is taking an incredible toll on the American nation, with no end in sight. This 'war' (which is actually an extended occupation of Iraq) has especially affected our most vulnerable citizens because its cost has vitiated domestic programs, stressed our military and their families beyond the breaking point (divorce and suicide rates in the military reached an all-time high during this initiative), debased our domestic economy to the point of impending ruin, and destroyed any vestige of our presumed prior status as a world leader on issues of human rights, freedom, and democracy, not to mention the suffering, death, shock, terror, rage and turmoil this embroilment has caused for the rest of the world, especially for human beings abiding in various parts of the Middle East, most notably, the citizens of Iraq.

This political-cultural-economic coup, this *third* shock wave, caused a psycho-social aftershock of immense proportions that left many of us confounded, but with eyes wide open. All of the traumas and discoveries taken together—acts of terror that were real, threats of terror that were manufactured, contra-democratic measures secretly introduced and implemented in the name of security, a vitriolic culture war at home cynically staged and directed by our presumed leadership, the failure(s) of government in the face of disaster, ongoing overseas wars of choice with minimal domestic visibility or accountability—force us to struggle with *risk*, *uncertainty*, and *disinformation* as motifs affecting our daily lives and altering our perceptions of *who we are* as a nation, not to mention the relationship between America as she is now and the rest of the world. The American landscape has been restructured and reordered, Barber (2001) tells us, as *Jihad* and *McWorld* leave anarchy in their wake, the very notion of democracy squeezed between the two. The product of this clash is a new American wilderness. As a result of these events, along with the constant and increasing anxiety of our citizens, we are now in a position where our identity as a (democratic) nation is at risk, if not altogether abdicated. This is the terrain of the *within*, and it has profound consequences for the public project of educating future citizens.

Second Piece: The Beyond, *a Fugue*[7]

If this was all we had to cope with, it would most certainly be challenging enough, but the times in which we live also offer externally-imposed complexities and ambiguities that make regrouping difficult as we seek a return to some sense of 'normalcy.' I think of these complexities and ambiguities imposed by the external world on the nation as the *beyond*, even though their effects are experienced internally. They also require serious consideration if we are to make sense of what is happening to our nation and to our place in the world. They complicate, and in some ways contradict, for instance, the call to 'educate for democracy' in our schools (e.g., Boston, 2005) and to re-envision and re-enact democracy as a way of being-in-the-world (e.g., Henderson and Kesson, 2004), and they do so at a time when these calls for more democracy and stronger democracy are most needed. This 'beyond' is complicated by the global context within which we are all now situated, its features having gone almost unnoticed (for Americans) in the face of so much domestic turmoil. This totalizing global environment—the civic-cultural surround within which we all live and labor—makes educating for democracy, however construed, an enormously complicated task.

These features include, *inter alia*: the wedding of a paradigm aligned with the production and distribution of wealth to one aligned with the production and distribution of *risk* (Beck, 1992), and all the ramifications of such a union;[8] an era of global *uncertainty* that limits both official and public thinking about education as a realm of possibility and results in a diminished role for schooling relative to social change (Porter, 1999); the increasing tendency of globalization to stretch both transnational possibilities and post-national space, intruding into the space of nation-states and eroding their symbol-ordering boundaries and capabilities (Appadurai, 1996; Barber, 2001, 2004; Bhabha, 1994; Habermas, 2001, 2006); and the unmitigated power of *image* to reshape and redefine reality (and schooling as a public project, which depends on some stabilized understanding of reality) in our times (Appadurai, 1996; Postman, 1986; Vinson and Ross, 2003). I describe these features in the following chapters and consider as well the implications of this beyond for the space of 'through education' as I contemplate contours of a curriculum for our times (see Chapter 9).

I argue, *first*, that post-9/11 America has become a prototype of the ultimate *risk society*—a "*catastrophic* society [in which] ...the exceptional condition threatens to become the norm" [emphasis in original] (Beck, 1992, 24)—which may also be characterized by a "loss of social thinking" (25) and by sudden political and social shifts as the public vacillates between hysteria and indifference. Control, in the risk society, is exercised by anonymous techno-economic powers that operate under the radar of democratic processes, but the innovations emanating from these powers drastically change daily life (54). In such a society, unseen side effects—increasingly made visible—are produced anonymously and therefore no one is held accountable. There is no closure, no resolution, and this keeps anxiety in the forefront of public thought and reaction, deeply impacting our ability as citizens to trust the risk experts charged with acting on our behalf and presumably in the nation's best interests, as well as our ability as citizens to believe in and/or respond to the 'exceptional condition' itself.[9]

Simultaneously, this risk scenario hinders us from getting to the root sources of the problems we face. We are, in short, left to fend for ourselves without any real gauge of where we are headed or what the future may hold. This surpasses anarchy—it reflects *chaos*. This is a condition that Beck characterizes as a "revolution under the cloak of normalcy" (186) where citizens lose their "cognitive sovereignty" (53) as the "anarchy (Arendt, 1981) of the (no longer) unseen side effect takes over power" (187). The risk society experiences a "profound systemic transformation" from non-politics to *sub*-politics" [emphasis in original] (190), a transformation within which "the political system is… threatened with *disempowerment* while its democratic constitution remains alive" [emphasis in original] (186). I cannot think of a more apt way to describe what has happened to/in post-9/11 America, but this 'disempowerment' has extraordinary consequences that cannot be ignored if we are to consider a curriculum of possibility for the future of democracy (Greene, 1971, 1988).

Second, due to both the erosion and the manipulation of the public sphere, we have lost our ability to become (and to remain) informed, let alone to communicate effectively across differences. To be in the know, we turn to our favorite partisan news-talk shows or web sites, where we can click on or tune in the perspective of choice, and hear what seems pleasing (even if scathing) to the ear. Consider the case of best-selling author Ann Coulter (2003, 2004), the Right's *provocateur extraordinaire*, whose marketing of hatred and venom towards liberals as the enemies of America has earned her public acclaim from the so-called Right and truly represents a phenomenon to be reckoned with in our times. Our politics have devolved to the level of show business (Postman, 1986), and not even show business in its best sense, as comedy or tragedy, but rather in its worst, as *soap opera*. Our culture has been reduced to a publicly viewed, 24/7 war of terror against deviance, including those who in any way resist or fail to accede to *normalization* (Vinson and Ross, 2003). Transgressions are paraded before us on a screen that provides non-stop coverage, but no prioritizing of issues. The effect of the juxtaposition of major news items with those that essentially have only entertainment value (if that) is to minimize the importance of everything. Value itself is deconstructed.

This is especially worrisome because we are driven by *hectic changes* (Beck, 1992, 185) and the anxiety they produce in a risk society, always working to catch up with a process that bombards us with change both randomly and continuously, exceeding our coping capabilities due to its extraordinary reach and accelerated pace. In essence, the Information Age mystifies choices and purposes through a glut of often meaningless data, obscuring actual realities 'on the ground,' and diverting attention away from them. Knowledge and learning are relegated to the status of information retrieval and data collection, while the need for *study* (see, e.g., Pinar, 2006a; Block, 2007) to empower critical moral judgment is undermined, countering the work of public intellectuals who reach for understanding and wisdom as the fruits of knowledge and who are capable both of decoding rhetoric and of discerning patterns of change and what they may portend for the future. In the midst of this enormous chaos, calls for schooling to advance and promote democracy—to prepare our young for greater civic engagement for the collective good—have become increasingly vocal. While the need is real, the irony is astounding.

Yet crucial questions related to such efforts emerge: questions, for instance, about how the young should be taught to think about our society, the world, and democracy in present context, and how they might be prepared to engage with the notion of democratized civil society in a global world. (In such times, how do we tell them, for instance, that if we don't find a path to this re-engagement we may well be facing, in the not too distant future, our worst science fiction nightmare?) We also need to consider what the potential outcomes of such efforts might be in a scenario where the public is not only *not* well-informed, but often purposefully *misinformed*, or, as Pinar (2004) sees it, 'mis-educated.' We must consider as well the political and cultural direction this turn should (or might) take under our present circumstances, a huge obstacle in a nation so clearly divided, not only from within, but from the rest of the West (Habermas, 2006; Micklethwait and Wooldridge, 2004), not to mention the rest of the world. These are all issues that would properly emerge in a context where the public sphere was open, clear, and free for civic debate and dialogue. Unfortunately, that has *not* been the case in post-9/11 America.

How *do* we teach our young here at home to think about our society, the world, and democracy in a time of such great division, hostility, uncertainty, and distrust? How do we teach them to approach difference in a time of fear-induced antagonism, the dissemination of outright hate, and anarchy? How do we teach them to sustain democratic attitudes and ideals when we are increasingly becoming *post-democratic* by virtue of mediated state-centric manipulation of the public mind, the invisible hand of techno-economic control, the promulgation of stringent security measures, and the proliferation of (not so) secret surveillance mechanisms? It seems important to consider these questions carefully as we contemplate ways to strengthen the sociopolitical dimensions of educational experience to advance and promote civic engagement amongst our young, and I argue here that any such initiative has to begin with some understanding of a working sense of the American nation: an autobiography that tells us something about our national identity, i.e., *who we say we are*.

Third Piece: Autobiography and Difference, a Rondo[10]

I offer here that we might start by approaching diverse understandings of the meanings of *America* and of being *American* as an autobiography of difference worthy of some exploration. Why use autobiography as an approach to the multitudes of problems we are facing today? Mailer (2003) supplies the rationale for this, while Pinar (1975, 1994, 2004) provides the (psycho-) analytic framework. In *Why Are We at War?* Norman Mailer (2003), attempting to explain a psycho-social disintegration in America following the events of September 11th, painted the American scene with these words:

> *What in God's name was happening?* It is one thing to hear a mighty explosion. It is another to recognize some time after the event that one has been deafened by it. The United States was going through an identity crisis. Questions about our nature as a country were being asked that most good American men and women had never posed to themselves before. Questions such as, Why are we so hated? How could anyone resent us that much? We do no evil. We believe in goodness and freedom. Who are we, then? (10)

For Mailer, what "kind of firm notion the ego attaches to itself" is not as important as the expectation that this notion will remain stable (i.e., that stability is what maintains our sense of identity), because stability "offers the psyche an everyday working notion of who we are" (11). But where that stability is "disrupted" or "pre-empted" (11), according to Mailer, "the effect is unmistakable," and one enters a situation where "the psyche is in a sprawl" (12). The series of shock waves surrounding September 11th created a serious psycho-social dilemma for *all* Americans:

> A mass identity crisis for all of America descended upon us after 9/11, and our response was wholly comprehensible. We were plunged into a fever of patriotism. If our long-term comfortable and complacent sense that America was just the greatest country ever had been brought into doubt, the instinctive reflex was to reaffirm ourselves. We had to overcome the identity crisis—hell, overpower it, wave a flag. (12)

This is precisely what Americans did, and, as Mailer points out, it was 'wholly comprehensible,' but it also made us excessively vulnerable to those willing to wave the flag (or wrap their agendas in it) most forcefully, and to declare most aggressively that they had the 'Right' answers to these (and other) very complex questions. This is a matter of no small importance for education.

Pinar's (1994, 2004) use of autobiography as a (psycho-) analytic framework for *currere*—the Latin from which the word curriculum derives, meaning 'to run the course' (Pinar, 2004, 35), alternatively interpreted as 'the course to be run' (Eisner, 2002, 25)—takes on increased saliency in a setting where the nation is experiencing an identity crisis. It becomes even more relevant in light of a decades-long culture war (Kincheloe, 1983; Kincheloe and Steinberg, 1993; Schlesinger, 1998; Shor, 1986), which I believe has become a recipe over time for developing a national form of multiple personality disorder, a disorder brought into high relief by the sudden, unanticipated events of September 11th. These horrendous events served, moreover, as *just one of three* shock waves for a substantial portion of the populace. This suggests to me that we have new terrain to explore, and that is my intention here. Whatever shape this terrain may take, it will be sure to impact the prospects for a democratic future, thereby shaping the future of curriculum as well.

I treat autobiography as the essential element of currere that it is, an element that can move us forward as we consider our situation both realistically and constructively, looking to the past and considering how to face the future, both past and present inherent (and complicit) in the future. Without working towards this end, any attempt to envision (let alone to enact) a curriculum for democratic purposes in *our times* will, I fear, be futile. *Currere* is used by Pinar (2004) as a verb (a gerund, actually), not a noun, helping us to see curriculum as a process of experiencing and understanding rather than as a fixed component of the educational experience. For Pinar, currere serves as well as a research method "whose aspiration is not only contribution to a 'body of knowledge' but contribution to the biographic-intellectual and thus political emancipation of those who employ it" (1994, 61). I transfer the notion of autobiography here from the individual or group to the nation taken as a complex whole, expanding the reach of autobiography by extending its method to the discursive terrain of 'nation-ness,' or national self-hood (Anderson, 1991; Appadurai, 1996; Bhabha, 1994) (see Chapter 4).

The nation, after all, is an *imagined community* requiring a narrative of autobiography (Anderson, 1991). Such biographies are constructed over time by a constant stream of remembering/forgetting (Anderson, 1991), and ours is currently floating in the deep waters of a post-national surround. This positioning complicates and contradicts our well-rehearsed renditions of our (democratic) identity as a nation, renditions to which we have become all too uncritically accustomed (Appadurai, 1996). Therefore, understanding the interrelations, or interconnectedness, between diverse iterations of *America* and *American* drawn from public, political, and academic discourses may be helpful both for deconstructing official 'conventional wisdom' (supported, in this case, by propaganda)[11] *and* for excavating the terrain of alternative possibilities. This is a vital task for the life of this democracy. Self-knowledge need not disintegrate into self-admiration or self-interest, despite the historic lure of both for mortals—but without understanding our own aspirations, without self-awareness and self-critique, how can we possibly proceed?

The texts selected for this study (with the exception of President George W. Bush's *State of the Union Address* in 2003) appeared within a sixteen-month period following September 11th. My intent was to take a snapshot of this moment in hopes that it might be helpful for framing democratic vision and imagination for post-9/11 America, situated as it is in a rapidly and radically changing world. In Pinar, what seems most essential to me is "the experience of knowledge creation... [which] represents movement, release from our arrest" (1994, 61). The purpose of this book, at least in part, is to question how we might emerge from a state of arrest into a state of "wide awakeness" (Greene, 1986, 2). Here, then, are some of the questions I seek to address in this (anecdotal) autobiography of our (democratic) nation at risk:

1. Who do we say we are as a nation? Who do we say we will become?
2. What can diverse narratives of our nation show us about our differences over the role of the state and varying responses to governance, especially questions of whether we sanction our government's control measures, how legitimately represented we feel ourselves to be, and whether we feel empowered to act on our own behalf?
3. How do we approach understanding different and multiple foundations for citizenship, i.e., how do they vary, why, and how do we respond to them?
4. What does it mean when powerful and organized groups proclaim that their truth is the *only* truth for *all* the people, and seek to enforce (their) consensus? What, if anything, are we prepared to do about it?
5. Is *Reason*, the core element of the Enlightenment project upon which many of this nation's ideals were based, beyond our reach in this "Fifty-fifty nation" (Micklethwait and Wooldridge, 2004, 94) with a "radical center" (Halstead and Lind, 2001, 16)? Can we *re-imagine* how reason might be put to work for a democratic future?
6. To what extent does our vista of the nation and of its relation to the world influence our thinking about our responses to governance and our sense(s) of belonging within the nation and world?
7. How can we prepare our young to envision and work towards a better world in the face of our own diversity, disagreements, and hostilities?

I decipher what different ways of framing answers to these questions might mean by mapping the disputatious terrain of post-9/11 American discourse and treating the exposition of this terrain as autobiography. My ultimate goal is to contribute to re-conceptualizing how we might truly educate *towards* democracy in present context. The map provides a civic-cultural portrait of America as it was discursively iterated following September 11th. This iteration serves as an autobiography of the nation expressed from multiple and contentious ways of seeing. I analyze the discourses to map a broad range of visions, or imaginings, of who we say we are as a nation, and what we say it means to be citizens, using a research genre from comparative education: social or comparative cartography, or social mapping (see Chapter 3). This range of visions is presented in a figure that illustrates their interrelations, and they are elaborated as 'cultures of citizenship' coexisting within the nation (see Chapter 7).

The interrelations of these cultures of citizenship point to some pressing problems for democracy in our times. Some reflect understandings that have been constant refrains in our past, while others are nascent perspectives signaling possibility, and yet others urgently demand the need for attentiveness, critical awareness, and strong, creative response. I use the mapping project to consider the challenges faced by curricularists dedicated to a future for democracy as we approach new conceptualizations of the meaning(s) of educational experience within a mediated state-centric risk paradigm in these uncertain times, and struggle against a new logic of disinformation that amounts to management of the public mind. This curriculum inquiry project aims to contribute something of value to the complicated conversation (Pinar, 2004) surrounding our nation and our times with an eye to reconceptualizing contours of a curriculum for post-9/11 America, the new American wilderness. This, then, is an outline of a curriculum based on the autobiography of a (democratic) nation at risk.

A 'Line of Flight' for Curriculum Inquiry

I engage with these issues by taking a 'lines of flight' approach, which Reynolds (2004) describes as

> (becomings) that allow, however contingently, briefly, or momentarily, for us to soar vertically like a bird or slither horizontally, silently like a snake weaving our way amid the constant reconfigurations, cooptations, and movements of the ruins. It is part of Deleuze's philosophy of multiplicities. (31)

This is a useful approach in this, our postmodern moment, where, according to Reynolds and Webber (2004):

We have moved through what Foucault (Rabinow, 1984) described as disciplinary societies in which people passed through various disciplinary institutions such as schools and factories that regulated habits, customs, and discourses to what Deleuze (1995) elaborated as control societies. (ix)

Reynolds and Webber note that such a "movement toward Empire has consequences in academic fields," and they highlight Lyotard's (1992) suggestion that in such times "there is a call in many disciplines to shut down experimentation and creativity" (ix). By way of response, the authors offer the approaches taken in their edited volume, work that "encourages and demonstrates creativity, multidisciplinarity, and lines of flight [as] a momentary space within Empire to express difference and hope" (ix). 'Lines of flight' research, then, is informed by "the authors' shared concern for viewing curriculum from alternative perspectives that are not method driven but instead are derived from the insights of a dis/position that seeks to disentangle curriculum from its traditional dependence on formalities" (x). Further,

> The authors have attempted to dwell in alternative methodologies such as textual analysis, discourse theory, hermeneutics, and poststructuralism while triangulating them with the important perspectives of race, class, gender, and sexual orientation. The chapters blur disciplinary boundaries and interweave curriculum theory with cultural studies, political theory, psychoanalysis, dance, technology, and other fields. All of this is done within an overall poststructural framework. (x)

I link this approach to *imaginative praxis* (e.g., Greene, 1995) as I ponder the contours of this post-9/11 curriculum, a curriculum potentially capable of opening to multiple 'becomings' while acknowledging their interrelations. My nomadic positioning and re-positioning—whether I am 'soaring vertically' or 'slithering horizontally'—is thus my response to the terrorizing practice of imagination exercised by those who attacked us. It is also my response to the terrorizing disciplinarities of those who (for now, literally) rule over us. This approach is a "disruption" that Reynolds and Webber (2004) assert is 'political in the sense that it opens space for "a 'line of flight' in power and meaning for the use of those who are marginalized or excluded" (5). The authors further venture that because

> such (research) practices about the status of pedagogic, representational, and research authority pulse with the power of individual imagination, they seem to force their way through the present densities of analytic production in efforts to articulate "why and how that-which-is" might no longer be "that-which-is" (Foucault, 1980). The sense of "that-which-is" becomes a sense of "what-can-be," always ready to just break loose (Jipson and Paley, 1997). (5)

Ultimately, I offer a metaphor, *opening a portal for democracy*, aimed at conceptualizing this sense of 'what-can-be'—as a 'curriculum of possibility' (Greene, 1971) in present context—to engender and sustain: *hope* to fight for a better world, *preparedness* against adversity of all kinds, and the development of *public will* for a democratic future. Once again, I say (with so many others): May America yet fulfill her aspirations for a democratic way of being-in-the-world grounded in faith for (and faithfulness to) democracy as it has been dreamed by so many (West, 2004). May Americans yet 'sing' this dream into being (Gough, 1993, 13).

Orientation to the Text

Part One reflects on theoretical dimensions of the study. Chapter 2 frames the use of autobiography as a research genre well-suited to address the multivocal claims to national identity in post-9/11 America, orienting my reader to the general concerns of the book. Chapter 3 introduces the comparative method partnered with autobiography here: social cartography, highlighting its positioning as a 'line of flight' approach (Reynolds and Webber, 2004) to curriculum inquiry. In Chapter 4, I elaborate Anderson's (1991) study of nationalism and Appadurai's (1996) study of cultural implications resulting from the transition to post-national space occasioned by global media and global migration, questioning what this means for our sense of the nation. I reflect on social imagination as a process that interacts with a public sphere that is transformed *by and in* post-national space, briefly attending as well to other readings (e.g., Barber, 2001, 2001, Bhabha, 1994).

Part Two presents an elaboration of the autobiographical work undertaken here. Chapters 5 and 6 present post-9/11 narratives of *America* and *American* in discourses that truly compose the autobiography. In Chapter 7, I present a mapping of these discourses as they converge into *cultures of citizenship*, which are treated as plateaus constituting a rhizome of intensified feelings reaching no climax (Deleuze and Guattari, 1987) and are elaborated in terms of the kinds of social space and social arrangements they envision and espouse.

Part Three highlights fragments of this 'complicated conversation' (Pinar, 2004). Chapter 8 sketches problematiques of the public sphere in our times, bringing together Porter's (1999) elaboration of an 'era of uncertainty' in education, Beck's (1992) theorization of a risk society paradigm, and various analyses of the techno-culture thesis, many of which examine Habermas' (1991) work on the transformation of the public sphere. Chapter 9 considers prospects for a curriculum of possibility (Greene, 1971) for the new American wilderness, looking to the past while exploring the present. I briefly review calls for critical pedagogies to engender more informed and engaged citizens: Greene's (1978) 'landscapes of learning' and her (1986) 'search for a critical pedagogy' and Pinar's (2004) work on autobiography as 'a revolutionary act.'

In the **Epilogue**, Chapter 10, I share some thoughts about where to go from here as I look at Twitchell's (2004) 'branded nation,' where national identity is marketed to us as a commodity, and question what a 'newly branded' post-9/11 America might actually mean. I wrestle with Ayers' (2005) question: how tolerant can we afford to be when intolerance is used to silence difference? Finally, I highlight the need to further explore the theory of authoritarian government formulated in Germany prior to the emergence of the Third Reich.

Part One

Theoretical Dimensions of the Study

2

Autobiography of Post-9/11 America

THE FRAMEWORK

> The air is getting thinner. Knowledge surveillance constricts narratives and talk. Maybe this is the work of meaning for the radical democratic possibilities of social science. To make sure there is discursive air to breath [sic], to reimagine, to critique, and to construct other stories of what could be. (Fine, 2002, 138)

> With a passion that was often missing in 2000, Mr. Gore on Saturday was forced to tell the party what should have been obvious. "Here in America, patriotism does not mean keeping quiet," he roared. "It means speaking up." ... The former vice president did his party a great service in reminding its leaders that Americans deserve outspoken advocates on more than one side. ...Dissent is not disloyalty. (Unleashing the Loyal Opposition, *The New York Times*, 2002)

It was a moment of silence that threatened to become a curriculum of silence, and that threat is with us still. It should be remembered, however, that September 11th, 2001, was also a moment in which public intellectuals displayed civic courage in the face of massive fear and confusion. Ideologues had assumed power over the nation and now turned the ship of state into hitherto uncharted waters without engaging in the honest and informed public dialogue that might have been expected to preface such a turn in a democratic society. Any sign of dissent from this turn would be met with a good deal of aggressive hostility both from the administration's supporters throughout officialdom and from those who supported them in or through state-centric media as well, especially television's talking heads in the mainstream media and the nationwide network of 'right-wing' radio talk show hosts. This reverberated across the many knowledge nodes in the public sphere as commentators (and university administrators as well!) noted the (*disagreeable?*) civic discord and measured it against the new American standard: unity at all costs, i.e., *unity-as-defense*. Although the silence is not the primary focus of this work, it should not be forgotten. It heralded the dawning of a national identity crisis, one that lingers still.

Therefore I acknowledge the silence and consider its implications for knowledge work as a prerequisite for considering emancipatory autobiographical possibilities offered by some discourses in that social moment. I also consider complexities of the socio-cultural, historical, techno-economic, and political terrain within which our epistemological views of the nation and of our civic-cultural surround were (and are yet) fractured and embedded. This terrain is composed by the act of producing knowledge, framed in multiple languages deriving from diverse perspectives and appearing in venues that compete for attention and influence. In this chapter, I address complexities of knowledge production, then, in relation to narratives presenting national autobiographic possibilities and also attend to venues where knowledge is produced and framed using languages that are incommensurate and that sometimes collide, producing tensions, conflicts, and raising new questions, rather than providing easy solutions.

The narratives considered here for autobiographical purposes are cultural artifacts drawn from various venues, some carrying more 'weight' (in both rhetorical *and* de facto power) than others: George W. Bush's (2003) *State of the Union* speech enunciating a new identity for the nation prior to the invasion of Iraq; an aggressive anti-dissident public advertisement by a powerful ideological clan seated at the right hand of power—William Bennett's group, 'Americans for Victory Over Terrorism' (AVOT); an academic journal dedicated to qualitative inquiry whose (invited) contributors reflected both personally and professionally on September 11th; and Op-Ed pieces from both a national newspaper of record in the mainstream press (*The New York Times*) and from a progressively-oriented website proclaiming itself an alternative to the mainstream (tompaine.com).

Public press (both print and electronic) and the university are characterized here as knowledge nodes of varying influence reflecting difference even when, as in the post-9/11 moment, they seek answers to common questions in response to a phenomenon experienced simultaneously by all. The Executive branch and its entourage, presumed to be conservative (but more appropriately framed as neo-liberal/neo-conservative), apparently felt they didn't need to ask questions; they simply affirmed that they had *the* answer. Unfortunately, they had control of the White House and Congress from the start, and had a powerful support group sitting on the Supreme Court as well (Toobin, 2007), giving them a trifecta of absolute power. With an intuitive sense of the darkness into which we were plunging, I undertook this curriculum inquiry project in 2001 because I was concerned with the growing power of a blatantly authoritarian government, with the disintegration of democratic structures, and with a tragic apparent weakening of our democratic aspirations as well, all features of the new American wilderness that I found deeply troubling. What troubled me most was the blanket of silence smothering dissent, an effect of terror that appeared to be uncritically sanctioned by the public, which posed the difficult question for me of *who we say we are*. Therefore the public and its imaginaries are my main focus in this work, rather than the forces of power, although I have scrutinized them somewhat as well (see Prologue).

In this chapter I elaborate the dilemmas inherent in knowledge production itself, first, in terms of its 'limitations,' and second, in terms of its general 'situating' within an amorphous and rapidly changing civic–cultural context. I consider the university, for instance, as an essential node of knowledge production, attending to other nodes in later chapters (print/electronic media in Chapter 4 and our new *virtual* public sphere, techno-culture, in Chapter 8). I do so in the hope that I might bring into clearer focus some of the dimensions of discourse that produced the autobiography of the new American wilderness elaborated in this text. First, however, I attend to the silence.

Silence and Silencing

There are many kinds of silence, but prolonged silence of any kind is deadly for those working in a pluralist arena. There is the silence that comes from within—from numbness, frustration, confusion, betrayal, or disillusion. There is the silence that comes from difference—from lack or loss of voice, of opportunity, of place. There is the silence that slowly creeps up on us as we recognize that we have acclimated ourselves to civic disengagement and sociopolitical voyeurism. There is the silence that comes from the sudden press of the fearful crowd for *Oneness* in a land where individuality has been a key normative value. Finally, there is the silence that comes from pressure from authority writ large to conform—i.e., to discard individual vision and conviction—under circumstances where everything around us tells us that *that voice* is the voice of power.

I take silence here to constitute a metaphorical curriculum-in-process, one that involves the whole nation and affects knowledge work struggling to define its character, to come into its own in the face of adversity. My concern for civic courage requires being able to see the construction of that curriculum as one that is composed of both internally *and* externally imposed elements—the *within-beyond*. The silence still surrounding the events of September 11th comes from varying directions, realities, and influences. It is a supremely important silence because *every* sentient American at some point confronted the same images and experienced the same trauma, although we each made sense of it in our own way. No matter what our differences and difficulties in sense-making—and that is where the curriculum of silence took hold—for this singular moment in American history, we *all* watched, immobilized by disbelief, as our nation came under attack. The spectacle was, after all, delivered via America's most ubiquitous medium: television (Danner, 2001).

The effect was to pull us into a space where we once again confronted the undeniable—namely, that we are a *nation*, despite our many differences and indisputable grievances. What made this realization so gut-wrenching was that, in a sense, it was in that moment—of shock, fear, and loss on so many levels—that we had the opportunity to 'rediscover' ourselves and to imagine ourselves (our nation) differently. In this sense, it was an opportunity to use the potential of the *regressive* and *progressive* moments (contemplating the presence in the present moment of both past and imagined future moments) in the autobiographical process (see Pinar, Reynolds, Slattery, and Taubman, 1995, 520; Pinar, 1994, 21-25). Responses to this opportunity, as we shall see, varied greatly. What was most noticeably prominent was the use of television as a delivery system: first, for the dispersion of effects of terrorizing attacks on New York City, Washington, D.C., and Flight 93; and second, for the overwhelming use of triumphal-nationalist rhetoric to market a new brand of post-9/11 American identity, a brand designed and sold to the people by their corporatist government (Klein, 2007) in collusion with mainstream media.

Within this scenario, there was a good deal of self-imposed silence. For those who perform knowledge work—i.e., for those for whom words, ideas, and images are our stock-in-trade—there may have been a sense of disjointedness between words to describe or make sense and feelings beyond either description or sense. For some, there was a sudden loss of meaningfulness surrounding their work. Kenneth J. Gergen (2002) articulates the latter:

> It was not only difficult to write but as well to read, teach, or carry out intelligent conversation. What difference did any of this make in terms of the greater agonies ascending to global prominence? Over time, I have returned to reflect more hopefully on our efforts... (186)

Kathy Charmaz (2002) frames the moment in the language of her students, who

> voiced their struggle to comprehend the unfolding realities and to understand their place in a changed world. They talked of the sudden meaninglessness of commodities and competition. They looked for solace within their families and religious faiths. They hoped for rapid resolution and an end to violence. Yet the hush of silence was also discernible. (189)

And yet, others felt this silence intruding from the external effects following September 11th. Hear, for instance, Mary Gergen (2002):

> I am waiting for the seal to crack on the seemingly unified stance regarding the curtailment of our old pre-9/11 inclinations. So far, I have not seen much resistance to the rising cries from government for new security measures and the restrictions on

civil liberties. I think of the people of Germany in another era who must have tolerated similar rulings in the name of their security. I long to hear some dissident voices. I think I hear them in the distance. Or do I? (151)

William L. Miller (2002), on the other hand, offers his 'hopefulness' as he contemplates complicating this silence and the enunciations producing it:

> We stand in the tortured silence with the hopefulness of waiting, with the fluttering, fragile faith of the butterfly. We resist the escapist calls for revenge against the evil ones, we know the evil of such dualisms. We have a different task with evil. We must acknowledge, complicate, and stir hope into the polluted sea of evil. (156)

Using the words of these and others who spoke out to critique or contradict the formulaic representations of America and of being American enunciated by those in power, I elaborate and then illustrate the textual wilderness of American autobiography in this moment. In short, I work here, to 'acknowledge, complicate, and stir hope into' a different body of water, the pool of discourse mirroring our varying senses of what America means and what it means to be American. I refer to this collective text, or *writing* (Barthes, 1989), as an intertextual field contesting this terrain of 'American-ness' as colliding and conflicting social imaginaries vie for space to be heard. This terrain is "the imagination as a social practice" (Appadurai, 1996, 31). These were the imaginaries of a nation undergoing an identity crisis in a moment of national trauma (Mailer, 2003), and I offer that they constitute a curriculum, one that I frame here via autobiography.

Limitations of Knowledge Production

'Locating' a Post-9/11 Curriculum

How are we to make sense of this 'new' reign of silence in American society—this curriculum that prevented us from publicly discussing the events of September 11th and their aftermath in a way that might have been more instructive, more constructive? And how can we allow talk about this moment to wither, when the images themselves presented *the entire nation* with an undeniable curriculum whose meaning is yet to be fully and openly explored? Most critically, where is the curriculum that might help us to break through the stifling hush? I approach these questions by mirroring the many faces reflecting our national persona to disrupt and complicate the triumphal-nationalistic turn our nation has taken. To do so is a way, in my thinking, to unleash the potential of the *analytical* moment—"description via conceptualization" (Pinar, 1994, 26)—in the autobiographical process.

Much of what has prevailed in the talk about unity, the nation, and its challenges relative to terrorism (especially talk emanating from our presumed leadership) has been essentially *triumphal*. Central to this enunciation is the claim that our nation (by the grace and with the blessings of God Almighty) has achieved democracy (i.e., that we have, in fact, triumphed as a beacon of freedom), and that we are well-served if we live (self-?) righteous lives, work hard, vote, embrace the prescribed wisdom upholding American exceptionalism, and put our faith in authority writ large to take care of the rest.

From my perspective, this *is* the silence, much like Lundgren's (1983) 'invisible' curriculum code (cited in Kemmis, 1986), where the values in play in our society and the questions they might raise (for educators, in Kemmis) are controlled by those who are deemed to know best and are even predigested for us, so that we no longer see what is at stake and what alternatives we might want to consider, let alone *imagine*.[1] In this work, then, I begin with the premise that this triumphal culture of citizenship constitutes an 'invisible' curriculum code that took center stage in a blatant display of rhetorical (and administrative) power over public discourse following September 11th, changing the language used to represent our nation dramatically, and altering as well the range of possibilities within which we have room to dream, room to imagine.

The Epistemology of Resentment

This triumphal view has, of course, always had an intimate relationship with power and capital. Bourdieu (1992), for instance, focuses on the power and capital behind positivist epistemology—especially its linkage with certainty as the privilege of a particular narrative of knowledge (science)—positioning this epistemological narrative against the backdrop of the politics of science. Drawing on the work of Bachelard,[2] who studied changes in scientific thought, Bourdieu offers that "epistemology is not a matter of ahistorical reflection," that "one develops more or less this or that principle of epistemology according to the state of the epistemological unconscious in the given society" (47). He provides us with this rendering of the ensuing problem:

> Many of the principles of positivist epistemology have no other function than to obstruct people who have ideas. They obey the logic of 'ressentiment,' in the rigorous, Nietzschean sense of the term: not being capable of inventing ideas, I will make sure somehow that those that have them will be culpable for having them. Behind epistemological choices there are social forces. We all know that violence hides beneath the most noble and pure *statements*. ...the taking of epistemological positions always involves the position in the scientific field of those who take them, and the type of capital which it commands... scientific strategies which are presented as absolute and

universal choices are often little more than rationalizations of their own limits. [Emphasis in original] (48)

The result of this 'rationalization of limits' is not only to bind those who 'obey the logic of ressentiment,' but also those who would push beyond such limits, transgressing against presumed 'certainties' to reach for new ideas. This may be especially true for those who work to understand and interpret social forces and to develop consciousness about knowledge/power relations (Foucault, 1980). This reinforcement of limits, Bourdieu argues, results in a 'mutilation':

> All this amounts to saying, 'You must be like me', which means: mutilated. Many of the actual debates in social science are debates of this type. They are debates which are organized around people caught within their pre-established limits. (48)

He supplies a useful analogy for considering how new vision is silenced within a scenario where debate withers or is directed towards the either/or, the false dichotomy (and thus becomes essentially powerless to effect change), never transcending its own limitations:

> Many epistemological conflicts are wars of religion. What for me is disastrous, is that all these strategies are self-mutilating. People struggle against each other, but for their own satisfaction, to pander to their own limits. This is the epistemology of resentment. (48-49)

This 'epistemology of resentment' plays a major role in the curriculum of this moment and we need to surmount this so that we can move towards a curriculum of voice that breaks free of the tensions of the past. Our so-called 'liberal' versus 'conservative' culture war has been going on for far too long (as has adversity towards various 'others' whom we manage to exclude as we think about the nation, a practice that cannot stand in these times). Further, we have transcended classical conceptions of both political categories (which have become mere labels as used in current political rhetoric) without realizing it, largely because we are ignorant (I speak of us as a public in general) of histories of thought that might have furthered our development as a 'civil' polity.

Moreover, we have yet to fully grasp the possibilities of pluralist democracy (see, e.g., Greene, 1995; Longstreet, 2000), and we have much to discover and experience in this domain if we can truly open to it in such a way as to promote our own civic-cultural development. The question at hand is this: how should education for such development proceed, given present context? We need now more than ever to develop new social imaginaries that can move us beyond this stagnancy in our civic development and this backwardness in our cultural understanding(s). It will be difficult to envision such imaginaries without the *regressive* element of autobiography, where we actively work to gain understanding of our past. I focus here, then, on civic courage and on its potential to break through the limitations that keep us from seeing with new vision who we (as a nation) could become, but I do so both by illuminating autobiography in the present and by exploring our past as I look tentatively and ambivalently toward the future.

Autobiography and 'Ideology-Critique'

The question of who we say we are as a nation, in fact, informs the core of this work. September 11th involved more than just massive fear and anxiety—it involved an identity crisis that would paralyze most of the nation's citizens as they struggled to overcome its effects. Mailer (2003), as noted (see Prologue), asserts that the result of that horrific social moment was to send our national psyche into a sprawl, and that the general response was a wave of patriotic nationalism to overcome the crisis. This, unfortunately, strengthened the hands both of those holding forth a triumphal view of the nation, and also of their behind-the-scenes political henchmen (e.g., Karl Rove, William Bennett, etc.), who were pushing an aggressive and *coercive* nationalism, which I have termed *hypernationalism* (Nicholson-Goodman, 2006, 2007). A nation with its 'psyche in sprawl' poses an alluring target for those looking to advance a particular ideological view, but some exercised civic courage, as noted above, and the floodwaters of dialogue about who we as a nation would, could, or should become could not be restrained completely. I work towards the elaboration of this 'psyche in sprawl' by applying the *synthetical* moment (Pinar et al., 1995, 521)—illustrated via "a conceptual gestalt" that is "finally visible" (Pinar, 1994, 27)—of autobiography in hope that it may ultimately reach its emancipatory 'end,' which is, of course, a new beginning.

I focus here as well, then, on civic-cultural struggle and a curriculum of possibility in this moment of social trauma. I approach this, however, by positioning autobiography as an essential feature of currere—the Latin from which the word curriculum is derived, utilized as a verb (as *doing*) in Pinar (2004), as the experiencing and understanding of *what it means* to run the course. It is impossible to locate the course, let alone to run it, when one has lost a sense of self. Worse yet, in this moment, an entire nation suddenly and violently lost its sense of self, stumbling as too many appeared to accept the easy answers proffered by those in power, rather than considering more thoughtfully the alternative possibilities some of our discourses offered. This has had serious consequences for our nation, for its citizens, and for the world.

Autobiography takes the foreground in this civic-cultural struggle because it complicates the conceptualization of this realm as *currere*. Currere "refers to an existential experience of institutional structures" (Pinar et al., 1995, 518) and was conceived as

> a strategy devised to disclose experience, so that we may see more of it and see more clearly. With such seeing can come deepened understanding of the running, and with this, can come deepened agency. (Pinar and Grumet, 1976, p. vii) (Pinar et al., 1995, 518)

It must be said that I am using autobiography in a political-philosophical manner that differs from its conception and development by Pinar, Grumet, Miller, and many others (see Pinar et al., 1995, 515-566), but this work hopefully demonstrates my concern for some of the same issues. Although I am working with a curriculum *not* situated within schooling, but rather in the public sphere as I draw from public, political, and academic discourses immediately following September 11th—and I believe that it is *this* curriculum that has greater import for how we educate ourselves and our children for a democratic future—the aspirations of autobiography and the method of currere have a role to play, I believe, in fostering the development of a healthy public sphere. I wish to address this difference in my approach by considering just a few commonalities.

First, while autobiography of the kind I am aiming at here does *not* attend to the individual emancipatory needs of teachers or students, it does echo some of the themes that emerged in autobiographical work as detailed in Pinar et al. (1995). Grumet's argument that currere acknowledges "Habermas' claim that the political language has driven ideas and impulses undermining its order out of its grammar and into the fragmentary language of the… unconscious" and that "any authentic public political opposition requires political struggle in the terrains of character and identity" (Pinar et al., 1995, 522) informs one of my major contentions, i.e., that a national autobiographical project (whatever its limitations may be) may contribute to the broader dialogue about how the currere of civic-cultural struggle may be constructively pursued, given some commonalities in our experiencing of the nation. The events of September 11th and its aftermath provided some common ground from which the texts taken to compose autobiography here speak, even as they disagree, forming a non-unified 'whole.'

Second, Miller's (1990) notion that "the process of creating an interpretative community in which lived experience can be discovered, expressed, and interpreted is one… of 'creating spaces'" (Pinar et al., 1995, 524) is not lost in this work, but resides in the "chorus" (Grumet, 1990, cited in Pinar et al.,

1995, 523) composed of public, political, and academic discourses contesting meaning in traumatic national autobiographic terrain during a specific social moment. While the space created here may appear to be distanced and abstracted from actual lived experiences of individual human beings, the 'complicated conversation' (Pinar, 2004) presented by these discourses in fact represents the differences, the confusion, the disillusion, and the fears of many in this moment. The autobiography they present to us of a (democratic) nation at risk, then, is by far more representational than the enunciation of national character, identity, and will proffered by those in power, even as the limits of their discourses are taken into consideration. Moreover, because these discourses offer multiple sensibilities and diverse vistas of the state of the nation, of its people(s), and of democracy's crisis in this post-9/11 moment, they reflect the pluralistic nature of our social being and becoming and offer up their voices: voices that reflect much of what the American people were feeling. Their voices, however, are *not* taken to be authoritative, but rather richly and thickly descriptive of public concerns overall, and of particular insights about, and ways of seeing, who we say we are or need to become, more specifically.

Finally, because this autobiography uses a perspectivist lens to reach for a sense of selfhood at the level of the nation, it embraces curriculum as *political text* (see Pinar et al., 1995, 243-314). This is not only intentional; it is unavoidable, given present context. At the same time, given that I have chosen to map this autobiography of the nation vis-à-vis discursive activity for the purposes of considering how to reconceptualize curriculum as a pathway to deeper understandings of civic-cultural struggle on the road to democracy, and that I have elected to do so based on a comparative method embracing postmodern sensibilities, this approach to autobiography speaks as well to curriculum as *poststructuralist, deconstructed, postmodern* text (see Pinar et al., 1995, 450-514). Both of these textual considerations play out fully in this study and in its articulation of a national discursive autobiography deconstructed in terms of a specific social moment and its multi-vocal (multi-textual) nature. This is a point that echoes throughout the work and is specifically addressed in Chapter 7, where the mapping project itself is elaborated.

For the purpose of mapping this autobiography, I focus on two features present in our discourses immediately following September 11th: first, varying epistemological conceptualizations—ways of seeing foundations of citizenship (*Orthodoxy*, *Reason*, and *Perspective*)—as grounds for being/becoming; and second, an axiological reading of modes of civic engagement (*Control*, *Representation*, and *Activism*) for self-defining within the collective and in relation to its governance. The writing of those who exercised civic courage attended to these features, albeit sometimes tacitly. The writing of those positioned within power—whose writing is fully explicit, albeit manipulative and misleading—is also included in this autobiography because their voices ruled the day as they sought to circumscribe or silence all others. And, sadly, their voices also represent *American* narratives that could not, and should not, be ignored.

Since any epistemological framing of the moment in question derives from 'the state of the epistemological unconscious,' it is necessary to deconstruct silence—to engage with our epistemological unconscious by analyzing our extant discourse(s)—in order to articulate civic courage as it emerged within such a scenario. While the task of attending to the epistemological unconscious of a nation is daunting, it seems to me that autobiography as a research genre is well-suited to approach this task, especially when partnered with a comparative approach to inquiry—comparative cartography, or social mapping. I approach this curriculum inquiry project, then, by exploring narratives that emerged in this moment, mapping their conceptual interrelations, and examining the autobiographical contributions they make in order to illuminate the civic-cultural surround *within* post-9/11 America. Thus, elaborating and mapping this intertextual field is construed here as a way to first *illuminate*, and then to *illustrate*, this autobiography of a nation in distress.

The Limits of Human Understanding

Introduction

While power showed its fist in a remarkably public way in this moment, it is also important to note that the silence cannot be construed as deriving exclusively from censorship; that would reduce and distort the curriculum. Bourdieu's discussion of the social constitution of our limits relative to censorship highlights the problem. Again, I extend a manner of reasoning utilized by Bourdieu from the study of science as a field of inquiry to the larger domain of our civic-cultural struggle(s) expressed via autobiography. I do so because the center of discussion is epistemology itself, an epistemology of purported self-knowing at the level of the nation. According to Bourdieu (1992),

> ...the limits of human understanding must be defined... in terms of their social constitution. At every moment, we are limited by social censorship. There are external censors, 'repressions', a term very much in vogue in the 1970s. Any scientific universe is full of instances of such censorship, which prevent certain things from being said. However, among the most rigorous censors, among those which are most difficult to get around, there are the internalized censors, the categories of thought which make a

> whole collection of things unthinkable, the categories of thought which determine that there is only black and white, and that grey areas do not exist. (48-49)

The rhetoric proffered by those in power in this moment indeed announced that there could only be black and white—i.e., that gray areas did not exist—but the questioning insisted upon by those exercising civic courage opened space for such gray areas (which always exist, acknowledged or not) to become part of the public conversation over time. In this text, then, I explore this 'silence' by attending to several layers of meaning construction—and obfuscation—that form some of the 'limits of our human understanding' vis-à-vis the nation. I look into the civic-cultural upheaval within which curricularists labor at this time, and pay particular attention to those venues whose discourses contributed alternatives to the *Orthodoxy* and *Control* espoused by triumphal discourse (and its hypernational vanguard, in a more *active* voice) in the autobiographical project we were (and are yet today) pursuing.

I problematize, in this chapter, the relationship between the public's desire for *belief* (and for its corollaries, *order* and *certainty*) versus the role of academics in the university setting pursuing inquiry that often reflects high levels of ambiguity and uncertainty. I also provide a brief review of caveats for knowledge work relevant to specific sites of knowledge production, or knowledge *nodes*. I employ a language that reconsiders citizenship from a cultural perspective and involves cultural qua political aspects of our varying senses of what it means to be citizens, which include issues of individual identity and of belonging, but also of collective coherence and community. I explore knowledge nodes, or venues, that are affected by this civic-cultural upheaval, especially their role in 'writing the history' of these events for the nation.

This leads me to consider discourse about the nation as an *imagined community* and the role of the media in shoring up the symbolic boundaries of 'nation-ness' (Anderson, 1991, 3). I also consider, albeit tangentially, the role of global electronic media in 'decentering' the nation, thus contributing to the erosion of the nation's symbol-ordering capabilities and to the emergence of new symbolic systems emanating from post-national "communities of sentiment" (Appadurai, 1996, 8) (see Chapter 4). Later, I explore the emergence of 'virtual democracy' and 'virtual community' as entities that are removed from specific localities of identity and/or belonging due to their positioning within a *virtual* mode of activity, and yet are heralded by some as viable avenues for reclaiming democratic space (e.g., Barber, 2004) (see Chapter 8).

My purpose in problematizing these knowledge nodes is to amplify understanding of social imagination as creative socio-cultural activity. My ultimate aim is to consider how new imaginaries may move us towards innovative social action to enhance the prospects of a democratic future—i.e., to achieve the *synthetical* moment in the autobiographical process, the moment where, having taken the elements of national autobiography apart for analytic purposes, we put them back together to achieve new understandings (Pinar et al., 1995, 521; Pinar, 1994, 26-27).

I frame the knowledge nodes explored here as the terrain through which a complex curriculum has worked, and continues to work, to shroud us in silence. To deconstruct the silence requires *excavating* (Foucault, 1972; Nicholson-Goodman and Paulston, 1996) the autobiographical possibilities embedded in this terrain, which I approach by bringing alternative narratives into the light and relating them to layers of meaning-construction that compose the civic-cultural surround as a space of struggle. This is the work of social (or comparative) cartography, or social mapping (Nicholson-Goodman, 1996, 2006, 2007; Paulston, 1993, 1995, 1996, 2005; Paulston, Liebman, and Nicholson-Goodman, 1996), which I address below (see Chapter 3). And yet, simply *seeing* components of this curriculum will not suffice in and of itself. Dialogue—of the unfettered and reflexive kind—is a core element of deliberative democracy (Gutmann, 1999), an element that we cannot afford to discard, especially in the face of post-democratic tendencies. Therefore, if we want to move beyond silence, we need to build a curriculum of voice—indeed, of many voices, one that engages us in social dialogue about this tragic moment and our responses to it from multiple perspectives. This text seeks to complicate the conversation (Pinar, 2004) in such a way as to expand that dialogue.

I also bear in mind Apple's plea for "alternative visions *bearing witness* to the negativity of existing patterns of interaction and knowledge to give this critique more power" and his assertion that "the knowledgeable critique, the standing in witness, is the prior act" [emphasis in original] (1975, 91). We need to explore how and to what extent we may ensure that our children have access to the tools of democracy, to educational and life experiences that equip them to sustain and defend authentic democratic vision, especially in times of crisis and adversity. Such an aim, I believe, requires critical, interpretive, and imaginative forms of inquiry and practice. My goals here are, then, to 'bear witness' to the silence, to attend to layers of meaning that dwell (and vie for legitimacy) in our national autobiography, and to investigate the role of *possibility* in 'cracking the seal' on our 'unified' stance (Gergen, 2002, 151), a stance that begged credulity from its inception, given our history of tensions, frictions, and outright conflicts. While we desperately need to exercise civic courage as citizens of a democracy in distress, our views of what that means and how we are to go about it differ (and will continue to do so) depending upon citizens' civic-cultural proclivities. The full range of such proclivities *define*, taken as a multifaceted whole, our sense of ourselves as a nation.

While our presumed leadership's politics and policies bear detailed scrutiny, they are only my concern here to the extent that they forged an oppressive civic-cultural surround based on the extreme self-interest of the privileged (reflecting an elite class-consciousness), a corporatist culture that held the people in check through secrecy, Machiavellian machinations, and unmitigated triumphalist bravado, even as the public was enduring its trauma(s) in the dark. We will be fortunate, indeed, if this ideology shows itself incapable of prolonging the effects it desires, as Klein (2007) suggests, but that does not mean the struggle is over, only that we will need to regroup along better pathways, to begin anew. Rather than reviewing this administration's 'legacy,' I foreground how citizens depict the meaning of such politics and policies, how this reflects national autobiographical propensities, and how such autobiographical work may impact the mutilation that occurs as a result of the epistemology of resentment currently in operation. I am concerned with the failure of the *public* and of the public sphere following September 11th, and of the national autobiographical propensities that make such a scenario possible.

It may be the case, in fact, that we are experiencing post-democracy as a nascent phase of totalitarianism, what Giroux (2004) calls 'proto-fascism' (9-32). Alarmingly, specific efforts have been made (and continue today) to target certain kinds of knowledge work for silencing where the agenda promoted by those in power is questioned or resisted (see, e.g., Lather, 2004; Lincoln and Cannella, 2004). The road to fascism does not lie far from the authoritarian pathway we are presently treading (although Arendt (1968) clearly delineates the differences between these power-centric formulations). While I fully appreciate the danger inherent in such negative tendencies, I offer that the silence has more than one face, and that its multiple facets need to be brought into view and considered publicly. I seek to accomplish this task by bringing discursive activity (*writing*) (Barthes, 1989) displaying civic courage to the foreground, a task that I believe is essential for curricularists in our times. I also bring forward the 'hidden' meanings of discourses of power, exposing their underpinnings to render them visible as they are re-conceptualized in relation to alternative discourses exhibiting civic courage.

It bears mentioning that academics, per Dahl (1999), "have a social and political significance" because they "rationalize, make a discourse of what is felt, known, etc." relative to "the members of society" (10). They are not "legislators," Dahl insists, that is, they do not "have much influence on the political situation and the social development" (10) of the nation. However, they are "probably the best interpreters and thermometers that we have access to" (11). According to Harvey (1996), perhaps more than any other group, academics "process and influence the reception of serious cultural products," focusing "rather strongly on the meaning and qualities of community, nation, and place" (325). Our knowledge work, then, serves reflective purposes in our endangered (democratic) republic worthy of respect, purposes that sometimes require a little courage, but we cannot pretend to be alone at the table, and we must find ways to open out, rather than close down, our multi-vocal dialogue. For this reason, I elaborate in this chapter the problematic situating of the university vis-à-vis public will.

Sites of Knowledge Production as Culturally-Situated Nodes

> I think that we are all provincials, enclosed in particular intellectual traditions, and that we are all threatened by a form of intellectual ethnocentrism. Perhaps it is because the systems of concepts… through which we organize reality are in part the product of scholastic traditions. If one wanted to advance a modern version of the theory of national character… it would begin, for me, with a theory of the educational systems in as much as they are formative of the structures of understanding, and constructive of our taxonomies. (Bourdieu, 1992, 39)

Having articulated my concerns about the silence within which knowledge workers labor today, I turn my attention now to segments of the public sphere—*knowledge nodes*—as venues that could have served effectively as sites of resistance to our 'new' reign of silence, but tragically failed to do so. The questions I raise throughout this work about these venues address tensions within our society that we never quite resolve; we simply cope with them in different ways at different times. They therefore present us with a forum for ongoing discussion.

The internal choices we face are always framed according to the dynamic realities and influences shaping the languages produced in the public sphere, with education caught in the fray of disputes over how meaning is made (e.g., what shape knowledge should take), but never truly controlling the dialogue itself. It is important not to confuse education with schooling, especially in our times, since the '(mis-)education of the American public' (Pinar, 2004) takes place on multiple fronts, while schools, teachers, students, parents, and sometimes entire communities serve on the front lines of the battleground. Meaning choices abound in the public sphere and constitute a menu of options for the work of social imagination. Even in these dark times they are capable of offering hope for engendering alternatives for social action. As such, they pose ontological choices for us as well, raising the all-important question—i.e., *who will we choose to become*, both for ourselves and for our young, with our fellow citizens, and in the world? Failure to address that question—based on the assumption that we already have the (correct) answer—is one major problem underlying the silence, as noted. For this reason, autobiographical work that both anticipates and makes space for difference and struggle holds promise for the work of social imagination.

As I lay the groundwork for this autobiography, I resolve to paint this rough portrait in broad brushstrokes, articulating a profile of civic-cultural concerns formed by the tensions driving the dynamics of present context. My goal here is not only to make visible particular manifestations of the epistemology of 'resentment,' but also to make visible alternative imaginings of our society. I raise such concerns for our general consideration because they are related, in both direct and indirect ways, to the civic-cultural upheaval within which these knowledge nodes operate. They indicate a messy, disputatious terrain that is not that far removed from its moorings in the past. In my efforts to make sense of various discourses addressing the contours of this terrain, I must acknowledge that I am wading in deep waters as I cross disciplinary boundaries. This task I undertake nevertheless as artist/citizen/scholar (Nicholson-Goodman, 2006), a stance reiterated here as I engage in a 'line of flight' (Reynolds and Webber, 2004) approach to curriculum inquiry to inform a praxis of imagination. As I explore discourses from multiple disciplines to inform the autobiographical project, I make no claim to contribute to scholarship outside of my field.

While autobiography as I frame it here is a study of the *within*, I augment the rich terrain of this post-9/11 excavation of the inward journey by examining as well complicating factors in the sociocultural and geopolitical spatial surround (the *beyond*) within which it is situated. Therefore, several external scenarios further complicating the civic-cultural surround within which this journey takes place—and exacerbating the tensions already fostered by our internal culture wars—also come into play in this text. This leads me to consider their reach and scope as a backdrop for our autobiographical disputes. First among these is the intrusion of global consciousness, which sometimes appears to be more conscious of *itself* than it is of the world, even though it more realistically reflects a hybridity produced at the intersection of the global and the local (Robertson, 1992). Second, the cultural politics of post-colonialism and post-nationalism have provided new and relevant optics for framing this surround (Appadurai, 1996; Barber, 2001; Bhabha, 1994). This is increasingly important as the global becomes both promise *and* threat (Barber, 2001) and the American public operates within a new ethos based on *fear* rather than possibility (Barber, 2004). Third, Beck's (1992) depiction of social and political change within a risk society paradigm shift shows an uncanny resemblance to our current transition to a security state paradigm re-ordered by the production and distribution of new kinds of risks and hazards (e.g., terrorist threats against the nation).[3] Finally, Porter's (1999) analysis of a global *era of uncer-*

tainty in education, which demonstrates its own tendency to re-order both public and official thinking about what schooling is for, leads him to conclude that a diminished role for schooling as an agent of social change is the result. The global advance of neo-liberalism and neo-conservatism as joint projects reflecting their own blurred boundaries appear to be at the helm of such re-orderings (Giroux, 2004; Harvey, 2005; Porter, 1999).

These external characteristics of contemporary life in a global context, compounded by increasingly disturbing internal dimensions of national life, deeply influence how we see ourselves as a nation and consequently play into our ways of seeing the role of education in society. They have become, in short, core elements in the shaping of our nation's autobiography and, as a result, in currere. Therefore, I attend to the knowledge nodes whose languages are used to derive the autobiography as affected segments of a national civic-cultural surround that is simultaneously subject to its own internal disputes, to the complications of the intrusion of global consciousness, to the refraction effects of imaginaries that are post-colonial and post-national in nature, and to some new features—introduced by a paradigm of risk and risk 'management'—of the contested terrain we call *home*.

Knowledge Production in Fragile Space(s)

Among the knowledge nodes explored in this study, the university is my primary concern, because it is a premiere setting for these internal disputes, for the intrusion of global consciousness and the refraction effects of post-national imaginings, and, increasingly, for the ultimate negative impact of the neo-liberal/neo-conservative global agenda as well. Universities are part of a global exchange that necessarily puts them at the center of this scenario. The kinds of knowledge work conducted within this setting have always depended upon intercourse with knowledge work conducted across time and space. The effects of this cannot be overstated. The academy is held accountable not just to the nation, but to the world of knowledge production in general in a way that causes our boundaries to be perhaps more porous than those of any other setting. Therefore, in a moment where those in power appear to increasingly espouse withdrawal to their own internal sense of what's right and appropriate for the world, rejecting any influence from beyond their imposed limits, the university is caught in a double bind—one formed both by its perceived position as a mediator of new understandings, and also as an institution whose knowledge is always and increasingly interlaced with influences from beyond the nation.

To briefly illustrate this point, let us consider Popkewitz and Brennan's (1998) discussion, in *Foucault's Challenge*, of a "new sea-migration of social theories from France and Germany" (5), theories that call for "different intellectual practices than those found in previous critical traditions in the social sciences" (6). Speaking of an emergent trend that looks at "the constitutive role of knowledge in the construction of social life," the authors explore "social epistemology"—"a specific scholarship that focuses on the relation of power, knowledge, and change" (8). They explain that

> Epistemology provides a context in which to consider the rules and standards that organize perceptions, ways of responding to the world, and the conceptions of "self." Concurrently, social epistemology locates the objects constituted as the knowledge of schooling as historical practices through which power relations can be understood. ... The conception of epistemology, then, is... an effort to understand the conditions in which knowledge is produced. (9)

My efforts in this text are attuned to understanding 'the conditions in which knowledge is produced,' an understanding without which we could neither begin to comprehend the curriculum being enunciated for us in the revised civic-cultural surround of post-9/11 America, nor the vision and potential of alternative autobiographical possibilities in this new American wilderness.

Popkewitz and Brennan offer that "social epistemology studies speech as effects of power" (9). Consequently, I treat the discourses from which our narratives of the nation are drawn as windows that show us particular *vistas* of national being/becoming as the 'effects of power,' and I scrutinize these vistas in relation to the power of the particular social imaginaries from which they draw breath. Popkewitz and Brennan assert that "knowledge of the world as 'learning' is not only about interpretation" (9), framing it additionally in these terms:

> The psychological visioning of the world is also a revisioning of the "self." ... A social epistemology enables us to consider the word *learning* not as standing alone, but as embodying a range of historically constructed values, priorities, and dispositions toward how one should see and act toward the world. (9)

This is consistent with Pinar's use of autobiography, and this work seeks—by analyzing and mapping social discourses to illuminate and illustrate post-9/11 American autobiography—to reach some understanding of the ways in which we might see the two-fold curriculum: the one that emerges from *within*, and also the one that surrounds us, the *beyond*. My ultimate purpose is to shed light on the possibilities offered by critical, interpretive, and imaginative discourses in relation to self, nation and world. In order to pursue this work, however, it is necessary to problematize various knowledge nodes, and here I employ this theoretical approach—social epistemology—because it approaches the study of knowledge *as social practice*. Popkewitz and Brennan locate social epistemology in the grander scheme of knowledge production itself:

> Social epistemological theory is... understood as situated within a broad, multidisciplinary conversation about the project of social science and history. This intellectual project is... a strategy to focus on theory as an epistemological problem; that is, it provides a way of orienting and of problematizing the social conditions in which contemporary social life is constructed... It is to treat theory, as does Bourdieu... as a "thinking tool"... (11)

I map and elaborate discourses that construct our ideas about who we are and how the world looks to us from within the post-9/11 nation, highlighting responses to enunciative power to view more fully what emerging alternative social imaginaries might have to offer. I attend to social epistemology here as I reach for autobiographical elaboration because:

> The strategy of a social epistemology... [makes] the problem of study that of the knowledge that inscribes agents. The terrain of social and educational theory is with a "critical," problematizing theory that focuses on the construction of knowledge itself... It makes problematic how the objects of the world are historically constructed and change over time. Such a strategy... is a political theory as well as a theory of knowledge, as the two are inseparable. The effect is to disturb narratives of progress and reconciliation, finding questions where others had located answers (Dean, 1994). (11-12)

The direction of this inquiry, then, is both epistemological *and* political in part because 'the two are inseparable,' but more importantly, because I 'disturb narratives of progress and reconciliation' cynically foisted upon us by those who sought to cement their vision of America in the public mind and to *enforce* their 'one true narrative' of being American in this moment. I engage with a multiplicity of perspectives as I work with autobiographical narrative(s) of the nation, rather than relying solely on this enunciation.

Further, I attend to the selected knowledge nodes as venues within which tensions emerge and often endure. Each constitutes a setting within which knowledge work is performed; each *contains* a set of disputes, or tensions, that interact, to some extent, with the larger sphere in which it operates. Each presents its own conundrums that must be grappled with in order to make sense of the knowledge work attempted within it, or produced by it. Finally, each node is instrumental in some way in contributing to the *range of possibilities* from which the work of social imagination may draw. What has been often noted in narratives about this moment is a rather general failure of imagination, and yet we have been seeking to make sense of the moment itself almost from its initial occurrence, in various ways and from multiple sites of knowing.

Competition for legitimacy between various rationales for making sense of the moment (in short, competing enunciations of what the events of September 11th and their aftermath *mean* for America)—and the predominance of an enunciation that sought to silence alternative ways of seeing—lie at the core of this work.

As a result, I seek here to provide at least some initial thoughts as well about the central issue of where imagination might lead us as it leads us beyond silence (see Chapter 9). My central concern in this respect is simply to sketch out the problematiques of what is seen as a period of civic-cultural upheaval for illustrative purposes. Further, by attending to social imagination as a form of social activity connected to social action, I seek to further complicate the knowledge/power nexus inherent in these venues and thus critique their legitimation, their validation. I begin this discussion by examining the university as social space.

The University as Social Space: Desire for Belief, Academic Freedom and the Power/Knowledge Nexus

> The impulse to intolerance arises out of the wish to believe, which is an ever present and powerful force in the human psyche. Never far from the surface in social interactions, it is a continual threat to democratic societies and to respecting fundamental principles of human decency. It attacks at every point of disagreement, insisting on conformity of every outward action, including speech, and frequently attempts to control the inner world of the mind as well. It is capable of producing the most vicious behavior human beings are capable of... (Bollinger, 2000, 35)

Admonitions or caveats about knowledge work are an important place to start in this deconstructive process, mainly because they provide us with a framing both of the nature of tensions within knowledge work itself and of the limitations within which we work. I work here with two essays about academic freedom from *Unfettered Expression*, a compilation of lectures given at the University of Michigan between 1991 and 1999 (Hollingsworth, 2000) to honor three of their faculty members summoned in 1954 by the House Un-American Activities Committee (HUAC) during an on-campus visit. Refusing to testify or claiming Fifth Amendment protection before HUAC in those McCarthy years, two professors had their appointments suspended, the third was censured. The resulting conference—*The Davis, Markert, Nickerson Lecture Series*—was established decades later, after all three had left the University of Michigan, two of them having left the country to distinguish themselves in Canadian universities. Not surprisingly, the lectures take academic and intellectual freedom as their theme.

The 'danger of belief' is identified by Bollinger (2000) as an element of "the fabric that is our culture," one that impacts our everyday lives (35). Asserting that "the daily acts of every one of us create an atmosphere far more powerful than the official acts we so often focus on" (35), Bollinger speaks of the connection between intolerance and the desire for belief—that 'powerful force in the human psyche' that threatens democratic society, offering further that "this wary vision of the human personality is a profoundly important theme" both in American traditions and in "Western political and social theory," especially in discussions of freedom of speech (35).

> The history of censorship of speech, and of persecution (or punishment) of those who hold and express those ideas, has produced some of the most eloquent and insightful observations about the human desire... to demand that others conform to your way of thinking and to rid the world of those who would not. .... But belief and the impulse to intolerance lead us not only to throw speakers into the flames... but also to insist on having our way in every decision about ordering the society. Writers of social and political theory, therefore, often also express the same fears about the hegemonic tendencies of belief. (35-36)

How do fears about 'the hegemonic tendencies of belief' play out in the pluralist, open-minded work of the academy, as compared with how they play out in everyday life? In Bollinger, is "the essence of life—the "collision of values"—a collision that can account for the "tensions of real life"? (39) After considering pluralism as an answer to this human dilemma, Bollinger resolves that in everyday life we see "an end to tolerance, an end to the open-mindedness of the posture of 'pluralism,' a point at which it is proper, even required, that one insist on having your way, insist that others comply" (39).

Turning his attention to the special role of the university (whose raison d'etre is not, according to Bollinger, based on principles that operate in everyday life), he claims that pluralism is nevertheless an essential component of academic life:

> ...the principle of academic freedom or intellectual and artistic values, involves a profoundly important process of suspension of belief, which produces an open mind and a sympathetic imagination that bravely explores the paths of human thought and experience, as well as nature, without reserve. It is not standardless; it is guided by notions of reason and truth. But it is continuously self-reflective... about what we take to be "reason" and "truth." Intellectuals, artists, scientists, are watchers—always looking for what seems to make no sense, for what's surprising, for what's foreign, for what's hidden. (43)

Bollinger asserts that another path to 'reason' and 'truth' exists, and situates knowledge work at the university in relation to this path:

> The life of action, of commitment to belief ...has its own way too of giving off the sparks of truth. But the approach of intellectual freedom is one distinctive method, and in a world so largely organized around the other approach the special character of the university is all the more useful to preserve, as wilderness is so much more precious in an urbanized life. ... Additionally, the special world of intellectual and artistic freedom in the university also stands as a fixed warning for the rest of society that the commitment to belief has its excesses and must be moderated with self-doubt. (44)

In Bollinger, the academy serves a special purpose in society, standing as a 'fixed warning' against the excesses of belief. Academic freedom is to be preserved and protected much in the same way we aspire to protect our wilderness spaces, and for very similar reasons. While a 'point' exists in *society* where conformity can be 'required,' per Bollinger, the university occupies a special social space, one where the process of suspended belief is more appropriate. There is, however, a cost involved.

Characterizing the university as home to a certain manner of knowledge work—the self-reflexive kind, the kind that questions its own limits—he sees this space as therefore separate from the 'real world.' Due to the special nature of its place in society, the university has something of inestimable value to offer. Nevertheless, he sees this social space as one that is highly vulnerable:

> The ideal of academic freedom is a way of life. It exercises and emphasizes certain sides of the personality, of the mind, and those parts, through exercise, gain strength and prominence. ... The suspension of belief, the openness to ideas ...is achieved only through a process that involves some mental distancing from the real world consequences of choices, from pain and suffering, in the way that a surgeon develops a numbness to the knife. Most importantly, the capacity for fixed commitment and decisive action tends to atrophy with a developed character of self-doubt and open-mindedness. And the capacities for dealing with a less-than-perfect world, and a less self-doubting world, are also diminished. (45-46)

Framing the university in this fashion, he articulates ambivalence between the will to act and the commitment to belief, on the one hand, and the development of self-doubt and sympathetic imagination, on the other. What he is struggling with here is the *sociopolitical* role of academics, and he ends with this caveat:

> ...we must understand... that the soul of academic freedom... resides not in particular rules or outcomes but in a spirit with which we approach life. It is a spirit that is born of a wariness of the dangers of belief, but that recognizes the importance of belief and commitment too. It is a spirit that while stretching in one direction, for perfectly good social reasons, lives comfortably with the disabling consequences of that course. Above all else, it seeks a capacity of understanding of the world, and of the consequences of our actions in it... (48)

In Bollinger, then, academics labor within a double bind—working for greater understanding supported by the principles of academic freedom, while appreciating the limitations of such a path. He apparently sees us as thus somewhat 'disabled' relative to belief and commitment. As noted, his special concerns for academic freedom have to do with the role of the university in upholding the spirit of academic freedom, a spirit that 'recognizes' its own inherent contradiction.

Pratt (2000) also concerns herself with the role and responsibilities of academics, but from a slightly different vantage point:

> Alexis de Tocqueville thought Americans the least philosophical citizens in the Western world but nevertheless a people of great certainties. Although they appealed only to the individual efforts of their own understanding, they did so with sublime confidence. The American practice "of fixing the standard of their judgment in themselves alone" led them to "readily conclude that everything in the world may be explained, and that nothing in it transcends the limits of understanding" (1956, 144). Whether in religion or politics, they found their assurances within themselves. The business of their science was to discover truth and put it into practice. Their plain and direct way of speaking assumed that language could tell it like it is. Their predilection for engineering rested on the certainty that... all things were commensurable. In 1831, perhaps only a prescient Frenchman like Tocqueville would have dared to deconstruct American certainties. (99)

Pratt's portrayal of the cultural surround derives from that famous visitor's description almost two centuries ago. Has America changed much since 1831? She doesn't appear to believe that it has, arguing that the nature of our society—represented by 'an equilibrium of contradictions'—runs like a continuous thread through to the present day, especially within the academy:

> In such a society both knowledge and opinion were held in an equilibrium of contradictions: knowledge one did not have was viewed with suspicion, but knowledge one did have was truth. ... Universities would, of course, be revered or reviled, depending on whether they confirmed one's knowledge and conviction or denied them. Academic freedom, the special condition that was to permit colleges and universities the free expression of ideas without threat of punitive action, carries within its traditions these same contradictions. For some, academic freedom is justified because faculty have truths to tell, and the truth and its prophets must be protected. For others, academic freedom is the condition necessary for the revision of truth by skeptics and dissenters from the accepted wisdom. Academic freedom then exists precisely because the truth is not certain, or stable, and the intellectual work of the academy is always to challenge our understandings. (99-100)

Pratt considers the period during which the newly formed American Association of University Professors (AAUP) were charged with preparing the

1915 "General Declaration of Principles" that was to define both "the principles and the practices of academic freedom" (104). It was a time when uncertainty appeared to be a central social theme, and she offers that

> From one perspective the history of academic disciplines in this century has been the story of certainties becoming unglued. "Things fall apart; the centre cannot hold," the poet Yeats writes in 1920, reflecting on a world whose principles of order seemed to be dissolving. In discipline after discipline we can trace the unfolding of scientific and theoretical developments that introduced uncertainty where certainty had once prevailed. (101)

She approaches academic freedom from the vantage point of working within uncertainty as well because of Lynne Cheney's (1992) "parting shot at the professoriate on leaving her post at the National Endowment for the Humanities" (100), a pamphlet entitled 'Telling the truth.' In this pamphlet, Cheney argues that without objectivity, without certainty, there is no basis for academic freedom, since the lack of truth leaves us only with opinions, "the advocacy of which translates as politics" (100). For Pratt, that assertion doesn't hold: "Cheney's logic is... profoundly American as she reflects the assurances Tocqueville described when she draws on her own understanding and from that point publicly and powerfully judges the world" (101). Pratt ignores the ideology behind Cheney's assertion, and instead characterizes Cheney's logic as *peculiarly American* in de Tocqueville's terms. More importantly, she critiques the ignorance or disregard Cheney shows for the 'principles and practices' she attacks, a disregard that reflects

> a deep misunderstanding of intellectual work. The nature of academic discourse and the freedom that protects it never depended in principle or practice on certainties. If truth were our currency, we would have little need for academic freedom... truth is not stable or absolute, and academic freedom protects the space in which to revise and reconsider it. Where "truth" cannot have, indeed must not have, the status of ideology or dogma, the highest standards of intellectual freedom must prevail—that is, the freedom to pursue alternative truth, to ask the shattering questions, to challenge the status quo, to critique hallowed beliefs, to expose error, and to redefine what knowledge is in light of new learning. In short, to be uncertain. The uniqueness of the academy in society is to house just these unsettling and always revisionary forays into the untrammeled spaces of thought. (101)

Pratt's defense of these academic 'principles and practices' does not lead her to place the academy on an ivory pedestal, however. Her purpose appears to be reflective—she pauses to consider our culpability as knowledge workers in contributing to the current ill ease manifest in society today. Acknowledging that the academy does not "always manage either to judge wisely or to withstand interference," she speaks about these discrepancies as well:

> If our principles and practices have always reflected a concept of academic freedom that protected both the truth claims and the truth questions, if academic freedom was always defined in communal decisions of participants in the field, how is it that we have sometimes faltered so far from our ideal, and how is it that a public that appears to grant us this space in thought so often thinks that we violate our own principles? The answer, I believe, lies in a loss of the traditional equilibrium or balance that stabilized disciplinary changes even when confronted with theoretical upheaval. In practice... until recently most academics in this century still wrote and published as if uncertainties were nonexistent. Now, they do not. The uncertainties that had in theory redefined the meaning of knowledge have now significantly redefined the nature of disciplinary work in many fields. (110)

Further complicating this scenario, Pratt turns to problems emerging from the power relations of institutions of higher learning themselves, which are undergoing rapid change.

> The traditional university, which was an instrument of emancipation through education, now also serves the economic and corporate power structure, which has little interest in the free exchange of ideas and little patience with the niceties of academic practice. The pace of change is unsettling, and many of the directions we see the university taking are unwelcome. (110)

Yes, Pratt argues, we are culpable, in that academics have conveyed knowledge as though its truths are singular, eschewing uncertainty and offering knowledge as though it could be known and communicated through a paradigm that is 'certain,' even though the opposite obtains, reflecting longstanding traditions of doubt and self-doubt. However, she continues, the eroding academic surround within which we work is also to blame, since the direction and pace of change are being imposed from outside the university, adding to its internal upheaval. For Pratt, the academy's relations with the public, on the one hand, and with the corporate order, on the other, lie at the core of this upheaval. This is not only a credible argument, but an essential one.

It is one thing to work with uncertainty as academics, suspending belief, questioning purpose, etc. It is something quite different, however, to deal with uncertainty where it collides with the desired 'aims' of the 'economic and corporate power structure' so prevalent in higher education now—what Pinar (2004) refers to as "this 'business' model of education" (xi). This is because this structure serves a Machine (Deleuze and Guattari, 1987) that tends to dismiss knowledge work where it fails to serve utilitarian ends, thus circumscribing entire areas of study except where there is some formulaic payoff. It is appropriate here to consider Apple's (1975) assertion that this utilitarian mode has powerful social and cultural influence:

> the dominant consciousness in advanced industrial societies is centered on a vulgar instrumentality—a logical structure that places at its foundation the search for certainty, order, the cooptation of significant social dissent, process/product reasoning, therapy to treat surface symptoms rather than basic structural change, and the search for even more efficient instrumentality. It, thereby, vitiates or redefines into less potent issues the political, ethical, and even esthetic questions of any moment. Hence, politics and manipulation become coequal; education and the guaranteeing of certainty in human interaction become synonymous. (90)

Conflating education with 'the guaranteeing of certainty in human interaction' may take on serious (and frightening) dimensions, undermining the university—and its tradition of academic freedom—as a social space dedicated to exploration and examination of multiple possible realities and truths. This conflict, in Pratt, produces a new collision, one that involves the public. She offers the following analysis, speaking both of present crises in knowledge work and of its future as well, with particular concern for the relationship between knowledge work in the academy and the American public's desire for belief in what she calls an "age of extremes" (113):

> Our universities are on a collision course with the American psyche because the public wants certainties, dividends, skills, information that will stabilize the future for our culture... our theoretical, philosophical, and scientific understanding is increasingly that the nature of knowledge is problematic and contingent. Increasingly, we shall need our academic freedom to protect the space in which to be uncertain, the space in which to hang possibilities that do not reconcile, the space in which to explore the connections that might be built between differences, the space in which to adjudicate an ethical outcome when opinions are in conflict. ... The tragic irony of our time is that at this historical moment in which consensus is a virtual impossibility, our society idealizes it, almost demands it, at the same time it makes television entertainment out of our discord. (113)

The critical dimension here is a struggle between desire for belief (*orthodoxy*), which tends towards silencing of difference, on the one hand, and suspended belief, expressed in open-mindedness and 'a sympathetic imagination,' which tends towards more authentic and more diverse understandings (*perspective*), on the other. Mediating between the two is left to long-standing traditions within knowledge work performed in the academy: study, research, theorization, experimentation, observation, argumentation, persuasion, and debate (*reason*) carried out by those whose lot it is to 'hold the fort' against incursions against and intrusions into the sacred territory of academic freedom.

Can we postulate, then, that knowledge and, by extension, knowledge-workers, are 'innocent,' apolitical, sufficiently 'distanced' from power? The response, from a number of directions, is negative. Apple (1975), for instance, asserts that "schools are not mirrors of society, they are society" (90), and, further, that educators are (or should be) critical actors as

> members of a larger collectivity whose values provide the fundamental framework for their thought and action. ...any critical act in an educational sense is by necessity an act that is critical of the dominant normative structure of the larger society. ...the sense that education is always moral and political activity in some degree must be the constitutive framework from which any committed educator can act. ... New ways of talk can only emerge from the dialectic of language and the generation of altered community. And this can only be generated if the negativity of the existing community is shown. (91)

Whereas Bollinger and Pratt argue that the university is a kind of 'sacred space' where academic freedom must be protected, Apple underscores the connectedness between educators and society and, most saliently, the role of public intellectuals in showing us 'the negativity of the existing community.' Seeing the act of 'educating' as 'moral and political activity' requiring 'the dialectic of language and the generation of altered community,' his vision is one that embraces 'everyday life,' and rejects Bollinger's isolated, other-worldly role in society for academics. His vision, therefore, may also be seen to foreshadow Pratt's 'collision course with the American psyche.'

Others urge acknowledgment of *location* within the knowledge/power nexus, along with disclosure of the implications of such locatedness, to protect this freedom. This argument is particularly cogent, for instance, in Blacker (1998), who tackles this problematique head-on, addressing Foucault's work as a discourse that has "particular relevance and importance to—and is even tailor-made for—intellectuals engaged in research within an institutional setting such as the contemporary university" (348). Arguing that "Foucault's more concrete remarks on ethics turn out to concern the subject position from which they are for the most part uttered, namely, that of the institution-bound intellectual," Blacker examines "the paradigm case... not unlike that of Foucault himself, Professor of the History of Systems of Thought at the Sorbonne," characterizing Foucault's position as that of "a purveyor of university supported and legitimated research" (350). From such a position, per Blacker, Foucault had to "be somewhat guarded in his prescriptions," not in the sense of keeping silent, but rather, in the sense of "a very deliberate circumscribing of the group to whom he addresses himself" (350). Blacker, however, is not ascribing the same disability to Foucault that Bollinger presupposes for all academics.

To the contrary, Blacker reiterates Foucault's positioning when he asserts that "a far more promising theoretical response is to concentrate on power's 'microphysics'" (356). Noting Foucault's "supposition that power operates at every level of the social body," he seeks to chart "a viable course for social change," and finds that "the proper level of analysis is a worm's-eye view"—i.e., that "power must be considered from the 'bottom up'" (356). Seeking a means to address the knowledge/power nexus from a micro-level positioning, Blacker offers that "at power's local extremities, its obfuscatory 'veil of administrative decency' to a great extent may be stripped away" (356) and he affirms Foucault's recommendation:

> "What is needed is a study of power in its external visage, at the point where it is in direct or immediate relationship with that which we can provisionally call its object, its target, its field of application" (Foucault, 1980, p. 97). (357)

Conceptualizing who we say we are as a nation, I argue, may best be approached via autobiography, revealing aspects of our being/becoming that reflect our responses to the 'external visage' of power applied in this social moment through the imposition of the *triumphal* narrative as an 'invisible curriculum code' (Lundgren, 1983, cited in Kemmis, 1986).

Blacker, further, offers two salient points worthy of note here: first, that "one's idea of what one is struggling against has a direct impact on what one *becomes* as one struggles," a notion that leads him, "from a strategic point of view" to urge that we should "get away from state-bound power theories"; and second, that "one who aspires to articulate emancipation must acquire a certain theoretical modesty" (357). He explains that

> Given power's (lack of a) nature, one should not expect to be able to utter much about it that holds universally. If the goal is an "autonomous, noncentralized kind of theoretical production, one... whose validity is not dependent on the approval of the established regimes of thought," one should not try to utter liberatory discourse from an authoritative subject position (Foucault, 1980c, 81). For instance, some of Foucault's most vitriolic remarks are aimed at theorists... who try to legitimate their ideas as "scientific"—thereby cashing in on science's aura of authority. One can, of course, still theorize, provided one is ever-mindful of the "tyranny of globalising discourses with their hierarchy and... privileges of a theoretical *avant-garde*" (Foucault, 1980c, 83). The point is that the theoretician... no longer represents a privileged site for articulating emancipatory discourse. (357)

Academics, then, per Blacker, are as deeply implicated in power structures as is the state or institution that wields its power from above. The difference is that where researchers will acknowledge the limitations their positioning places upon them, they may conceptualize and situate their work in such a way as to preserve both its integrity and its authenticity. Qualitative inquiry, in general, is based on this notion. Such an acknowledgment affects both the manner in which knowledge work may be approached and the limitations within which it may be conducted. Here the knowledge-power nexus dictates to some extent what the knowledge worker may do and how she may do it to avoid the contradictions between the writing itself and 'privileges of a theoretical avant-garde.'

The 'theoretical modesty' to which Blacker refers—the avoiding of enunciations of universal applicability by adopting the more modest scope of examining social life, social thought, etc., from a 'worm's-eye view'—informs this study and is hopefully evidenced in its execution. At the same time, the need to balance theoretical modesty with the prospect of challenging the hegemonic enunciation of power in post-9/11 America places me on a theoretical tightrope as I engage in the moral-political activity of illuminating and illustrating this autobiography. Therefore, the methods of approach I employ here are of utmost importance, just as disclosure of self in relation to my notion of changed community is essential. The moral-political aspects of this study are threaded throughout the text, and are explicitly addressed as I introduce social mapping as a mode of analysis (see Chapter 3). For the purpose of disclosing self in relation to community, my opening and closing narratives should indicate how conducting this work reflects my sense of 'altered community.'

3

Social Cartography

A 'LINE OF FLIGHT' FOR CURRICULUM INQUIRY

Because social cartography allows the comparison of multiple views and contested codes in heuristic constructs, it will also have potential to serve as a metaphorical device for the provisional representation and iconographic unification of warring cultures and disputatious communities. Every social map is the product of its makers and open to continuous revision and interrogation. In the process of mapping meaning, the subject is seen to be mobile and constituted in the shifting space where multiple and competing discourses intersect. ...the mapper is articulated around a core self that... is nonetheless differentiated locally and historically. Social mapping, in this view, makes possible a way of understanding how sliding identities are created, and how the multiple connections between spatiality and subjectivity are seen to be grounded in the contested terrain between discourse communities... (Paulston, 1996, xxi)

Power... is not solely based upon material dimensions, but also involves the capacity to throw into question established codes and rework frameworks of common understanding. ...we should seek to form an appreciation of the ways in which 'ordinary' understandings become constructed, of issues of interpretative conflict and semiotic plurality more generally. However, this cannot be achieved without also appreciating how dominant systems and institutions seek to establish the power of master codes, meaninglessness and dominant viewpoints. ... Such notions arguably join together sociology's attempt to map the 'big' transformations of modernity with cultural studies' attempt to capture more subtle shifts within meaning and aesthetics. (Stevenson, 2001, 2)

Social Cartography as Curriculum Inquiry

Rhetoric and reactions following the horrific events of September 11th, 2001, have underscored some of the most basic tensions in American civic-cultural life, tensions that were already seriously impacting education and promise to have serious import for the public educative experience both at present and into the future. What began with a brutal attack directed at our people and our institutions mushroomed, in terms of national response, into a thorough thrashing of our national ideals, values and principles—and those who sought to uphold them—with much of the world watching. A new 'master code' was enunciated for 'the people,' one that constituted a prescription for our self-interest based on a dismissal and discouragement of difference (vocalized as dissent)—the ubiquitous call for 'unity'—as the administration undertook a new global 'war on terror,' a prescription that most Americans (the polls told us) appeared to accept in that moment. Additionally, the contradictory use of terms like 'freedom' by the administration to render them meaningless and to obscure the actualities underlying values-talk (Lakoff, 2006) may have further clouded our judgment in a difficult scenario.

As a public we did not pause to consider sufficiently—let alone critique—what that master code actually meant for us as a nation, and many Americans have been taken by surprise at the conditions predominating here at home as a result, and in our foreign engagements and relations as well. Government fraud and governmental failure, in other words, were compounded by the failure of the public itself, an event that should neither escape our notice nor our concern as curricularists. As a consequence, for Americans the world is a different place now; that is, the world changed as a result of our responses to September 11th, and we may have changed as well. Once familiar terrain has become a landscape that is barely recognizable, and solutions to our many dilemmas elude us at present. New maps are needed in order to navigate this new American wilderness. Mapping, as noted above, has "potential to serve as a metaphorical device for the provisional representation and iconographic unification of warring cultures and disputatious communities" (Paulston, 1996, xxi). Therefore, it serves my purposes as I explore a range of autobiographical visions at the level of the nation to examine who we say we are.

Following September 11th, the struggle over national ideals, values, and principles was propelled, in part, by a radical neo-liberal/neo-conservative posture that positioned a specific vision of America promulgated by those in power—an America that is predatory, self-righteous and protective only of its own interests—as the regulator of the global community, ready to strike out at any who questioned or opposed this vision, both around the world *and* here at home. For too many, the threat this repositioning of America posed was obscured by secrecy on the part of our government and an artful use of manipulative and misleading rhetoric that led to confusion and dismay amongst our people. Decisions about how best to respond to such attacks riveted the attention of the nation to media representations designed to show us who we are and what we think. Anyone who watched television news, or who read daily newspapers during this time, moreover, was subjected to a steady diet of civic-cultural skirmishes—usually over meaningless matters and minutiae—in an endless procession. In addition, the public was treated to a constant stream of right-wing diatribes, sometimes cloaked by a questioning posture, sometimes blatantly accusatory, in which the 'left-leaning liberals' were characterized as 'un-American,' even 'anti-American.' The effect was to claim America as a space peculiarly belonging to the 'Right.' This circumstance was produced, in part, by a proactive New Right agenda that sought to move the country towards an ultra-conservative orthodoxy and to impact and eventually transform all major institutions in the process (Barry and Lobe, 2002). The effects of this re-envisioning and repositioning of the public educative experience, moreover, have yet to be fully explored, let alone fully fathomed.

What I see is that we 'dissidents' succeeded, in terms of responding to September 11th, only to the extent that we realized that those of us who are *not* situated within the New Right lack a singular—or a definitive—'answer' to this crisis. We were continually and publicly blamed by this cultural/political faction for not accepting *unquestioningly* the solutions proffered to us by those at the highest levels of power, as though those in power *were* America. Our 'problem' appeared to be that we had as many 'answers' as we had points-of-view, and in the face of risk, disinformation, and uncertainty, we failed to coalesce in a way that could counter the prevailing public rhetoric. This strengthened the de facto power of the Bush-Cheney administration's radical revolution. The irony should not be lost on us, since we generally look to our alternative discourses for some sense of where a revolution consistent with democracy might find its moorings. In an autobiographical approach taken to be a 'revolutionary act' (Pinar, 2004), we might expect to find such moorings, and that hopeful expectation propelled this study towards a search for such moorings, however slippery the ground might be. What the public was offered instead by the administration was the persistence of striated thinking in smooth space, along with a rather expansive deterritorialization (Deleuze and Guattari, 1987) of our ongoing civic-cultural struggle.

In effect, we who dissented were made to appear to be something 'other than' American, and I am concerned, of course, with the source of the designation itself, but more so with its deadening effects on social imagination as a spur to alternative visions. In the 2008 pre-election civic-cultural climate, an awakening has appeared to emerge at last, but the threat that 'solving' the problems will be left in the hands of an incoming administration by an uncertain and ill-informed public still looms. Further, the complexity of the problems we face is enormous, and we have yet to address, even at a surface level, the implications for education of this new American wilderness, i.e., the outcome(s) of this failure of the public, which was a failure of democracy as well (Shenkman, 2008). In fact, the question of how to reconstruct and revitalize the public educative experience so that democracy is strengthened, rather than minimized, is perhaps the most urgent issue to confront.

Mapping provides a means for confronting this question, tending as it does towards "provisional representation and iconographic unification of warring cultures and disputatious communities" (Paulston, 1996, xxi); autobiography provides the ground, which is neither firm nor fixed, but rather, slippery, deterritorialized, and uncertain. The task of mapping such terrain, therefore, involves acknowledging, from the start, that the mapping is tentative, incomplete, and offers a *portrait* of the moment rather than a model for what we should see. In this sense, mapping autobiography may be seen as 'cognitive art' (Paulston, 1993, 3; Paulston and Liebman, 1996, 14), although social mapping has not yet truly produced anything approaching what might concretely resemble an art form. Perhaps the best term for this research genre is 'artful inquiry.' I use it here as a mode of curriculum inquiry that employs 'imaginative extrapolation' (Eisner, 2002, 153) to pursue autobiography (Pinar, 1975, 1994, 2000, 2004; Pinar et al., 1995) at the level of the nation.

The curriculum that emerged following September 11th tended to impose and reinforce a silence, as noted, that emanated from the privileging of a narrative of extraordinary political power. Many of us, in fact, exhibited the effects of the all-too-human fear of seeking alternative footing in an atmosphere where, on the one hand, the risk attached to dissent appeared to be too great and, on the other, information and imagination to feed alternative vision(s) were lacking. In this curriculum inquiry project I therefore explore our relationship with American 'ideals, values and principles' as elements of national autobiographical iteration, focusing on constructs of *nation* and *citizen* in the process. The question raised is: Who do we say we are, or will become, as a nation, as we move through this 'moment of silence' and seek a more democratic curriculum, a curriculum of voice? Considering variations in our internal responses to being terrorized—the changing shape of the terrain of our national narrations of selfhood (both conscious and unconscious) in this moment—and raising the question of whether we are approaching *post-democracy* in our thinking about the nation, its ideals, values and principles are thus foremost in my thinking.

My reasoning is that the future curriculum of civic-cultural struggle will be most deeply affected by these internal responses to the public educative experience and that they therefore require exploration. Such explorations should stimulate mappings that can contribute to our understanding(s) of the moment. The civic-cultural struggle I map here as autobiography is an episode that took place in a deeply troubled terrain—in the face of fear, anxiety and uncertainty. Those who engendered critical dialogue in this moment exhibited civic courage, and that courage should also inform currere in the future (i.e., as part of its past), particularly the currere of the struggle for national identity, or selfhood. Since such struggles are hardly new to Americans' understandings of their nation's past and present, two questions emerge: first, whether the struggle can be conducted in a more constructive way, given its troubled history and contemporary complication(s), and second, whether the struggle itself might be put to beneficial use as the ground (slippery though it may be) for educational growth. I believe this is what advocates for deliberative democracy, for instance, intend (see, e.g., Gutmann, 1999); it is also what Lakoff (2006) sees as our heritage when he declares that "America has been a nation of activists, consistently expanding its most treasured freedoms..." (3).

I therefore offer here that the struggle will and should continue, but that understanding its dimensions and dynamics in an intertextual field composed in the present and considering its linkage(s) with the past are crucial to any envisioning of a future for democracy. Present and past taken together, after all, constitute a means for articulating *continuity*, on the one hand, and *rupture*, or change, on the other. These considerations propel this curriculum inquiry project in the direction of mapping the terrain to show the interrelations of competing and conflicting iterations of post-9/11 American national being/becoming.

Social Mapping and Autobiography

> Today, long dominant goals and assumptions underlying modern theories of education and society are undergoing a ravaging subversion. Post-structuralist, post-modernist, post-patriarchal, post-Marxist—yea, post-everything it would seem—theories push forth new ways of seeing grounded in, paradoxically, anti-essentialist and anti-foundationalist ideas. Social relations and basic notions of reality and knowledge production undergo fragmentation, and many find themselves confused and disoriented in a shifting intellectual landscape with new knowledge communities speaking seemingly incomprehensible research languages. Surprisingly swift and unexpected, this rupture is also imploding the study of educational change. Now no metanarrative, or grand theory, be it positivism or humanism, functionalism or Marxism can credibly claim hegemonic privilege and the right to fill all the space of truth or method. (Paulston, 1996, 3)

I have chosen here to partner a comparative method variously called 'social cartography,' 'comparative cartography,' or 'social mapping' (Nicholson-Goodman, 1996, 2006, 2007; Paulston, 1993, 1995, 1996, 2003, 2005; Paulston, Liebman, and Nicholson-Goodman, 1996) with autobiography (Pinar, 1975, 1994, 2000, 2004; Pinar et al., 1995). I employ this approach to provide a *visual* portrayal of conceptualizations of the nation in relation to the discursive civic-cultural surround, highlighting *difference* in the struggle for autobiography. In this comparative approach, contested discursive terrain is mapped by juxtaposing selected conceptual elements of the discourse to produce a visual arrangement of the interrelations of varying claims, or iterations. This works to provide an enlarged, inclusive, and enriched understanding of the 'situatedness' of claims made within the terrain. The aims of social mapping are (a) to open space for an expansive conception of dialogue and thus for inclusion of difference, (b) to reinscribe the claims within contested terrain so that their conflict positionings and meanings are made lucid as they become visible in figural form, and (c) to level the discursive playing field by juxtaposing the grand narratives, or metanarratives, of modernity with mininarratives at play in a wide-ranging intertextual field, a field thus reflecting postmodern sensibilities.

The mapping project is positioned in this study, however, as a vehicle for the larger project of curriculum theorizing,[1] or curriculum inquiry: namely, locating the contours of a curriculum hidden within the 'silence' noted above. This is a curriculum that emerged in a time of national crisis, of fear and anxiety about the future, *and* that emerged within a troubled context—the context of internal division resulting from a decades-long culture war and from a history that has necessitated group identity politics as recourse against a hegemonic narrative of *what was, is, and should be*. It emerged as well within a moment where internal doubt had arisen over issues of representation (see Prologue) and a crisis had already begun to emerge over issues of 'belonging' as some engaged in a *new* project of group identity- and community-formation, which was due, first, to the recognition of Western history as imperialist and colonizing, and second, to the emergence of post-colonial discourse about globalization itself (Appadurai, 1996; Bhabha, 1994) (see Chapter 4). Both of these trends speak directly to civic-cultural struggle and its attendant concerns. Curriculum inquiry linked with this particular moment, then, has to engage with a surround that was filled with horror, loss, and dismay—even as it acknowledges that such problems are, in fact, not new, but rather *preceded* the events of September 11th, and that their legacy—now felt more intensively—is implicated not only in the past and in the present state of affairs, but in future prospects for democracy as well.

The public sphere—the arena in which citizens in a democracy engage each other in public conversation and acquire information and understandings vital to civic-cultural participation—was already eroding prior to September 11th (see, e.g., Gitlin, 1993), but this erosion was dramatically accelerated in this moment of social trauma. Since venues in the public sphere provide the narration, the public sphere is itself a major theme in this work. I therefore problematize the following: a) the university as a social space for academic freedom that exists in a tense relationship with public desire for belief, as noted (see Chapter 2); b) print and electronic media that are eroded, commodified, and manipulated so that symbolic power over our sense(s) of who we are or will become is clouded, complicated, and contradicted in our encounter with post-national contingencies (see Chapter 4); and c) an electronic public sphere that is *virtual*, and thus presents us with possibilities, but represents a 'thin' community of 'cool' talk that may only *simulate* political participation, presenting further complications (Turner, 2001, 29), and that poses dangers as well, as a *spectacle-surveillancee* paradigm emerges as the 'new disciplinarity' for educators (Vinson and Ross, 2003) (see Chapter 8).

One reason for considering these *problematiques* is because I explore discourses of possibility selected from these venues in this work. The alternative discourses represent a set of subdialogues situated within the public sphere from: a special 9/11 edition of *Qualitative Inquiry*, an academic journal, Op-Ed commentary from *The New York Times*, and Op-Ed commentary from a self-proclaimed 'progressive' website, tompaine.com. These venues were selected to incorporate discourses displaying civic courage in the larger body of writing, discourses that were willing to confront a blatant attempt to silence opposition. Of course, writing that effectively seeks to enact silence is also included: President George W. Bush's (2003) *State of the Union Address* and advertising by a right-wing anti-dissident group called Americans for Victory Over Terrorism (AVOT).

In order to narrow the study, my selection was limited (with the exception of the *State of the Union Address*) to a period from September 11th, 2001 through January 7th, 2002. I must acknowledge that while much has been said about 'structured silence,' this study focuses on civic courage in the *discursive* terrain to approach this civic-cultural struggle and the social imaginaries represented in the upheaval surrounding (and complicating) the fray. In essence, this is a study of American psycho-social narratives purporting to represent *America* (nation) and *American* (citizen) as they compose autobiography. Therefore I focus my energies on these two constructs—*nation* and *citizen*—because they appear to me to be the singular features of this moment that will have the most impact on future educative experience(s), both within schooling and outside its walls, and on future civic-cultural struggle as well.

Further, because print (and electronic) media 'shore up' the epistemological 'boundaries' of the nation as a social construct, I have also problematized the nation as an *imagined community* to open space for understanding the phantasmagoric nature of our constructs of 'nation' and what they mean (Anderson, 1991). This is essential for understanding our varying constructs of 'citizen' and what they mean. Our understandings of these constructs were circumscribed by much of the rhetoric coming from the administration and its entourage and then, as noted, further enhanced, disseminated, and legitimated by mainstream and 'right-wing' media. At the same time, the intrusion of global electronic media into public consciousness necessitates that I attend to the *limits* of the nation resulting from this intrusion as well (Appadurai, 1996) (see Chapter 4). These limits are important because they speak directly to the erosion of civic-cultural symbolic boundaries and to the emergence of imagination as *global* cultural practice, which can be as terrorizing as it may be promising (Greene, 2008), as the events of September 11th and their aftermath so dramatically demonstrated.

Because social mapping involves the 'situatedness' of the mapper relative to the phenomenon under study (the space from which I see what/as I see), the need for self-disclosure arises. Part of this work, then, involves problematizing self (working to disclose persona) to expose the mapper's ways of seeing. To accomplish this, I have included intermittent autobiographical anecdotes to disclose how my persona contributes to and shapes the mapping project, but this is kept to a minimum in this work. I partner the qualitative-interpretive genre of social mapping, then, with illuminatory and emancipatory discourses of curriculum inquiry to open space to consider critical, interpretive, and imaginative praxis. As a mapper, I locate myself within this qualitative-interpretive mode of inquiry to focus on *illustration* for the purposes of illumination, but that does not prevent me from thinking about curriculum in emancipatory terms.

Finally, I craft the work in a manner that follows an aesthetic sensibility. While the crafting and its attendant weaknesses are my own, I follow Eisner's (2002) thinking about what and how the arts might contribute to the 'culture of schooling' as I pursue a unique blend of aesthetic sensibility and scholarship in this study that has implications for schooling, but draws from and locates itself in the public sphere as the larger site of civic-cultural struggle. This book is necessarily, therefore, moored to a different conception of learning from what so ubiquitously prevails in our schools. Eisner contrasts this mode of learning with a more traditional model:

> I am talking about a culture of schooling in which more importance is placed on exploration than on discovery, more value is assigned to surprise than to control, more attention is devoted to what is distinctive than to what is standard, more interest is related to what is metaphorical than to what is literal. ...an educational culture that has a greater focus on becoming than on being, places more value on the imaginative than on the factual, assigns greater priority to valuing than to measuring, and regards the quality of the journey as more educationally significant than the speed at which the designation is reached. I am talking about a new vision of what education might become and what schools are for. (16)

I ask my reader to bear these features of the study in mind as you make your way through the book. I ask you to understand that the mapping project, like the larger project of autobiography as curriculum inquiry, is not an end unto itself. It is, rather, an entryway to something more: to processes of exploring, encountering surprise, finding the distinctive, thinking metaphorically, looking to become, imagining, valuing and journeying through this moment of *dread* in an effort to transcend it. Ultimately, it is about 'locating' currere in this moment and thinking about how to communicate its contours in a way that might help learners both understand *and* transcend the moment. It is additionally an effort to draw on imagination as praxis and to call attention to social imaginaries that may enable the young to craft a future that exceeds the limitations of the present.

Terminology/Genealogy of the Study

In this study, I do *not* clarify what I mean by 'the events of September 11th and their aftermath.' This is intentional. Chapters 5 and 6 are 'readers' that provide a 'cultural record' of discursive response(s) to this horrific moment in American history. I allow these readers to provide their narratives of this moment untrammeled by any constraints I might impose (beyond selection). Just as the attacks on the World Trade Center, the Pentagon and the plane we refer to as 'Flight 93' were part of this moment, so were many other events. Some of these were highly visible; some occurred 'behind the scenes.' I let the discourses detail and define what belongs to this moment. Since my intention here is to map civic-cultural disputes about this moment in an effort to articulate a national autobiography, the discourses must necessarily provide the substance, first, of the disputes themselves, and second, of the autobiography as it emerges through the struggle.

There are three terms used in this study that require some initial explanation so as to avoid excessive confusion or frustration on the part of my reader: *civic courage*, *social imaginaries* and *the New Right*. I briefly introduce my use of these terms here, and ask my reader to bear in mind that I expect, to some extent, that fuller meanings will become self-evident as the study unfolds. Although this is intended as a scholarly work, it nevertheless contains the same elements, hopefully, as any good narrative would, and I depend on these elements to assist my reader in making sense of the work. I begin with a brief explanation of my use of the term 'civic courage.'

When I speak of *civic courage*, I am using Giroux's sense of this (Kincheloe and Steinberg, 1993) as the ability and willingness to confront one's own difference in civic matters. In the context of this particular moment, speaking out against the prevailing rhetoric was made problematic because the nation was under attack; essentially, it was deemed more appropriate to unite behind the prevailing rhetoric than it was to engage in debate or dialogue. Dissent was made even more problematic by virtue of the fact that *representation* of difference disappeared. Given the extraordinary circumstances, those who had courage to dissent were on their own if they spoke out against the 'master code' of a new post-9/11 American identity or questioned the 'meaninglessness' (Stevenson, 2001, 2) so pervasive in the apparently non-sensical language spoken by the administration, a language that used a form of double-speak to cloak the 'theft' of progressive American ideas for its own purposes (Lakoff, 2006, 7). The party ostensibly representing these citizens became (in the name of bipartisanship) 'lap-dogs' for the administration, and hence there was no support for questioning, let alone for genuine oppositional thinking. This was further complicated by the fact that progressives showed little understanding of what the intended shift in meanings portended (Lakoff, 2006, 8).

Little space was open for genuine questioning of what had happened or why. Little space was open for questioning our leadership and the positions being taken by them in response to the attacks. The result was a collapse of support for difference, leaving a one-party system with a very strong party line in control. As the media echoed the tone of the administration, all questioners, those who ventured beyond the limits of the prevailing rhetoric, were labeled, and sometimes shouted down, as 'unpatriotic,' 'anti-American,' 'soft on terrorism' and even ultimately, as 'traitors.' The general public tone (as conveyed by the media) was not just triumphal—it was, rather, characterized by coercive nationalism. Therefore, oppositional discourse involved considerable risk-taking. It was as though America was under a 'spell,' a spell that was only breached, it seemed, when former Vice President Al Gore spoke out in public and "roared" his conviction that "patriotism does not mean keeping quiet, but rather speaking up" (Unleashing the Loyal Opposition, *The New York Times*, April 15, 2002). To put this in perspective, we need to realize that it took *eight months* after the national tragedy before this 'ground' was broken on its surface, another *five years* before the 'foundation' for public questioning was firmly set by the 'rolling disclosure' of abuses of power (see Prologue). For many, it was a very long (and excruciating) wait.

The use of the term *social imaginaries* (Appadurai, 1996) comes into play because we live and work in a world of meanings constructed in multiple sites and under diverse circumstances. I neither wish to become entangled here in the wealth of literature that looks at 'reality' as problematic nor to engage in philosophical inquiry into the nature and existence of reality. That simply is not my purpose in this work. Nevertheless, we cannot help but confront the basic evidence, displayed in everyday life, that our 'known' world is dependent upon, and flooded with, both rhetoric and images that shape, constrain, expand, distort, etc., our sense(s) of what is 'real' or 'true' and what ought to be valued. This applies not only to the everyday world, but also to major constructs, like *nation* (as Benedict Anderson (1991) makes clear) and *freedom* (as Lakoff (2006) makes clear), and therefore to our civic and cultural forms of sense-making. This requires some further explication, which I provide by way of an abridged genealogy of some of the thinking behind the study.

In the 1970s, as a student of political science at Hunter College (CUNY), I was introduced to Mannheim's (1936) *Ideology and Utopia*. He speaks of the political as it intersects with 'cultural aspirations':

> In political discussion in modern democracies where ideas were more clearly representative of certain groups, the social and existential determination of thought became more easily visible. In principle it was politics which first discovered the sociological method in the study of intellectual phenomena. Basically it was in political struggles that for the first time men [sic] became aware of the unconscious collective motivations which had always guided the direction of thought. Political discussion is... more than theoretical argumentation; it is the tearing off of disguises—the *unmasking* of those unconscious motives which bind the group existence to its cultural aspirations and its theoretical arguments. To the extent, however, that modern politics fought its battles with theoretical weapons, the process of unmasking penetrated to the social roots of theory. [Emphasis mine] (39)

It was, however, his clarification of the political-epistemological element in both ideology and utopia as trajectories of thought and belief that most fully captured my attention, since

> The original German edition of *Ideology and Utopia* appeared in an atmosphere of acute intellectual tension marked by widespread discussion which subsided only with the exile or enforced silence of those thinkers who sought an honest and tenable solution to the problems raised. Since then the conflicts which in Germany led to the destruction of the liberal Weimar Republic have been felt in various countries all over the world, especially in Western Europe and the United States. The intellectual problems which at one time were considered the peculiar preoccupation of German writers have enveloped virtually the whole world. What was once regarded as the esoteric concern of a few intellectuals in a single country has become the common plight of the modern man. (x)

As a child of the world war that followed the destruction of the Weimar Republic and ensuing Nazi rule, I found Mannheim's thinking helpful for naming and clarifying doubts that had originated in a time and space where I lacked the capacity to articulate what was so troubling to me. He considers the deeper meanings of these two tendencies, beginning with ideology:

> The concept "ideology" reflects the one discovery which emerged from political conflict, namely, that ruling groups can in their thinking become so intensively interest-bound to a situation that they are simply no longer able to see certain facts which would undermine their sense of domination. There is implicit in the word "ideology" the insight that in certain situations the collective unconscious of certain groups obscures the real condition of society both to itself and to others and thereby stabilizes it. (40)

At the opposite end of the political-epistemological spectrum lies utopian thinking:

> The concept of *utopian* thinking reflects the opposite discovery of the political struggle, namely that certain oppressed groups are intellectually so strongly interested in the destruction and transformation of a given condition of society that they unwittingly see only those elements in the situation which tend to negate it. Their thinking is incapable of correctly diagnosing an existing condition of society. They are not at all concerned with what really exists; rather in their thinking they already seek to change the situation that exists. Their thought is never a diagnosis of the situation; it can be used only as a direction for action. In the utopian mentality, the collective unconscious, guided by wishful representation and the will to action, hides certain aspects of reality. It turns its back on everything which would shake its belief or paralyse its desire to change things. [Emphasis in original] (40)

As a student in the late 60s and early 70s, I embraced activism as a means to address specific issues that had pricked my conscience enough to require critical response. The civil protest advocating a moratorium on the war in Vietnam (among other issues) in Washington, D.C., for instance, was one site of response, but it was there that I first encountered the brute force of 'the police state,' and came to see that power had nothing but contempt for the 'citizen.' It was there that a certain degree of cynicism about government first made itself felt in my political psyche. My understanding of the need for critical response to wrong-minded policies was there confronted by the raw fact of power and its capacity for thwarting public response. This was a turning point in my thinking, which moved me from naïve activism to new horizons of consciousness as my primary focus and my own internal project. Thus it was Mannheim who first alerted me to the basis from which my later work as a doctoral student engaged in mapping divergent perspectives in social thought (itself embedded in contested terrain)—including both ideological and utopian strands—would emerge.

Further on in my studies, I was also deeply impressed by the work of Berger and Luckmann (1975). Their patterning of meaning systems for the social construction of reality helped me to see how the power of cognitive structures and coherent systems of thought could organize, and potentially be used to organize for us, how we perceive reality.[2] More recently, Walter Truett Anderson's (1990) work provided me with a genealogy of this field of inquiry, along with insights about the nature of changes in belief and in 'beliefs about beliefs' (3) in the postmodern world that confronts us now. These discourses lurk behind my thinking about both Benedict Anderson's work (1991) on the concept of the nation as an 'imagined community' and Appadurai's (1996) work, which draws from Anderson and extends the discussion from national to post-national exigencies and their effects on social imagination as cultural practice (see Chapter 4).

It is in Appadurai (1996) that I find the clearest conception of 'social imaginaries' as they pertain to the events and aftermath of September 11th. It is Appadurai who 'makes sense' for me of how a group like *Al Qaeda* comes to be and, more importantly, comes to enact what it has allegedly enacted, using social imaginings as "fuel for action" (7). It is Appadurai who assists me to think about what that means for our own sense(s) of *America* and of being *American*. The social imaginary is, perhaps too simply put, the use of the imagination as *social practice*—that is, its use as a means of fashioning and re-fashioning our identities, not just at the individual level, but at the national, transnational, or post-national levels as well. Appadurai, for instance, approaches social imaginaries as the means for global and anti-global creation of "communities of sentiment" (8).

The third term I use frequently throughout this study is the *New Right*, and this is actually quite complex and therefore deserves some preliminary discussion. The New Right is not simply a political party (although it is usually associated with Republicans), or even a political position or philosophy. While this is a coherent group with a large membership, a variety of common issues and values, a sophisticated model of organization, and its own media and academic/institutional outlets (see, e.g., Micklethwait and Wooldridge, 2004), it is nevertheless a *faction*, one that nevertheless embraces the total transformation of culture in America in order to have things *its way* in American society (see, e.g., Barry and Lobe, 2002; Schlesinger, 1998; Shor, 1986).

It is important to note, however, that the New Right is not a monolith; rather, it is a factional movement in American social, cultural, and political life. This faction has, in fact, various component groups composed of citizens who do not necessarily agree on all issues—but as a movement they have artfully and persuasively used their rhetoric to advance a crisis in morality in general and in education more specifically that much of the public appears to 'buy.' Additionally, because they utilize a 'populist' language to promote their views, they have shown themselves capable of drawing adherents from left, right and center, and their general public acceptance and their current intimate linkage with power make their ideology both civically and culturally troubling for me. I therefore work in this study to 'situate' their positioning vis-à-vis civic debate using narratives of and critical responses to the New Right. Situating this faction in terms of public space is vital for bringing the issue of civic courage into focus.

This, then, is the context—or *contextual moment*—within which this study is situated. It is because of my abiding concern for our young that I approach the study from the focal point of a nation whose psyche is 'in sprawl' (Mailer, 2003). It is because of my abiding concern for the nation that I approach the study from the focal point of constructs of social imagination: multiple meanings of the *nation*, and multiple approaches to the being/becoming of the *citizen* that in this moment strained for space within which to find voice. It is because of my abiding concern for freedom's fate that I approach the study at all.

Intent, Organization, and Rationale for Selection of Venues

My intention here is to analyze selected fragments of a public dialogue that began immediately after September 11th, and to map the interrelations of these *subdialogues* with an eye to locating a curriculum of possibility within the multilayered intertextual field they form, a field that denotes autobiography at the level of the nation. I look at a small portion of the public reaction that ran counter to the 'conventional wisdom' advanced by the administration in the early period, specifically, from September 12th, 2001–January 7th, 2002. This was the moment before repression set in, before the 'master codes' (Stevenson, 2001, 2) were fully proclaimed, the reconstruction fully enacted. All too soon, we, the American public, foolishly allowed our leadership to make us 'feel safe' in the face of the fear and anxiety we were feeling, and silence fell like a thick, dark, lingering fog. The rhetoric emanating from the White House certainly was designed to provide an illusion of safety, despite its ultimate outcomes, intended and otherwise. Consequently, I turn my attention first to the master codes themselves, and then to a small number of venues generally engaged in a counter-rhetorical dialogue displaying civic courage in this social moment (see Chapters 5 and 6).

I focus on a triad of sites of civic debate that appear to me to be useful as a sample of what some had to say as they expressed reservations about, fear of, or total rejection of the proposed national course of action in terms of both domestic and foreign policies that could purportedly add to our security at home. My hope is to illustrate how they saw who we say we are or will become as a result of September 11th. Furthermore, I look to these subdialogues to provide imaginaries that might enhance and enliven imagination in such a contextual moment for the purpose of theorizing what our curriculum of civic-cultural struggle might look like in the future.

My intention here is twofold. First, by elaborating the subdialogues that contributed to an initial discussion of environment and response following September 11th, I hope to outline aspects of the discourse that underscore civic courage in the face of attack and extreme fear. I expect this sketch to yield some thoughtful insights for the question of what could be communicated about these events and America's early response to them. Second, by mapping various understandings of the civic-cultural struggle, I hope to provide a portrayal of American autobiography that includes the *refusal* of the '*es muss sein,*' of the 'given' (Greene, 1988, 10), which is an exemplar of civic courage, a courage intimately connected with the internal wartime response of American citizens *and* reflective of what a parent culture in a democratic society might seek to communicate to its young.

The response I refer to cannot therefore be characterized in terms of the external response of our governmental authorities, since they pursued an agenda that was largely hidden from the public. Rather, the characterization that interests me is envisioned here in terms of the internal responses of our people to the reshaping of a nation and its ideals as we took on a new, and poorly understood, position in the world community, and did so in a moment of national crisis. This is, I believe, what is most likely to impact public educative experience in the future. My hope is that by providing a portrayal of the interrelations of these discourses, I may contribute something to curriculum inquiry relevant to the events that are reshaping our lives as individuals and the life of America as a nation. Mapping civic courage, the kind of courage that is most needed in a democracy, is a primary concern, then, in this curriculum inquiry project.

Social Cartography and Discursive Knowledge Production

Social mapping provides a *visual* portrayal of the dimensions of dispute within any given contested terrain, and requires some explanation. My approach in this study will be to provide an elaboration of the texts in each of these venues, followed by a figural mapping of the intertextual field they form, taken together as part of a larger, though unseen, 'whole.' In other words, I provide an analysis of the interrelations of these discourses that may alert my reader both to the conceptualizations involved and to how they intersect to form sliding identities indicating possibilities for new dialogue and for change. I map dimensions of being/becoming within these subdialogues to reveal the potential of the civic courage they display for the autobiographical project and discuss their implications for further curriculum inquiry.

Social maps are a way to visually portray the interrelations of complex and sometimes heated dialogues, bringing into the open both the visible and the not-so-visible aspects of what is being disputed. This method, cultivated by Rolland G. Paulston for the purpose of enhancing understanding of social and educational change in the field of comparative education, is based on its relation to Foucault's (1972) approach to 'a general history of knowledge,' which involves 'excavating' particular sites of knowing, or ways of seeing phenomena located within a social milieu. Foucault explains that "in our time, history is that which transforms *documents* into *monuments*," and "deploys a mass of elements that have to be grouped, made relevant, placed in relation to one another to form totalities, thus aspiring to the condition of archaeology" (7). Nicholson-Goodman and Paulston (1996) acknowledge the problem:

> What Foucault details here, within the parameters of a history of knowledge, is the disruption, or deconstruction, of a history based on a linear notion of progress. For Foucault (and for others sensitive to this transformation), this has led to a new set of problems for the general (as opposed to the traditional) historian of knowledge. (100)

This set of problems emerges because while "a total description draws all phenomena around a single centre—a principle, a meaning, a spirit, a worldview, an overall shape; a general history, on the contrary, would deploy the space of a dispersion" (Foucault, 1972, 10). This dispersion occupies a space of contestation and exhibits internal ruptures as well. For Nicholson-Goodman and Paulston (1996), the crux of the problem is this:

> The task of explicating (or excavating) the space of a dispersion is complexified by the specialization, or fragmentation, of knowledge communities and their subject matter. Further, those following this sensibility, whose varying approaches are generally gathered under the umbrella term postmodern deconstruction, work within a milieu that is neither well understood nor apprehensible through prior research forms or agendas. Fulfillment of the promise of apprehending dispersion requires access to new modes or tools for excavation. (100-101)

The authors offer social cartography as a means to provide this access, to serve as one potential 'new mode' for excavation.

Social maps provide such tools, indicating the researcher's arrangement of meanings vis-à-vis a particular phenomenon—an arrangement that portrays the space under discussion and locates, within the broader array of meanings, indicators that can assist readers to make sense of the terrain as a partially visible 'whole.' Mouat (1996) speaks to fragmentation and its resulting disorientation in terms that indicate the need for mapping abstractions:

> The postmodern era began with a dawning awareness that "reality" is composed of disconnected fragments. As early postmoderns sought reconnection, they discovered that the concrete representation of interrelationships between and among fragments often eludes expression. As the struggle to discover and express interrelationships intensified, it became apparent that the *abstract* representation of interrelationships is often possible when their *concrete* representation is not. Therefore, social cartography as mapping abstractions arises initially as a vehicle through which to express, in highly condensed, abstract form, the interrelationships between and among elements of systems which are not amenable to concrete description. [Emphasis in original] (82-83)

This approach, then, may be helpful as it provides insights into the layers of fragmentation and/or contestation occurring within any particular discursive domain. It is my express hope that its usefulness in the contextual moment under study here will become evident as my reader ponders and critiques the map, and applies the implications and complications of its autobiographical trajectories to curriculum theorizing about this moment.

However useful the map, this is *not* an approach that claims innocence, or value-neutrality. Harvey (1996) notes both the significance of mapping as a political tool in power struggles over knowledge and the utility of the *imaginary* within mapping:

> The discursive activity of "mapping space" is a fundamental prerequisite to the restructuring of any kind of knowledge. All talk about "situatedness," "location" and "positionality" is meaningless without a mapping of the space in which those situations, locations and positions occur. And this is equally true whether the space being mapped is metaphorical or real... Mapping is a discursive activity that incorporates power. The power to map the world one way rather than another is a crucial tool in political struggles. Power struggles over mapping... are therefore fundamental moments in the production of discourses. ... The imaginary (thoughts, fantasies, and desires) is a fertile source of all sorts of possible spatial worlds that can prefigure—albeit incoherently—all manner of different discourses, power relations, social relations, institutional structures, and material practices. The imaginary of spatiality is of crucial significance in the search for alternative mappings of the social process and its outcomes. (111-112)

This 'search for alternative mappings of the social process and its outcomes' is foremost in my thinking throughout this study. So is 'the power to map' as 'a crucial tool in political struggles.' Social mapping, then, acknowledges its discursive-political power, but focuses on the excavation itself ('digging' through layers of the terrain) and seeks to highlight the spatial reach of the imaginaries involved. The spatial reach of extant imaginaries signals what is crucial to 'other stories of what could be' (Fine, 2001), and is, in my view, a vital component of democratic thinking.

I utilize 'the imaginary of spatiality' here to portray the interplay of particular discursive positions that highlighted civic courage to counter the orthodoxy of triumphalism and, more so, of coercive nationalism (identified on the map as *hypernationalism*) and what that courage has to teach us. The success of the project depends upon being able to locate a multiplicity of alternative ways of seeing, or positionings, through which we might exercise civic courage as we make sense of the surround. The usefulness of the project depends upon the extent to which it is germane for other scholar-practitioners in the field. Observations and conclusions drawn should assist us in thinking about curriculum, and in theorizing how best to approach communicating this historic moment.

Paulston (1993) argues for "the utility of mapping knowledge perspectives as a kind of cognitive art, or 'play of figuration' to help orient educators to knowledge communities and their cultural codes, and to reinscribe earlier modernist vocabularies into post-modern ways of seeing and representing educational change knowledge" (3). This 'play of figuration,' Paulston asserts, also serves as a site of resistance to the dominant discursive mode, the hegemonic portrayal of reality for any given site of knowing or way of seeing: in this case, the constraints of orthodoxy in imposing autobiography to serve its purposes in the moment under consideration. This 'cognitive art' is also a form of metacognition, thinking about how we see and interpret cultural codes and, more importantly for Paulston, portraying them in visual interrelation in a "*hermeneutic of imagination*" (1996, 354) where we must see where we (mappers) stand as well. According to Paulston and Liebman (1993), when

> applied to education, social maps help to present and decode immediate and practical answers to the perceived locations and relationships of persons, objects and perceptions in the social milieu. The interpretation and comprehension of both theoretical constructs and social events can then... be facilitated and enhanced by mapped images. (39-40)

Is social mapping a 'definable' research method? Is there some prescribed formula for the process of social mapping? I would argue that this would defeat the purpose of social mapping and change the nature of the approach *qualitatively*. Christina and Nicholson-Goodman (2002) described the mapping process this way:

> Social maps are built from the ground up, but also float on the breezes of rumination. In other words, while the knowledge (and self-knowledge) work involved in conceptualizing the map is intensive, the actual mapping (production of the product) is somewhat of an epiphany, involving that serendipitous moment where the knowledge work leads to deep understanding. (9-10)

Is a methodology that relies on 'epiphany' useful, practical? I believe this is common in many fields, scientific inquiry not the least of them. That epiphany is itself, additionally, very much like what Garman and Piantanida (1999) describe, in *The Qualitative Dissertation*, as 'Coming to a Conceptual Leap':

> During the process of slogging, researchers try out various forms of data analysis and display or the crafting of texts. At issue is far more than a neat or clever organization of the material. Inherent in this conceptual grappling is the process of generating knowledge, of interpreting the phenomenon under study, struggling to create authentic portrayals of those meanings. The aha moment represents a conceptual leap in which the researcher sees the essence of the study and how the pieces fit into a larger, coherent portrayal of the phenomenon under study. (172)

While there is no prescription, no formula for the mapping process, it is not an arbitrary approach to inquiry. The mapper is responsible for providing an elaboration, analysis, or exegesis of texts and of demonstrating sufficient warrant for a particular organization or arrangement of meaning, and the map itself is open, of course, to critique and to reinscription by the reader. This is a form of qualitative-interpretive inquiry requiring deep reading of texts for analysis, and substantive reflection on the part of the researcher vis-à-vis authenticity and conceptualization.

Further, the researcher acknowledges her space of belonging within the hermeneutic circle of the researched phenomenon by situating herself within the map's parameters, disclosing in some way how it is that she comes to be positioned where she is on the map. Because of this, Paulston (1996) notes that

> future efforts to represent and compare the growing complexity of socio-educational phenomena will require a generosity of spirit and a deepening of self-understanding that may leave many behind. ... A hermeneutic approach helps us realize that objects and events are inseparable from the process of apprehension (i.e., the imaginative process) within which they are formed. So if we are to fruitfully analyse and compare how things in the world take on meanings, it will be necessary to understand better the diverse imaginative enactments that produce meaning. ...It is now time for ...educators ...to question how our choice of ideas and forms of representation influence our views of how reality is constituted and construed, how meaning and value are created and imposed on an otherwise unruly world. (363-364)

I offer that this approach to curriculum inquiry may be useful to scholar-practitioners as a way of opening to variations of meaning within a particular social milieu: in this case, layers of meaning in our civic-cultural struggle over our internal national response(s) to the events and aftermath of September 11th, involving our own being/becoming as a nation.

Social mapping serves a number of purposes. First, it operates from a postmodern sensibility about the 'now' of experience, displaying an understanding of the conditions which have led to the postmodern rupture with prior (fixed) notions of 'progress' and 'reality.' Second, it exhibits awareness and sensitivity to issues emanating from the cultural collisions resulting from globalization, especially acknowledging and understanding the 'Other'—and seeing ourselves as 'other'—and the need to make space for a diversity of voices and visions. Third, it represents a re-valuing of introspection and reflection in knowledge work that is neither solipsistic nor narcissistic, but makes space for the mapper's self-disclosure in relation to the terrain mapped. Fourth, social mapping suggests a transition from research as 'science' to research as 'art form,' allowing the 'ludic play' (Usher and Edwards, 1994) of cognitive art in academic work as a form of cognitive resistance to assumptions of objectivity—providing portrayal, rather than presuming value-neutrality. Fifth, it emphasizes dialogue, and the value of all participants in the discursive mode, seeking to ensure inclusiveness as a vital element of keeping the work fresh, sensitive to social change, and open to new voices and visions. Finally, it moves us from the purely textual towards the visual in discursive analysis (albeit within limits), displaying inclusiveness and sensitivity to new forms of meaning construction that no longer take place solely through words, but increasingly through the proliferation of images.

Social mapping, then, seeks to level the playing field in a discursive terrain, balancing the metanarratives (the 'grand narratives' of valorized voices) by including the mini-narratives that may have their own logic and value, but may not get as much play in the discourse. Additionally, this method empowers portrayal of highly complex webs of meaning within particular contested discursive terrain in a fairly sophisticated manner, and does so in a way that values reflection, postmodern sensibilities about the 'now' of experience, the 'art' of qualitative-interpretive research as a form of resistance to presumed 'objectivity,' and the contribution of the image to the dialogue. Finally, it identifies its own bias, its own position relative to the mapping, creating space for further critique and dialogue. In short, this is a reflexive research genre.

Since I must also acknowledge that as a mapper I am 'in' the mapping (i.e., in a space of preferred perception), and that in a hermeneutic sense the mapping emerges 'through' me, I locate myself on the map (i.e., relative to other texts), using an icon (a star). I provide self-disclosure through personal anecdote, allowing my reader insight into my persona as mapper. I do so to open space for critique of the power relations between the mapper as a site of knowing, and the map itself as a portrayal of the interrelations of the discourse. Put simply, the map serves as a heuristic, and is neither a model nor an established ordering of meaning. It represents one way of seeing how meaning may be arranged, and invites the reader to join a dialogue of comprehension, of sense making. At the same time, mapping serves as a tool for conceptualizing—and reconceptualizing via reiteration—how we might think about the subject under study.

4
'Nation-ness,' Nationalism, and Post-National Space

Before turning to writing about *America* and being *American* in post-9/11 national-autobiographic discourse, it might be helpful to understand the dilemmas of conceptualizing 'nation' and 'citizen' as social constructs constituting categories of being and becoming in present context. In order to approach this autobiographic work in terms of the nation, I consider first how nationalism emerges and secondly, the context within which it is presently situated. This, it should be noted, is itself a disputed terrain. In this chapter, I provide some basic insights into analysis and argumentation about *nation-ness* and nationalism as cultural phenomena, as well as dilemmas nation-states face in post-national space and the role of nation-ness in legitimizing the state. Therefore, I lay out in some detail Anderson's (1991) anthropological framing of the concept of nation and the origins and spread of nationalism as products of historical shifts in Western thinking about the world. I focus on those features whose traces are most evident in our discourses today about the nation, concentrating here on Anderson's conceptualization of factors contributing to the emergence of national consciousness such that it became possible "to 'think' the nation" as "a fundamental change... in modes of apprehending the world" (22).

Anderson highlights the importance of print culture to a nation's sense of itself as a living entity. His reflections lead us through a series of events related to understanding nationalism as a Western concept: first, its origins in historical shifts away from notions of the sacred (religious community and rule by divine right); second, its emergence as a force that took its original shape from struggles within the *creole* states of the Americas—states that were "formed and led by people who shared a common language and common descent with those against whom they fought" (37)—and then spread across the world, adapting to exigencies of locality as it spread; and third, its tendencies both as a qualifier *of* culture and as qualified *by* culture.

Appadurai (1996) extends Anderson's work by moving from a consideration of print culture to global electronic media and global migration in order to theorize the contemporary rupture of the nation-state in its symbol-ordering form. He provides a complex analysis of global flows in a post-national world, where hybridization of the global and the local is negotiated at the intersection of global media and its images, on the one hand, and the effects of global diasporas, on the other. Appadurai, like Anderson, uses an anthropological lens to illuminate global-hybrid impacts of imagination as social practice, a practice that is fashioned, distributed, acted upon and reacted to across the world in our times. I select these two texts to provide an anthropological framing of the work of social imagination: in Anderson's work, as an approach that theorizes nationalism; in Appadurai's work, as an approach that theorizes the *limits* of nationalism.

I follow this with a brief discussion of alternative views of this civic-cultural terrain in terms that attend to changing meaning(s) of nation-ness and the dramatically altered place of the nation-state (and nationalism as a derivative) in post-national space. I am compelled to acknowledge that Appadurai's (1996) notion of the 'unleashing of the imagination' (31) on a global scale—and the resulting proliferation of civic-cultural struggles impacting America both from *within* and *beyond* the symbol-ordering boundaries and capabilities of the nation-state—may also be an unleashing of the terror of other imaginings, creating a type of chaos that potentially undermines the fragile frame within which the nation, at least ideally, endures as our best possible entry to a potentially better future (although Barber (2001) disputes this claim). This is particularly (though not exclusively) true for triumphal tales of who we are and who we will become. The imaginative work of which Appadurai speaks forms its own counter-narratives as it negotiates between individuals (as 'sites of agency') and what now may be seen as "globally defined fields of possibility" (31), opening space for considering the *limits* of the nation and of nationalism, not to mention the complication (and contradiction) of civic-cultural constructs situated within this terrain. The effects of such counter-narratives deeply impact the nation's autobiography, as we shall see.

Bhabha (1994), additionally, proposes a "cultural construction of nation-ness as a form of social and textual affiliation" (201) as he seeks to locate culture in "the complex strategies of cultural identification and discursive address that function in the name of 'the people' or 'the nation' and make them the immanent subjects of a range of social and literary narratives" (201). In this study, these 'complex strategies' inform the core text of autobiography, and they are the 'social and literary' stuff that reflects what we variously seem to believe we, as Americans, are made of. Taking Anderson's work into account and moving beyond it with a critical eye, Bhabha provides a conceptualization of negotiated "intersubjective and collective experiences of *nationness*" as those that emerge in the "interstices... the overlap and displacement of domains of difference" [emphasis in original] (2) as he points to "a more transnational and translational sense of the hybridity of imagined communities" (7). It is my express intent that the autobiography resulting from discursive analysis and mapping of post-9/11 writing as a nation's autobiography should be oriented to this 'translational sense,' but that it should emerge from *within* domestic discourse.

A final view, for my purposes here, of our self-understanding and of the positioning of the nation relative to the world may be found in Barber (2001), who argues that globalization has bifurcated into a power struggle between 'wild capitalism' (*McWorld*) and 'wild terrorism' (*Jihad*) (xxiii), two forces visibly in conflict and yet, in actuality, feeding from the same trough and fostering anarchy together as the world they bequeath to us spins out of control (5). In the process, according to Barber, the nation-state is pushed towards irrelevance, since the disruption of sovereignty and the unraveling of nation-state autonomy are the combined product of these two world forces. Given that the autobiography under consideration here is unique to post-9/11 America, Barber's text cannot easily be ignored in discussing changing conceptions of the role and status of nation and of citizen.

These specific texts strike me as being particularly significant for this work, since they attend to the central dilemmas of the construction of public beliefs about the nation and their relationship with *constancy* (or continuity) and *change* (or rupture). My purpose here is to reflect on the power of public beliefs shaped by the cultural surround within which they are embedded, yet impacted as well by media stimulations of moral imagination—most specifically, stimulations that are situated within media representations of current national and nationalist 'realities,' but, increasingly, also with media representations of global, or globalizing, 'realities.' I use this exploration to highlight and problematize media representations relative to our national social imaginaries (which are heterogeneous, not homogeneous) and as a way to situate questions about preparing citizens in this rapidly changing nation and world in the face of simultaneously post-national *and* anti-democratic trajectories. I begin with a detailed account of Anderson's work as a way to immerse my reader in the complex language and terrain of discourse about nation-ness, nationalism, and the nation.

Anderson: Nation-ness and Nationalism

> ...unlike most other isms, nationalism has never produced its own grand thinkers...This 'emptiness' easily gives rise, among cosmopolitan and polylingual intellectuals, to... condescension. Like Gertrude Stein..., one can rather quickly conclude that there is 'no there there.' ...even so sympathetic a student of nationalism as Tom Nairn can nonetheless write that: '"Nationalism" is the pathology of modern developmental history, as inescapable as "neurosis" in the individual, with much the same essential ambiguity attaching to it, a similar built-in capacity for descent into dementia, rooted

in the dilemmas of helplessness thrust upon most of the world (the equivalent of infantilism for societies) and largely incurable.' (Anderson, 1991, 5)

I begin here by considering Anderson's (1991) anthropological inquiry into the nature of "nation-ness" (3) and the origins and spread of nationalism. For Anderson, nationalism appeared in the West as a new form of consciousness produced at the intersection of capitalism and the concept of 'print,' or 'print-capitalism' (39), in an historic shift requiring a new "secular transformation of fatality into continuity, contingency into meaning" (11). His work highlights some of the concerns of national autobiography as I am using it here: establishing and maintaining a national psyche intertwined with and dependent upon the work of social imagination (past, present, and future) often expressed or contained in public media serving as knowledge nodes. His inquiry therefore lends insight into the place and role of print media in the autobiography itself, problematizing our dependency on this medium as one arbiter of national identity.

Anderson explores "nation-ness" and nationalism as "cultural artefacts" capable of arousing "deep attachments" (4). For Anderson, "the 'end of the era of nationalism,' so long prophesied, is not remotely in sight," and he acknowledges that "nation-ness is the most universally legitimate value in the political life of our times" (3). However, explaining its origins and analyzing its meaning as a phenomenon has proven, Anderson argues, to be "notoriously difficult" (3). His starting point, then, is "to offer some tentative suggestions for a more satisfactory interpretation of the 'anomaly' of nationalism" as he searches out the cause(s) for the "profound emotional legitimacy" (4) invested in notions of 'nation-ness' and nationalism.

Commenting on perplexities encountered in attempts to theorize nationalism, he finds three paradoxes: first, "the objective modernity of nations to the historian's eye versus their subjective antiquity in the eyes of nationalists"; second, "the formal universality of nationality as a socio-cultural concept"; and third, "the 'political' power of nationalisms versus their philosophic poverty and even incoherence" (5). While the first two of these paradoxes are important to note, it is the third that most fully engages my attention here, in large part because I am attending to questions about the coherence of our sense(s) of ourselves as citizens of post-9/11 America in this moment and about the effects of this moment on our social consciousness—or lack thereof—as members of the nation and the world. The fact that the 'political power' of nationalism paradoxically coincides with its 'philosophic poverty and even incoherence' is, then, an important point in this conversation.

Anderson proposes that "nationalism has to be understood by aligning it, not with self-consciously held political ideologies, but with the large cultural systems that preceded it, out of which—as well as against which—it came into being" (12). He highlights "the religious community" and "the dynastic realm" as cultural systems in the process of decomposing both prior to and during the Enlightenment period of Western civilization (12). He attributes this decomposition to a number of factors. With regard to the religious community, these factors include: explorations of the world beyond Europe, which "abruptly widened the cultural and geographic horizon and hence also men's conception of possible forms of human life" (16); a "territorialization of faiths which foreshadows the language of many nationalists" (17); and a "gradual demotion of the sacred language itself" (18) such that "the sacred communities integrated by old sacred languages were gradually fragmented, pluralized, and territorialized" (19). With regard to the dynastic realm, Anderson points out that "the automatic legitimacy of sacred monarchy began its slow decline in Western Europe" in the seventeenth century (21), so that "after 1789 the principle of Legitimacy had to be loudly and self-consciously defended, and, in the process, 'monarchy' became a semi-standardized model" privileging an emergent European notion of the *limits* of monarchy (21). The principle of legitimacy played an active role as well in the struggles of the creole nations of the Americas, a role that continues today, especially in present context.

Equally important to Anderson's anthropological analysis is a shift in "apprehensions of time" (22). Citing Auerbach, he elaborates the medieval and sacred (Christian) notion of time as "wholly alien to our own," or (per Benjamin, 1973, cited in Anderson) as "Messianic time, a simultaneity of past and future in an instantaneous present" (24). A closer look at 'Messianic time' is worth taking into account. Auerbach provides the elaboration:

> ...the here and now is no longer a mere link in an earthly chain of events, it is *simultaneously* something which has always been, and will be fulfilled in the future; and strictly, in the eyes of God, it is something eternal, something omnitemporal, something already consummated in the realm of fragmentary earthly event. [Emphasis in original] (Auerbach, cited in Anderson, 24)

Anderson's explanation of the shift to modern time signals the intrusion of something new into our temporal sensibilities:

> What has come to take the place of the mediaeval conception of simultaneity-along-time is, to borrow again from Benjamin, an idea of 'homogeneous, empty time,' in which simultaneity is ...transverse, cross-time, marked not by prefiguring and fulfilment, but by temporal coincidence, and measured by clock and calendar. (24)

The importance of this transformation, he argues, "can best be seen if we consider the basic structure of two forms of imagining which first flowered in Europe in the eighteenth century: the novel and the newspaper" (24-25).

Anderson examines both national literature and the daily national newspaper as 'cultural products' (33) that cement our sense of ourselves as members of a particular national civic-cultural community entwined together in a social project called history, which is always in the making. He defines a nation as "an imagined political community—and imagined as both inherently limited and sovereign" (6) and goes on to explain the rationale for this working definition:

> The nation is imagined as *limited* because even the largest of them ...has finite, if elastic, boundaries, beyond which lie other nations. No nation imagines itself coterminous with mankind. ... It is imagined as *sovereign* because the concept was born in an age in which Enlightenment and Revolution were destroying the legitimacy of the divinely-ordained, hierarchical dynastic realm. Coming to maturity at a stage of human history when even the most devout adherents of any universal religion were inescapably confronted with the living *pluralism* of such religions, ... nations dream of being free, and, if under God, directly so. The gage and emblem of this freedom is the sovereign state. ... Finally, it is imagined as a *community* because, regardless of the actual inequality and exploitation that may prevail in each, the nation is always conceived as a deep, horizontal comradeship. Ultimately, it is this fraternity that makes it possible ...for so many millions of people, not so much to kill, as willingly to die for such limited imaginings. [Emphasis in original] (7)

In Anderson, the question that haunts is, again, the source of power behind the "profound emotional legitimacy" (4) of the nation, a power that, in the West, can only be granted by 'the people.' Anderson is not specifically concerned, then, with the power of the state, but rather with the power of the nation as an *imaginary*—one that is both civic and cultural in derivation and is situated within the consciousness of the people as it is articulated in print culture. He seeks to theorize the conditions under which the nation develops a 'selfhood' (an *autobiography*), and appropriates time as one element in his construction of the process:

> The idea of a sociological organism moving calendrically through homogeneous, empty time is a precise analogue of the idea of the nation, which also is conceived as a solid community moving steadily down (or up) history. An American will never meet, or even know the names of more than a handful of his 240,000-odd fellow Americans. He has no idea of what they are up to at any one time. But he has complete confidence in their steady, anonymous, simultaneous activity. (26)

Central to this construct of national selfhood, then, is an illusion of communal activity that lies beyond sight, but not beyond assurance. Time, in Ander-

'Nation-ness,' Nationalism, and Post-National Space 83

son, is the guide rope along which we all make our way through history 'together,' and the accompaniment of our fellow countrymen and countrywomen is an assumed certainty based on confidence.

Anderson examines the daily national newspaper as a cultural product, and acknowledges "its profound fictiveness" (33).

> If we were to look at a sample front page of, say, *The New York Times*, we might find there stories about Soviet dissidents, famine in Mali, a gruesome murder, a coup in Iraq, the discovery of a rare fossil in Zimbabwe, and a speech by Mitterand. Why are these events so juxtaposed? What connects them to each other? Not sheer caprice. Yet obviously most of them happen independently, without the actors being aware of each other or of what the others are up to. The arbitrariness of their inclusion and juxtaposition... shows that the linkage between them is imagined. (33)

The fictive nature of the newspaper as cultural product doesn't appear to hamper its effectiveness in telling us our story—the story of our nation and world—in spite of arbitrary and imagined linkages between stories. Why do we consult the newspaper? Where is its promise? Anderson provides an answer:

> The date at the top of the newspaper, the single most important emblem on it, provides the essential connection—the steady, onward clocking of homogeneous, empty time. Within that time, the 'world' ambles sturdily ahead. The sign for this: if Mali disappears from the pages of *The New York Times* after two days of famine reportage, for months on end, readers do not... imagine that Mali has disappeared or that famine has wiped out all its citizens. The novelistic format of the newspaper assures them that somewhere out there the 'character' Mali moves along quickly, awaiting its next reappearance in the plot. (33)

According to Anderson, we read the news to tell us the state of things and content ourselves with the thought that somehow we have been informed by virtue of having read it in print. The twin illusions of progress and reliability ensue; the framing involved evokes both certainty and calm, even where the events reported display a world gone mad. We are comforted even in alarm. But there is a "second source of imagined linkage," one which "lies in the relationship between the newspaper, as a form of book, and the market" (33):

> The obsolescence of the newspaper on the morrow of its printing... creates this extraordinary mass ceremony: the almost precisely simultaneous consumption ('imagining') of the newspaper-as-fiction. ... The significance of this mass ceremony... is paradoxical. It is performed in silent privacy... Yet each communicant is well aware that the ceremony he performs is being replicated simultaneously by thousands (or millions) of others of whose existence he is confident, yet of whose identity he has not the slightest notion. Furthermore, this ceremony is incessantly repeated at daily... intervals throughout the calendar. What more vivid figure for the secular, historically clocked, imagined community can be envisioned? At the same time, the newspaper

> reader, observing exact replicas of his own paper being consumed by his ...neighbors, is continually reassured that the imagined world is visibly rooted in everyday life. ...fiction seeps quietly and continuously into reality, creating that remarkable confidence of community in anonymity which is the hallmark of modern nations. (34-36)

The significance of the daily news as a product for mass consumption cannot be overstated. Many of our convictions, as well as our misconceptions and knowledge gaps, result from our ongoing consumption of such fictive narratives in print culture, now complicated by our consumption of fictive narratives put forward by electronic media. Democracy and its freedoms serve the purpose of binding us together through principles that we esteem and espouse. And yet, day after day, we read about abuses of power, without it ever resulting in our conscious dissolution as the citizenry of a nation. How do we 'know' the nation we call America—through a 'remarkable confidence of community in anonymity'? Where is the fount of national consciousness—that source of wisdom and self-actualization—that gives us our sense of history, of continuity?

While some would argue that our history is a given—a prescribed set of facts that, summed neatly together, tell us who we were, where we came from, what we fought, killed and died for, and what held us together, Anderson has a different take on this:

> All profound changes in consciousness, by their very nature, bring with them characteristic amnesias. Out of such oblivions, in specific historical circumstances, spring narratives. ... The photograph... is only the most peremptory of a huge modern accumulation of documentary evidence... which simultaneously records a certain apparent continuity and emphasizes its loss from memory. Out of this estrangement comes a conception of personhood, *identity*... which, because it cannot be 'remembered,' must be narrated. ...the narratives of autobiography and biography flood print-capitalism's markets year by year. ... These narratives... are set in homogeneous, empty time. Hence their frame is historical and their setting sociological. (205)

Anderson is speaking here about the ways we have of 'remembering' our nation's narrative—a history which is told to us by documents "amassed and turned into monuments" (Foucault, 1972, 8). In this, our print culture plays a major role, bringing us living imagery and an ongoing narrative, where history is continually revised, albeit incrementally, based on the *materiel* involved, but also, on the time and place of telling. Print culture (including electronic forms) has become an impressive site for the knowledge industry to disseminate its work at the global level, but we have yet to make full use of its democratic potential (Barber, 2007). It produces a living legacy of narrative, strengthened or embellished by works of fiction and non-fiction included in our national literary treasure, but this is a treasure that should grow in its inclusivity and provide access to all. Struggles over canonical claims to preserve and circumscribe the literary scope of this treasure are just one outcome of disputed 'remembering/forgetting.'

Anderson points us to the example of the American Civil War in terms of how it is taught to our young. In this case, he observes that

> A vast pedagogical industry works ceaselessly to oblige young Americans to remember/forget the hostilities of 1861-1865 as a great 'civil war' between 'brothers' rather than between—as they briefly were—two sovereign nation-states. (201)

His point is that the nation, like a person, requires a narrative of identity and that such a narrative recasts historic realities, reflecting 'characteristic amnesias.' Take, for instance, Mark Twain's American classic, *Huckleberry Finn*. Anderson supplies an analysis of an element behind the story line of this piece of national fiction that merits our attention, and to set the stage, speaks of the realities of the historic period in question:

> ...on the one hand, the American states were for many decades weak, effectively decentralized, and rather modest in their educational ambitions. On the other hand, the American societies, in which 'white' settlers were counterposed to 'black' slaves and half-exterminated 'natives,' were internally riven to a degree quite unmatched in Europe. Yet the *imagining* of that fraternity ...shows up remarkably early, and not without a curious authentic popularity. [Emphasis mine] (202)

The fraternity to which Anderson refers here is a remembered/forgotten 'brotherhood', the fraternity required for nationhood. Twain created, despite the historic struggle, and against all contradictory evidence,

> the first indelible image of black and white as American 'brothers': Jim and Huck companionably adrift on the wide Mississippi. But the setting is a remembered/forgotten antebellum in which the black is still a slave. (203)

As if by a sleight of hand, then, this American classic, written in 1881 (following the end of the Civil War and the Emancipation Proclamation), places its readers in a world where fraternity is evident, despite the oppressive realities of race relations and the brutal practice(s) and legacy of slavery. It does so as well in spite of the historic fact of the most costly and vicious war ever fought on American soil. It could be argued that Twain's work succeeded in becoming a classic *because* of its fictive narrative of fraternity as we knew it should be, creating a figure of the ideal in a 'new' national consciousness, despite the abhorrent realities surrounding (and embedded within) its telling. What is the effect of such a literary device?

> These striking nineteenth-century imaginings of fraternity, emerging 'naturally' in a society fractured by the most violent racial, class and regional antagonisms, show as clearly as anything else that nationalism... represented a new form of consciousness—a consciousness that arose when it was no longer possible to experience the nation as new... (203)

Twain's classic represents the narrative imagining of a fraternity yet to be realized, and yet capable of being celebrated even in its *absence*. Whether this is desirable is certainly questionable, but to some extent, the imagining of this fraternity was critical to the imagining of an America united after the Civil War, and it was this imagining that contributed to the 'new' national consciousness that, for some, constituted the true emergence of America *as nation* (see, e.g., Lind, 2001; Urban and Wagoner, 2000).

Appadurai: Post-Nationalism and the *Limits* of the Nation

> The image, the imagined, the imaginary—these are all terms that direct us to something critical and new in global cultural processes: *the imagination as a social practice*. ...the imagination has become an organized field of social practices... and a form of negotiation between sites of agency (individuals) and globally defined fields of possibility. This unleashing of the imagination links the play of pastiche... to the terror and coercion of states and their competitors. The imagination is now central to all forms of agency, is itself a social fact, and is the key component of the new global order. [Emphasis in original] (Appadurai, 1996, 31)

Appadurai signals the intrusion into this national consciousness, more than a century later, of effects of globalization that indicate the *limits* of the nation. Appadurai provides "a theory of rupture that takes media and migration as its two major, and interconnected, diacritics and explores their joint effect on the *work of the imagination*" [emphasis in original] (3). I focus here largely on his argument as it relates to global electronic media, which "decisively change the wider field of mass media," offering both new resources and new disciplines "for the construction of imagined selves and imagined worlds" (3). He offers that varying effects of this mediation—e.g., "the telescoping of news into audio-video bytes" (3)—are immediately absorbed into our discourses, creating a scenario where "electronic media... tend to interrogate, subvert, and transform other contextual literacies" (3). What interests me primarily here is their immediate absorption into public discourse, thus effecting a transformation, serving as "resources for experiments with self-making in all sorts of societies, for all sorts of persons" (3). This picture is complicated as well, he contends, by mass migration.

"As with mediation, so with motion," declares Appadurai, and for him this migration "is juxtaposed with the rapid flow of mass-mediated images, scripts, and sensations," destabilizing "the production of modern subjectivities" (4). The result is that "we see moving images meet deterritorialized viewers" to create "diasporic public spheres, phenomena that confound theories that depend on the continued salience of the nation-state as the key arbiter of important social changes" (4). It appears that a faultline has opened between the Western concept of the nation and its adherents, on the one hand, and a variant of the nation that he terms a 'community of sentiment' (8). Such communities transcend national boundaries as their organizing feature and include terrorist groups *and* multinational corporate giants, as well as transnational and global organizations and movements. Consequently, Appadurai argues that a shift has occurred "in which the imagination has become a collective, social fact" and "the basis of the plurality of imagined worlds" (5). Yet we know that strong, even coercive nationalism arose following September 11th, and that nationalism is still very much alive. *Some* may have moved beyond the nation-state, the nation as territorial construct, and nationalism itself, but *none* have moved beyond civic-cultural striving.

This development is central to the core notions addressed in this work, since it is the work of social imagination that propels national identity, the nation as a community imagined together. However, the development of collective social imaginaries based on global 'mass-mediated images' and global migration "often provokes resistance, irony, selectivity, and, in general, *agency*," so that "terrorists modeling themselves on Rambo-like figures (who have themselves generated a host of non-Western counterparts)" serve as just one example showing that the media image is "quickly moved into local repertoires of irony, anger, humor, and resistance" (7). For Appadurai, imagination as social cultural practice "has a projective sense about it, the sense of being a prelude to some sort of expression," and can therefore "become the fuel for action" (7). This captures my attention as it holds out both danger and opportunity with the same gesture, and thus speaks of possibility. In fact, he depicts the space of imagination today as "a staging ground for action" (7). If that is the case, then this is a faculty we cannot fail to nurture in our young; but we must be clear that imagination as Appadurai uses it is not the same as fantasy, and we need to take care that imagination is fostered within an inclusive and constructive moral fabric (Greene, 2008).

Global media and migration, then, affect the creation and promotion of imagined communities of various types, including terrorist groups, who aim to carve out a place for themselves in opposition to existing nation-states. The result, Appadurai declares, is that "the monopoly of autonomous nation-states" has been broken, and "the transformation of everyday subjectivities" is now both "a cultural fact" and is as well "deeply" political, "through the new ways in which individual attachments, interests, and aspirations increasingly crosscut those of the nation-state" (10). This is both a reaction to and an outcome of the failure of the nation-state to accommodate difference in a more constructive way, thus leading to the emergence of identity politics as a means to counter oppressive cultural practices.

"Throughout the world," he argues, as states are "encompassing their ethnic diversities into fixed and closed sets of cultural categories to which individuals are often assigned forcibly, many groups are consciously mobilizing themselves according to identitarian criteria," creating a scenario where "culturalism, put simply, is identity politics mobilized at the level of the nation-state" (15). "The ethnic violence we see in many places," Appadurai suggests,

> is part of a wider transformation …the conscious mobilization of cultural differences in the service of a larger national or transnational politics frequently associated with extraterritorial histories and memories, sometimes with refugee status and exile, and almost always with struggles for stronger recognition from existing nation-states or from various transnational bodies. (15)

For Appadurai, the essential ethical question is this: "what mechanism will assure the protection of minorities, the minimal distribution of democratic rights, and the reasonable possibility of the growth of civil society?" (19). He makes no pretense to having answers, but works to diagnose why the answers are so elusive. Looking for "alternative possibilities to the strategy of defining some nation-states as healthier than others and then suggesting various mechanisms of ideology transfer," he notes that "even where state sovereignty is apparently intact, state legitimacy is frequently insecure," and thus that "debates about race and rights, membership and loyalty, citizenship and authority are no longer culturally peripheral" (20).

He puts forward what he calls "difficult concessions: first, that the political systems of the wealthy northern nations may themselves be in crisis, and second, that the emergent nationalisms of many parts of the world may be founded on patriotisms that are not either exclusively or fundamentally territorial" (21). This is the space of post-national complication, contradiction, and disruption or displacement of the nation itself. This rupture between nationalism and place is fundamental to understanding our post-9/11 world, as well as the dynamics of our own national and nationalist narratives. Those on the 'Christian Right' here at home, for instance, also turn their eyes to a *beyond* disconnected from earthly place—and connected instead to some conceptualization of God's Heaven—but they attach their concept of the nation to this estrangement, reifying and deifying America as God's instrument.

'Nation-ness,' Nationalism, and Post-National Space   89

What Appadurai prescribes is closer analysis of "*diasporic public spheres*" [emphasis in original] (21), and he offers this rationale as he considers the link Anderson (1991) made between mass mediation and imagining the nation, asserting that

> ...there is a similar link to be found between the work of the imagination and the emergence of a postnational political world. ...as mass mediation becomes increasingly dominated by electronic media... and as such media increasingly link producers and audiences across national boundaries, and as these audiences themselves start new conversations between those who move and those who stay, we find a growing number of diasporic public spheres. (21-22)

For Appadurai, these diasporic public spheres are "the crucibles of a postnational political order" since their discourses are driven by "mass media ...and the movement of refugees, activists, students, and laborers" (22-23). As he explores the limits of the nation-state in the face of this diasporic escalation, he asserts the possibility that this "emergent postnational order" will be "based on relations between heterogeneous units," which might include: social movements, interest groups, professional bodies, nongovernmental organizations, armed constabularies, and judicial bodies (23). The challenge, he concedes, is to determine whether "such heterogeneity is consistent with some minimal conventions of norm and values" not requiring "strict adherence" to the social contract as it was conceived in the modern Western nation-state (23). He offers that the results may be mixed:

> This fateful question will be answered...by the negotiations (both civil and violent) between the worlds imagined by these different interests and movements. In the short run... it is likely to be a world of increased incivility and violence. In the longer run ...we may find that cultural freedom and sustainable justice in the world do not presuppose the uniform and general existence of the nation-state. (23)

Appadurai is not alone in considering the possibility that the nation-state is obsolete as the sole arbiter of civic-cultural identity. Barber's (2004) elaboration of *CivWorld* as an antidote to being squeezed between Jihad and McWorld also includes the central notion that

> in a world where there are diseases as well as doctors without frontiers, corruption and prostitution as well as Interpol cops without frontiers, and terrorists and wars against terrorists as well as peacemaking NGOs without frontiers, the time has surely come for *citizens without frontiers*. Without them, lex humana will remain a dream and such formal international governance institutions as can be contrived will be without substance or effect. Without them, global education, global cooperation, global law, and global democracy are empty phrases. The paradox is that global citizens are most

> likely to be produced by the global education, global cooperation, global law, and global democracy that global citizens produce. [Emphasis mine] (230)

This notion of 'citizens without frontiers' is interesting as a critical feature of Barber's *CivWorld* and speaks a language of possibility, which is highly desirable in our times, but a major caveat appears to be necessary here. One of the complications Appadurai encounters in his thinking about "the central problematic of cultural processes in today's world" (29), a complication that is foremost in my thinking about the 'global citizen' as well, is this:

> Marshall McLuhan, among others, sought to theorize about this world as a "global village," but theories such as McLuhan's appear to have *overestimated the communitarian implications* of the new media order (McLuhan and Powers 1989). We are now aware that with media, each time we are tempted to speak of the global village, we must be reminded that media create communities with "no sense of place" (Meyrowitz 1985). The world we live in now seems rhizomic (Deleuze and Guattari 1987), even schizophrenic, calling for theories of rootlessness, alienation, and psychological distance between individuals and groups on the one hand, and fantasies (or nightmares) of electronic propinquity on the other. [Emphasis mine] (29)

As a result of this particular feature of the global village as a mediated construct, special attention is given by Appadurai to "nostalgia without memory," one of the "central ironies of the politics of global cultural flows" (30). He reflects on the thought that in the United States,

> the past is now not a land to return to in a simple politics of memory. It has become a synchronic warehouse of cultural scenarios, a kind of temporal central casting, to which recourse can be taken as appropriate, depending on the movie to be made, the scene to be enacted, the hostages to be rescued. (30)

"In the cultural styles of advanced capitalism," he asserts, this

> apparent increasing substitutability of whole periods and postures for one another… is tied to larger global forces, which have done much to show Americans that the past is usually another country. If your present is their future …and their future is your past… then your own past can be made to appear as simply a normalized modality of your present. (31)

Appadurai contends that "the issue is no longer one of nostalgia but of a social *imaginaire* built largely around reruns" [emphasis in original] (30), so that the U.S. "is no longer the puppeteer of a world system of images, but is only one node of a complex transnational construction of imaginary landscapes… now mediated through the complex prism of modern media" (31). In short, this transformation of our public discourse as an effect of global media and migration reflects a far greater transformation where 'a simple politics of memory' (30) is displaced by this notion of 'substitutability' at the global level in such a way that civic-cultural perspective may dictate the choice of *materiel* for narratives we choose to remember/forget in the process of autobiography at the level of the nation.

The role of democracy as the premiere signifier for America becomes arguable, and even rather arbitrary, in such terrain. Barber (2001) affirms this point when he notes that we are "squeezed between... opposing forces"—between Jihad and McWorld, or "wild terrorism" and "wild capitalism" (xxiii)—in such a way that "the world has been sent spinning out of control" (5). This is consistent with Mailer's (2003) sense of the national identity crisis that Americans were thrown into following September 11th, a crisis that signaled the ensuing 'squeeze' in unanticipated and terrorizing terms. Barber raises a question that can no longer be avoided by those of us who are watching a world consumed by wildfires born of rage, hate, and a lust to kill, on the one hand, and greed, corruption, and absolute indifference to human suffering, on the other: "Can it be that what Jihad and McWorld have in common is anarchy: the absence of common will and that conscious and collective human control under the guidance of law we call democracy?" (5)

Appadurai, however, is neither concerned with anarchy nor with democracy, but rather with a very different problem: "the tension between cultural homogenization and cultural heterogenization" where "there is always a fear of cultural absorption" since "one man's imagined community is another man's political prison" (32). This tension resides not only at the global and at transnational levels, but is crucial and central as well to the issues surrounding national identity *within* post-9/11 America. Bhabha's (1994) work, *The Location of Culture*, is instructive in that it returns us to the notion of the *limits* of the nation as boundary, as border, as a thing which is capable of being transgressed and therefore of being redefined in response to the ever-present threat of 'cultural absorption.' After briefly considering Bhabha's writing about the *beyond* in civic/cultural life, I return, finally, to Benjamin Barber's (2001) work, *Jihad vs. McWorld*, to consider what this tension between competing imaginaries means at its extreme, and what it indicates for the future of democracy, for the nation, for citizenship as category and for culture as 'squeeze.'

Bhabha: Beyond Civic/Cultural Homogeneity and Hegemony

What is theoretically innovative, and politically crucial, is the need to think beyond narratives of originary and initial subjectivities and to focus on those moments or processes that are produced in the articulation of cultural differences. These 'in-between' spaces provide the terrain for elaborating strategies of selfhood—singular or communal—that initiate new signs of identity, and innovative signs of collaboration, and contestation, in the act of defining the idea of society itself. ... It is in the emergence of the interstices—the overlap and displacement of domains of difference—that the intersubjective and collective experiences of *nationness,* community interest, or cultural value are negotiated. [Emphasis in original] (Bhabha, 1994, 2)

Bhabha (1994) speaks of the "social articulation of difference" in terms of its role as "a complex, on-going negotiation that seeks to authorize cultural hybridities" (3). Its potency, for Bhabha, lies in its peripheral positioning relative to authority and power, where it is

> resourced by the power of tradition to be reinscribed through the conditions of contingency and contradictoriness that attend upon the lives of those who are 'in the minority.' The recognition that tradition bestows is a partial form of identification. In restaging the past it introduces other, incommensurable cultural temporalities into the invention of tradition. This process estranges any immediate access to an originary identity or a 'received' tradition. The borderline engagements of cultural difference may as often be consensual as conflictual; they may confound our definitions of tradition; realign the customary boundaries between the private and the public, high and low; and challenge normative expectations of development and progress. (3)

"Political empowerment," Bhabha writes, "and the enlargement of the multiculturalist cause," derive from "questions of solidarity and community from the interstitial perspective" (4). He points to issues of identity and belonging as "the signs of the emergence of community envisaged as a project," a project that incorporates both vision and social reconstruction as it "takes you 'beyond' yourself in order to return... to the political *conditions* of the present" [emphasis in original] (4). Assessing the significance of post-foundational discourses (i.e., poststructural and postmodern), Bhabha argues that their value is that they make us aware of "the epistemological 'limits' of... ethnocentric ideas" and of their role as "enunciative boundaries of a range of other dissonant, even dissident histories and voices" (6). Therefore, he critiques the notion of "homogeneous national cultures," arguing that

> the consensual or contiguous transmission of historical traditions, or 'organic' ethnic communities... are in a profound process of redefinition. ... This side of the psychosis of patriotic fervour... there is overwhelming evidence of a more transnational and translational sense of the hybridity of imagined communities. (7)

Displacement and disjunction (and the diasporic public spheres they hint at and ultimately reveal) are key themes in Bhabha, and speaking of a "'new' internationalism," he sees "the 'middle passage' of contemporary culture" as "a process of displacement and disjunction," where there is no longer an appropriate space for a totalized experience (8). This creates a scenario where "cultures are being produced from the perspective of disenfranchised minorities" to reflect 'national' propensities, and he argues that rather than "producing... a pluralist anarchy," they actually open to a "changed basis for making international connections" (8)

Bhabha presents a critique of Anderson's work on nation-ness and nationalism that is situated via "critical comparativism," asserting that the "currency" of work in this field "is no longer the sovereignty of the national culture conceived as Benedict Anderson proposes as an 'imagined community' rooted in a 'homogeneous empty time' of modernity and progress," but reflects more accurately "a radical revision in the concept of human community itself," as evidenced in the fact that this new geopolitical space "is being both interrogated and reinitiated" (8). Part of this process, according to Bhabha, involves the need for the "Western metropole" to "confront its postcolonial history, told by its influx of postwar migrants and refugees, as an indigenous or native narrative *internal to its national identity*" [emphasis in original] (9). For Bhabha, the West needs to face its past and open to 'dissonant' and 'dissident histories' as voices to be included in the reconstruction of national identity. As he sees it,

> to dwell 'in the beyond' is... to be part of a revisionary time, a return to the present to redescribe our cultural contemporaneity; to reinscribe our human, historic commonality; *to touch the future on its hither side*. In that sense, then, the intervening space 'beyond' becomes a space of intervention in the here and now. [Emphasis in original] (10)

His sense of "the borderline work of culture" necessarily requires "an encounter with 'newness'" that "creates a sense of the new as an insurgent act of cultural translation" (10) This translational sensibility "renews the past, refiguring it as a contingent 'in-between' space" even as it "innovates and interrupts the performance of the present" so that the convergence of past and present "becomes part of the necessity, not the nostalgia, of living" (10). For Bhabha, this is *art*; in this work, it is *autobiography*.

Noting Hobsbawm's (1975, 1987) work on "the history of the modern Western nation from the perspective of the nation's margin and the migrants' exile" (200), Bhabha offers an illuminating portrayal of the nation as *metaphor*:

> The emergence of the later phase of the modern nation, from the mid-nineteenth century, is also one of the most sustained periods of mass migration within the West, and colonial expansion in the East. The nation fills the void left in the uprooting of communities and kin, and turns that loss into the language of metaphor. Metaphor... transfers the meaning of home and belonging, across the 'middle passage'... across

those distances, and cultural differences, that span the imagined community of the nation-people. (200)

Asserting that nationalism is not his main concern, that he is, in fact, writing *against* "the historical certainty and settled nature of that term," he sees instead the need to "write of the Western nation as an obscure and ubiquitous form of living the *locality* of the culture" (200), and offers that

> This locality is more *around* temporality than *about* historicity; a form of living that is more complex than 'community'; more symbolic than 'society'; more connotative than 'country'; less patriotic than *patrie*; more rhetorical than the reason of State; more mythological than ideology; less homogeneous than hegemony; less centred than the citizen; more collective than 'the subject'; more psychic than civility; more hybrid in the articulation of cultural differences and identifications than can be represented in any hierarchical or binary structuring of social antagonism. [Emphasis in original] (200-201)

For Bhabha, neither class hierarchy nor ideological or partisan division, then, accounts for nation as metaphor, but rather displacement.

Bhabha's disclosure of purpose, his rationale for taking this approach is, as noted above, that he is "attempting to formulate... the complex strategies of cultural identification and discursive address that function in the name of 'the people' or 'the nation' and make them the immanent subjects of a range of social and literary narratives" (201), having proposed a "cultural construction of nationness as a form of social and textual affiliation" (200). Unlike Bhabha, Barber (2001) focuses on the relations between present context, the nation as the location of citizenship, and the threat to democracy.

Barber on Anarchy and Democracy: *Jihad vs. McWorld*

> As the world enters a novel stage of shadowed warfare against an invisible enemy, the clash between Jihad and McWorld is again poignantly relevant in understanding why the modern response to terror cannot be exclusively military or tactical, but rather must entail a commitment to democracy and justice even when they are in tension with the commitment to cultural expansionism and global markets. The war against terrorism also will have to be a war for justice if it is to succeed... (Barber, 2001, xi-xii)

> The language of justice was surely the appropriate context for the American response, but it will remain appropriate only if the compass of its meaning is extended from retributive to distributive justice. (Barber, 2001, xii)

Barber's (2001) prescient narrative of the state of the world (originally published in 1995), *Jihad vs. McWorld*, reaches broadly to capture a multitude of influences—domestic, international, transnational, and global—fashioning present context. *Jihad* is used in Barber to indicate "the forces of disintegral tribalism and reactionary fundamentalism," while *McWorld* is used to indicate "the forces of integrative modernization and aggressive economic and cultural globalization" (xii). Barber asserts that collision between these movements "has been brutally exacerbated by the dialectical interdependence of these two seemingly oppositional sets of forces" (xii), with democracy squarely at risk:

> In *Jihad vs. McWorld*, I warn that democracy is caught between a clash of movements, each of which for its own reasons seems indifferent to freedom's fate, and might suffer grievously. It is now apparent... that democracy rather than terrorism may become the principal victim of the battle currently being waged. (xii)

Updated in 2001, this text is a narrative of the now, not of some threatening future. Given the broad reach of the text, and because Barber's focus is democracy and its survival in present context, I draw in this chapter only from those textual threads that speak directly to the nation, to nation-ness, to citizenship, and to culture in these times, all of which are subservient to his concern for democracy.

Barber discloses a search for "new foundations" for both citizenship and democracy in the clash between "the fractious forces of Jihad and the spreading markets of McWorld," both of which effectively cut "the legs out from under democratic institutions" (219). His characterization of this phenomenon, this "clash," situates democracy in relation to the *need for* the nation, while situating citizenship as being more closely linked to democracy itself:

> ...the clash of Jihad and McWorld foments a new world disorder in which democracy is occluded. The nation-state certainly has not in and of itself guaranteed a democratic civil society, and is probably something less than an indispensable condition for the flourishing of free women and men. After all, democracies of one kind or another arose in small city-state polities—for which they seem ideally suited—before there were nation-states... However, in the last several hundred years, democratic and egalitarian institutions have... been closely associated with integral nation-states, and citizenship (democracy's sine qua non) has been an attribute of membership in such states. (119)

For Barber, "the consequences of the dialectical interaction between [Jihad and McWorld] suggest new and startling forms of inadvertent tyranny," and, equally important, this new form of tyranny "is indirect, often even friendly" (220):

> Alexis de Tocqueville first captured its character 160 years ago when he wrote: "fetters and headsmen were the coarse instruments that tyranny formerly employed; but the civilization of our age has perfected despotism itself... Monarchs had... materialized oppression; the democratic republics of the present day have rendered it as entirely an

> affair of the mind.... [T]he body is left free, and the soul is enslaved." The ideology of choice seems to liberate the body... but fatally constricts the possibility of real freedom for the soul... (220)

Although the triumphal discourse following September 11th (and its hypernational accoutrement) was anything but 'friendly' to those *not* willing to yield to its orthodoxy, America is subsumed under the category of McWorld in Barber (a category that markets itself as benign and beneficent, as does triumphal discourse). In Twitchell (2004), 'Brand USA' (295) may even be cause for celebration (297). In either case, a new 'brand' under this authoritative regime poses the threat not only of 'indirect tyranny,' but of more sinister and blatant forms, as we have seen.

Barber's sense is that this entire scenario, for Americans, is complicated by a civic-cultural struggle that revolves both around issues of national identity and of how we are situated in relation to the world:

> As if still in the nineteenth century, America has persuaded itself that its options today are either to preserve an ancient and blissfully secure independence that puts us in charge of American destiny, or to yield to a perverted and compulsory interdependence that puts foreigners and alien international bodies such as the United Nations or the World Court in charge of American destiny. (xix)

Explaining that "In truth, however, Americans have not enjoyed genuine independence since sometime before the great wars of the last century" (xix), Barber insists that

> Interdependence is not some foreign adversary against which citizens need to muster resistance. It is a domestic reality that already has compromised the efficacy of citizenship in scores of unacknowledged and uncharted ways. (xix)

I argue here not only that 'the efficacy of citizenship' has been 'compromised,' but also that the category of the civic as a whole has been deterritorialized in such a way as to leave the 'psyche in sprawl' (Mailer, 2003). It is from this vantage point that I work to illustrate an autobiography of post-9/11 America and to illuminate the emergence of a number of problematic issues, most importantly the extent to which national identity is fragmented and disputatious, revealing pluralist imaginings of our nation and varied understandings of what it means to be American.

Concluding Thoughts on Nationalism in Post-National Space

Theoretical work on the nation, nation-ness, and nationalism is useful because it frames present context in new terms and, more importantly, with new vision. This matters because the emergence of post-9/11 America was propelled in part by violent attacks attributed to a 'transnational sodality' (bin Laden's Al Qaeda) whose aims and purposes, apart from spawning fear and terror, are not well understood, and because this was augmented by the systematic obfuscation employed by the Bush-Cheney regime that worked to confound America's conscience and blatantly undermined democracy in the name of security. The intrusion of such agendas into our consciousness as a nation has changed us and will continue to do so, probably in some fundamental and unexpected ways, for some time to come. The effects of their social imaginings, in short, have impacted not only our material and social realities—our new 'need,' for instance, for 'homeland security' and our apparent willingness to trade our liberties for some illusion of 'safety'—but also our national imaginaries of character, will, identity and purpose. The effects, in internal response, are far-reaching and are likely to challenge our imaginative powers more deeply than any prior attack or event ever could. My answer to this is not only to work from an authentic (albeit anecdotal) autobiography of the nation, but to advance as well the cause of critical, interpretive, and imaginative praxis.

The American nation may well rise to these challenges brilliantly, and the challenges posed by this scenario may, in fact, bring out the best in us, rather than the worst, if we—and the term 'we' is highly problematic—can bring our imaginative powers to the fore. The effects produced by this new awareness of adversity need to be closely scrutinized and reexamined with theoretics that can serve as new 'thinking tools' (Popkewitz and Brennan, 1998, 11). We need to consider what tools might be engaged to defuse, offset, divert, etc., the intended impacts of both Jihad *and* McWorld. In short, we need an entirely new work of social imagination to attend to post-9/11 America, an America that needs to be revived, informed, aligned and engaged with its new task—resisting and defying terror, *in all its forms*. In this lies a genuinely new curriculum perhaps yet to be conceived, one that should be undertaken with energy, humility, and gravity by curricularists, our new *warriors* in the work of social imagination. Such a call to arms requires an authentic dialogue.

Schooling is at the forefront of the public sphere, insomuch as it lays the groundwork for future possibilities by preparing society's change agents, its future citizens. Schooling, however, is not an autonomous site for this project—Porter (1999), for instance, sees a diminished role for schooling in this *era of uncertainty*—and educators are currently operating under heavy restraints. Nevertheless, responsibility cannot be forfeited to the events of the moment. Therefore, I am compelled to urge that we explore multiple avenues for pursuing understanding, with an eye to renewing efforts towards the socio-cultural and political education, *first*, of ourselves, and *then*, of our young. However we choose to view our own contextual moment, our perspectives are constructed out of the weavings of psycho-social, cultural, regional, ethnic, racial, religious, class, embodied and gendered identities that are further fragmented and impacted by the geopolitical. These identities are always and everywhere local, although they are shaped by their own histories, which may transcend local, and often even national, distinctions. Therefore, our consciousness always involves greater gestalts of community than those that materially surround us. Print culture may intrude into the local a sense of the national and global, but it is certainly not the only medium which does so.

Appadurai asserts that "culturalist movements... are the most general form of the work of the imagination and draw frequently on the fact or possibility of migration or secession" (15). Such movements therefore "are self-conscious about identity, culture, and heritage," which are part of their "deliberate vocabulary as they struggle with states and other culturalist focuses and groups" (15). We need to recognize and address the fact that the civic and cultural institutions constituting our public sphere transcend national boundaries, and that transnational intercourse may sometimes place these institutions in precarious circumstances in our times. At the forefront of this kind of scenario are our universities, which are of necessity deeply enmeshed in transnational dialogue and cooperation (as are some of our 'faith-based' organizations and 'new' social movements). Appadurai points out how vulnerable the national framework—and its institutions—are to this positioning:

> ...diasporic public spheres are frequently tied up with students and other intellectuals engaging in long-distance nationalism. ... Religions... now pursue global missions and diasporic clienteles with vigor... Activist movements involved with the environment, women's issues, and human rights generally have created a sphere of transnational discourse... Major transnational separatist movements... conduct their self-imagining in sites throughout the world, where they have enough members to allow for the emergence of multiple nodes in a larger diasporic public sphere. (22)

A question that has consistently been raised is whether the nation can be protected from terrorism without sacrificing democracy. How social change plays out in educative terms is a matter of tremendous importance. As a nation, an imagined community, the question must be raised: *Are we living in a post-democratic era?*

Appadurai, as noted, contends that the U.S. is "no longer the puppeteer of a world system of images" (31). This characterization bears on something of great magnitude—the renewed energy and influence of 'others,' individuals (including corporations), identity groups, other nations, and 'communities of sentiment' alike, in terms of images proliferated across the globe, their meanings, effects and influences—for thinking about the autobiographic process at this national level. Describing the ongoing battles over meaning in terms of the *limits* of the nation, Appadurai theorizes tension between the actual, administered body of the state and the imaginary, collectively embraced entity we call the *nation*, a relationship that is "embattled" everywhere such that

> in many societies the nation and the state have become one another's projects. ...while nations (or more properly groups with ideas about nationhood) seek to capture and monopolize ideas about nationhood ...separatist transnational movements, including those that have included terror in their methods, exemplify nations in search of states. ...each of these represents imagined communities that seek to create states of their own or carve pieces out of existing states. States... are everywhere seeking to monopolize the moral resources of community, either by flatly claiming coevality between nation and state, or by systematically museumizing and representing all the groups within them in a variety of heritage politics that seems remarkably uniform throughout the world... (39)

I bear in mind here Blacker's assertion that "one's idea of what one is struggling against has a direct impact on what one *becomes* as one struggles" (357). I am suggesting that since we are dealing with a novel social force, a 'culturalist' effect of the social imaginary of others, we would do well to try to understand it. However, since what we *become* as we struggle is the central focus of this work, let me now return to those dimensions of the discussion. In the next section, I take up the matter of *who we say we are* or *will become* in post-9/11 America.

Part Two

Autobiography and Civic-Cultural Struggle

Introduction

AUTOBIOGRAPHY AS CURRERE

Introduction: Autobiography of a Nation as *Currere*

The texts elaborated in the next two chapters form a record of civic-cultural struggle in the moment immediately following September 11th, providing us with some priceless historical glimpses. They give us access to vistas of social thought inhabiting public space at the time, and some are alive to possibility and radiate imagination, enriching this work immensely as they articulate diverse narratives of our national autobiography and thus testify to our pluralism. Although I have had to select just a few pieces from a larger body of writing for my purposes in this book, they offer a rich description that is invaluable. They form a *currere* of this moment as American voices offer their hopes and fears for our nation in the moment where the threat to the (democratic) nation—to America as we had known it—first reared its ugly head in a manner that rendered it visible to the public eye. Texts are taken to reflect vistas of post-9/11 America; vistas are grouped according to how they depict civic-cultural struggles over autobiography. Vistas enunciated by power (*triumphal* and *hypernational*), vistas that sanction control (*voyeurist*), as well as vistas that reflect (more or less passive) *consciousness* of control (*vigilant* and *pluralist*) are presented in the next chapter, Part I of the autobiography (see Chapter 5). Vistas reflecting alternatives to control (that is, reflecting active resistance to or re-appropriation of the message(s) of control) (*globalist*, *reparationist*, and *communitarian*) are presented in the following chapter, Part II of the autobiography (see Chapter 6).

I invite my reader to experience the moment under study, then, through the 'storylines' of these texts and to listen for *who they say we are*, or *will become*. They reflect Pinar's (1975) notion of *currere*: that is, the sense in which these texts embody—however differently, however disputatiously—what it might mean to 'run the course' of our experiencing of public selfhood as educative (Pinar, 2004, 35) and as a means to help us "understand the human impact of culture's struggle for self-description," (Kincheloe, 1998, 130). This is a central feature of the terrain explored in this work. These texts offer up their part in the struggle to portray America in a troubled contextual space—the civic-cultural surround of the new American wilderness. As such, they form a curriculum that invites us to consider alternatives to the powerful hegemonic enunciation of 'Truth' for the nation that emanated from the voice of power and from those who sought to enforce it.

I begin with a selection of excerpts that reflect *Orthodoxy*: first, President George W. Bush's *State of the Union* Address (2003); and second, the *public* discourse of Americans for Victory Over Terrorism (AVOT, 2002). It should be noted that these two articulations of vision are supported by extraordinary power in present context. This weights their enunciations heavily, and this weight sits on the shoulders of *all* Americans, even more so since it has translated into devastating material social realities, both at home and abroad. Other voices had to compete with their power to be heard in this moment, and exhibited civic courage as they did so, given the 'mood of the nation' as depicted by the media and circumscribed by the enunciation(s) of power.

Following an elaboration of these two texts, I re-frame this moment based on alternative discourses addressing the "central questions posed by *currere*": namely, who we say we are or will become (Kincheloe, 1998, 130). I have fashioned this work so that we might 'see into' alternative imaginaries that attempt to answer these questions in terms of the nation as an imagined community and citizenship as we exercise it to form, maintain, and/or transform that 'community.' The central point is that *it is our task* to form, maintain, and/or transform our nation. I do not pretend that these alternative imaginaries are constructs that will hold over time, but credit them with displaying courage in their willingness to voice their civic difference in a tightly constrained environment during a traumatic moment. It is essential to bear in mind Kincheloe's caution that

> As a perpetual struggle, the curriculum of Pinar's *currere* is never a finished product that can be finally mastered and passed along to an awaiting new generation. Such a perspective protects the curriculum from the all-too-common fragmentation of modernist pedagogies, as it focuses our attention on the lived realities, socio-political encounters, and the identity formation of individual human beings. (130)

Eisner (2002) suggests that "what is missing from American schools is a deep respect for personal purpose, lived experience, for the life of imagination" (77). I concur. Pinar's *currere* extends beyond the schools, however, and "concerns the investigation of the nature of the individual experience of the public" using an "analytical synthesis" of phenomenology, psychoanalysis and aesthetics (Kincheloe, in Pinar, 1998, 129). Kincheloe explains Pinar's reasoning:

Introduction

> Pinar argued that we are better prepared to approach the contents of consciousness as they appear to us in educational contexts. Such exploration allows us, Pinar argued, to loosen our identification with the contents of consciousness so that we can gain some distance from them. From our new vantage point we may be able to see those psychic realms that are formed by conditioning and unconscious adherence to social convention. (129)

I look explicitly here at 'unconscious adherence to social convention'—and to its breakdown—to find contours of a curriculum embracing new imaginaries. My criteria for selection of texts, therefore, were attuned to answering the following questions: (1) did the text advocate or portray some vista that might offer understanding of America in this social moment? (2) did the text offer some imagining of what exercising citizenship—*enacting* civic courage—in this social moment should mean or require? and/or (3) did the text hold out some alternative offering that might contribute to moving us away from this post-democratic moment via new imaginaries? Texts included here attended to at least two of these three criteria, although they may have done so tacitly.

I sought, in my selection, to ensure that a multiplicity of perspectives were included. Often the expression through which these imaginaries found play was tacit, since the imaginaries are in many cases embedded within the telling of a tale, the sharing of reminiscences, or the construction of an intertextual play of verbal images. Where I am dealing with commentary (e.g., *The New York Times* and tompaine.com), there is an added dimension. Approaching texts that often aim to *entertain* as much as they do to inform, inspire, or advocate something complicated my thinking about how to position them within the intertextual field of the greater collective text. Ultimately, I used what I read as their *descriptive vision*—their portrayal or critique (a vista) of new post-9/11 American realities—to inform the map's contours. As a result, texts do not necessarily correspond with an author's positioning; what I am looking at here is the vista itself.

For each text, I begin with excerpts that highlight how the social moment is depicted, and then briefly elaborate the truth- and value-claims of the text. I use this elaboration to flesh out autobiography and to inform the contours of the map (see Chapter 7) as I look for distinct features of the vista portrayed—first, an epistemological 'foundation' for citizenship, and second, a particularly valued mode of civic engagement. I derived three perceptual codes for each of these two conceptual organizers from discursive analysis of the texts: foundations for citizenship are represented by *Orthodoxy*, *Reason* or *Perspective*; modes of civic engagement are represented by *Control*, *Representation* or *Activism*, each of which I briefly outline here for purposes of orientation to the autobiography that follows.

Orthodoxy involves believing or accepting that 'Authority'—the administration, the system, hegemonic belief, religious tenets, or God—should define the nature of the nation in such a way as to conflate nation and state, i.e., to render them one and the same. *Reason* involves believing or accepting that the nature of the nation should be defined or construed according to its founding principles of civic debate and civic conscience, so that the nation depends on the public sphere for its being, its nature, its will. *Perspective* involves adhering to a gestalt of community not corresponding with the nation, something either broader or more particular, complicating or contradicting the circumscribed notion of the nation as a discrete entity. Each of these 'foundations' reflects a different epistemological code of identity and belonging within the nation, as well as differing bases for coherence and different senses of community.

Related to these epistemological codes, or foundations for citizenship (which are 'truth claims' that tend to define our thinking about the nation), there are also axiological codes—preferred modes of civic engagement (these are 'value claims' that tend to define our thinking about civic responsibility). *Control* signifies valuing 'government *for* the people,' such that texts located in this domain reflect a 'sanctioning' of the administration itself or of the system in general. *Representation*, on the other hand, signifies valuing 'government *of* the people,' such that texts located in this domain reflect an appreciation of the need for a public negotiation of legitimacy to support the system as a whole and a sensitivity to inclusion in the represented whole. Finally, *Activism* signifies valuing 'government *by* the people,' such that texts located in this domain reflect the right of and need for citizens *to be empowered to act* in accordance with public needs, desires, and aspirations.

These categories are neither neat nor discrete; they overlap and interweave. They are nomadic, deterritorialized tendencies exhibited by public, political, and academic writing in this moment, but they provide coherent pathways through the chaos of being/becoming, ways of seeing what was being experienced vis-à-vis the nation and its citizens in the face of social trauma and the emergence of a threat to the nation *and* to democracy. Further, the interrelations of particular foundations for citizenship and particular preferred modes of civic engagement led me to consider whether there was a more sophisticated way to conceptualize the perceptual codes that had emerged. This I navigated by analyzing the juxtaposition of foundations for citizenship with preferred modes of civic engagement. My goal was to provide a clearer sense of meaning, along with a more authentic way of approaching the vistas offered by the texts themselves, especially where a foundation for citizenship and/or mode of civic engagement was tacit rather than explicit. From this juxtaposition I inferred from these vistas, then, *cultures of citizenship*. I derived eight cultures of citizenship from these texts: *triumphal, voyeurist, vigilant, pluralist, globalist, reparationist, communitarian,* and *hypernational*.

Texts are organized in this chapter so that each section addresses a space where codes converge. At the center, or root, of the map lies the convergence generally perceived to have been envisioned by the Founding Fathers, the *Reason-Representation* convergence, which Americans have at least tacitly claimed as their founding faith, but from which we have wandered as we pursued other visions, having seen the historic limitations of the original. So it is to be expected that these cultures of citizenship stray, to greater or lesser degrees, from the center, and they do not disappoint in this regard. This dispersion outwards from the center represents a *diasporic public sphere* (Appadurai, 1996), the deterritorialization (Deleuze and Guattari, 1987) of both culture and citizenship.

A Word about 'Alternative' Venues

The 'Partial Special Issue: 9/11 Reflections' of the *Qualitative Inquiry* journal was produced, by invitation, as a response to this social moment from within a broad, but thickly-defined community of scholarship. Norman K. Denzin and Yvonna S. Lincoln used the following language as they invited commentary:

> Yvonna and I are stunned, appalled, and grieved by the attacks on the World Trade Center and the Pentagon and sorrowing not only for the loss of life but for the loss of opportunity, for the loss of love, and for the temporary loss of the ability of dialogue to work through problems of hatred and religious intolerance. ... We are also deeply concerned about the implications for an interpretivist social science that has left us with so little by way of understanding how or why this could happen. Our invitation to you is to join with us ... to talk about the terror, about its implications for an interpretivist social science, and about ways in which a radically reformulated social science directed toward communitarian ethics and social justice might address our understanding of this horror, and perhaps our ability to resolve those issues that have seemingly created the circumstances that prompted this attack. (133)

Additionally, they characterize contributions as statements that strengthen "*Qualitative Inquiry*'s commitment to the belief that interpretive scholars have the moral responsibility to record and analyze such events as those of 11 September and to do so because a genuine democracy requires no less" (134). I took that moral responsibility to heart as well, determining to 'record and analyze' diverse responses to the 'national psyche' in sprawl (Mailer, 2003) in that moment. *Qualitative Inquiry* was one of two print venues from which I drew texts for the autobiography.

The other print venue was *The New York Times*, often referred to as a 'national newspaper of record.' The *Times* responded to the needs of a city that had come under attack and had suffered untold horror, shock and loss—all of it displayed and sent around the world through the image machinery of global electronic media—as it created new print spaces for the emerging needs and crisis of the nation, as well as of New Yorkers themselves. At the same time, the paper managed to maintain Op-Ed pages that were consistent in tone and quality with pre-September 11th offerings, not losing its edge as the voice of conscience and criticism, or what used to be called 'the loyal opposition.'

Finally, I drew from writing on a 'radical' website (that is how it portrayed itself relative to mainstream discourse): tompaine.com. This website came to my attention because of its advertisements on the Op-Ed pages of *The New York Times*, and these ads made a case for the failure of mainstream media to reflect the nation's need for alternative vision(s) in this time of national crisis. This website prides itself on a 'common sense' approach to American discourse, and its ads 'announced' that the people had a need for 'real' information and insights that were not only thought provoking, but sometimes also shocking. This website describes itself as a 'public interest journal' that was "inspired by the great patriot Thomas Paine," who "used his talent to advance the cause of liberty and democracy against distant and unaccountable rulers." Its stated mission is "to enrich the national debate on controversial public issues by featuring the ideas, opinions, and analyses too often overlooked by the *mainstream media*" [emphasis in original] (www.tompaine.com/about.cfm).

The opening vignettes in the chapter that follows offer an analysis of *triumphal* and *hypernational* narratives. These two cultures of citizenship were *enunciated* and/or *enforced* by power, and therefore the analysis is straightforward and brief. Following these analyses, the elaboration of autobiographical writing representing alternative cultures of citizenship is more fully developed. For that reason, each culture of citizenship occupies its own space, respectively, in each of the chapters.

5

A Post-9/11 American Autobiography

PART I

Triumphal Discourse

The following excerpt provides us with a triumphal narrative of post-9/11 America that asserts consensual agreement about the historical character of the nation, about our 'arrival' as a democracy, about our status as a world leader, and about our destiny as a people. Further, this narrative makes assumptions about our cultural beliefs and values, assumptions that only apply realistically to those espousing a form of nationalism now popular with the so-called 'Christian Right.' This excerpt is drawn from President Bush's *State of the Union* Address on January 28, 2003, enunciating a triumphal view of both the nation and its citizens. This text is consistent with other speeches used by the President, but is more dramatic, since it was presented to the nation just before our actions in Iraq. Here are the words spoken by President George W. Bush:

> Many challenges, abroad and at home, have arrived in a single season. In two years, America has gone from a sense of invulnerability to an awareness of peril, from bitter division in small matters to calm unity in great causes. .... And we go forward with confidence, because this call of history has come to the right country. .... Americans are a resolute people, who have risen to every test of our time. Adversity has revealed the character of our country, to the world, and to ourselves [sic]. .... America is a strong nation and honorable in the use of our strength. We exercise power without conquest, and we sacrifice for the liberty of strangers. .... Americans are a free people, who know that freedom is the right of every person and the future of every nation. The liberty we prize is not America's gift to the world; it is God's gift to humanity. .... We Americans have faith in ourselves, but not in ourselves alone. We do not claim to know all the ways of Providence, yet we can trust in them, placing our confidence in the loving god behind all of life and all of history. May he guide us now, and may God continue to bless the United States of America.
>
> (*The Washington Post Company, 17, www.washingtonpost.com/ wpsrv/onpolitics/transcripts/bushtext_012803.html*)

What are the claims of this discourse? The first claim is that we are experiencing 'calm unity in great causes.' The effect of such an enunciation is to isolate those who feel neither calm nor unity, as well as those for whom such unity (or the pressure to unite under this regime) indicates potential danger. Further, this text asserts that our 'bitter division' (prior to September 11th and now magically transformed) was only in 'small matters.' One has to wonder how people become 'bitter' over '*small* matters' [emphasis mine]. This amounts to a dismissal of difference that manifests as *control* over the positioning of the citizen vis-à-vis the crisis itself. Another claim is our exceptionality as a 'resolute people' given to honor and strength 'who have risen to every test of our time.' This new 'test,' the 'call of history', therefore, has—in this enunciation— 'come to the right country.' This vista is a place where the honor and strength of the American people reside in our (consensual) belief that freedom comes from God, and that we can move forward with confidence in God's purposes and Divine will, and in our nation as God's 'blessed' instrument for accomplishing His will. The accusation that the Bush-Cheney administration—and America's wars of retaliation—amounted to a Christian crusade against Islam found its rationale in this kind of enunciation, and fairly so, given the language used to frame the crisis and its resolution, protests against such accusations notwithstanding.

In this America, the character of our country has been revealed, both to ourselves and to the world, and we are *not* found wanting. This America not only has great strength, but is 'honorable' in its use of that strength. We are exceptional in this rendition of our national character, because we 'exercise power without conquest,' and because 'we sacrifice for the liberty of strangers.' In this America, the people are free, and understand that freedom as 'the right of every person and the future of every nation.' This freedom, however, doesn't come from us. This freedom comes as 'God's gift to humanity,' a gift God gives *through* us. We have faith in ourselves because we have confidence in 'the loving god behind all of life and all of history.' This 'loving god' has blessed us, and our civic courage amounts to trusting that *He* will continue to do so as we remain true to these doctrines. If we remain true, then we may be triumphant. In this narrative of the nation, the state and the nation (as a reflection of a united and like-minded people) are 'faithful servants' of God; they are one.

The President speaks not just as head of state and Commander-in-Chief of the armed forces, but also as the voice of the people. Although President Bush speaks for only *some* of the people, the enunciation itself *pretends* to speak for the whole. The effect is to 'silence' those not inclined to unite under this banner of self-proclaimed goodness, nobility of purpose, and divine sanction, a banner whose effect is to exert control over alternative possibilities for characterizing the nation and its response to terror. The foundation for citizenship is

Orthodoxy; the mode of civic engagement is (assumed) *Control*. The culture of citizenship advocated for the nation is *triumphal*.

This is the weighted enunciation prevailing immediately following September 11th and echoed in the public and political speech of each of the administration's cast of players—from President Bush and Vice-President Cheney to Secretaries of State and Defense to lesser White House spokespersons—as well as in the public and political speech of the then-ruling Republican Party in both Houses of Congress, and in the public rants of right-wing media outlets (e.g., Fox News personnel and 'conservative' radio talk show hosts across the nation). This enunciation is not just President Bush speaking *to* the American people. It is President Bush—and the machinic assemblage (Deleuze and Guattari, 1987) behind him—speaking *on behalf of* the American people, and speaking not just to us, but *to the world*. Therefore, what is most noticeable in this enunciation is the incredible arrogance of its re-presentation and re-definition of national identity.

Hypernational Discourse

One text that clearly shows *coercive* nationalism, or *hypernationalism* (Nicholson-Goodman, 2006, 2007), is the writing of a group called 'Americans for Victory Over Terrorism' (AVOT). This group, from its inception, proclaimed America's policies blameless and announced its intention to "support democratic patriotism when it is questioned" and "take to task those groups and individuals who fundamentally misunderstand the nature of the war we are facing." This group also declared that the threats America was facing were partially internal, and that the internal threat was embodied in "those who are attempting to use this opportunity to promulgate their agenda of 'blame America first'" (*The New York Times*, WK, March 10, 2002).

The Chairman of AVOT is William J. Bennett, former Secretary of Education. Interestingly, he was also a signatory of the 1997 Statement of Principles of 'The Project for the New American Century' (PNAC). This is a group with a 'Reaganite agenda' focused on a policy of U.S. global supremacy backed up by militarism and unilateralism, a group that had difficulty moving its agenda forward publicly *prior* to September 11th, 2001 (Barry and Lobe, 2002, 2-4). However, they have found it much easier to have their way in a post-democratic, post-9/11 America. Other signatories included Richard B. Cheney, Donald Rumsfeld, Paul Dundes Wolfowitz, Jeb Bush, Elliott Abrams, Frank Gaffney and a number of other "right-wing luminaries" now sitting at the right hand of the ultimate seat of power (Barry and Lobe, 2002, 2). All of them, including Mr. Bennett, have been regular guests on major cable networks' news/talk shows following September 11th: e.g., *Hannity and Colmes* on the Fox channel, CNN's *Situation Room*, and Chris Matthews' *Hardball* on MSNBC.

Their message is clear: this group would target liberals and others whom they considered 'dissidents' and intimidate anyone who questioned administration policies. Their ad did more than promise to harass and demonize those who questioned their orthodoxy; it also promised that the culture war that had been raging since the 1970s would be brought into the public forum via media and used to castigate dissenters in the courts of public opinion, taking advantage of the 'mood of the nation' (which they helped to create) to have their way. The language used in their ad advanced the belief that liberals and other 'dissidents' constitute a threat to the nation because of their "hatred for the American ideals of freedom and equality" or because of their "misunderstanding of those ideals and their practice." Those who declined to accept the orthodoxy of this faction were, therefore, either characterized as 'America-haters' or as ignorant about what America stands for. AVOT's avowed goal was "to defeat ideologies that support" terrorism, and liberals and others who dissented from the orthodoxy were included in that category. "The central focus of our activity," the ad declared, "is public opinion." The most accessible route to public opinion, it should be noted, is 'through education.' The foundation for citizenship is *Orthodoxy*. The preferred mode of civic engagement is (anti-dissident) *Activism*. The culture of citizenship advanced for America by this writing is *hypernational*.

Voyeurist Discourse

Arthur P. Bochner (2002), in 'Love Survives,' recounts the images of the day as he recalls that "the faces and forms of the dead" included a "rainbow of ethnicity and social class," workers of all kinds, "the men and women of everyday life." (166). He uses a cinematic framing, moving from scene to scene, refocusing the lens as he transitions from one scene to the next. He rehearses again the images that impacted us all as television screens replayed this horrific scene over and over again, but he juxtaposes them with others, less well examined, for purposes of critique. The first of two close-ups is a critical look at rage, which he paints in terms of "faces red with anger," raised fists, and puffed-out chests (166). The desire expressed in this rage, and associated in their thinking with allegiance to the nation and "readiness to fight for freedom" is vengeance of major proportions, the kind where we "blow them—the enemy—off the face of the earth" (166). Bochner concludes the scene by noting that they see retaliation as justice; he speaks of healing and of achieving social justice as more appropriate responses.

The second close-up is a scathing shot of *control*. It begins with the "warmongers" finding "their justification" in the deaths of so many. As the generals step forward, we are told to make ready for a long, "unconventional war," "a different kind of war" (166). The President's voice echoes in the background, proclaiming the terrorists "evildoers, cowards," as Bochner rehearses the litany of verbal assaults coming from this voice, many of them using a langue peculiar to Hollywood images of cowboy justice (166). Ultimately, off-screen voices begin to question, and receive only silence in return as the scene fades out. Emerging from his reverie, Bochner confronts his (our?) desire for the Hollywood ending as he reflects on the 'what-might-be' (Reynolds and Webber, 2004) that has been discarded in the scenario as it has played out, and wishes for "the happy ending" where hunger, despair, and hatred are absent (167).

In Bochner's vista, America is diverse, a rainbow of ethnicity and social class, deeply suffering. We are misrepresented by red, angry faces calling for revenge and retribution, generals appearing to be in control, our president dividing the world into friend or foe, threatening annihilation to the latter. This America, however, is attuned to fantasy, to the Hollywood happy ending, and has no answers except its rage, no reality except its incapacity to understand as it wonders about its guilt.

Maureen Dowd (2001), in 'Going Really Postal,' frames the government's responses to the anthrax attacks in terms derived from popular culture as she considers parallels with the town council in *Jaws*, who, fearing that "panic will spread and business will suffer," encourage us to "go back in the ocean before they've figured out how to fight the shark" (*The New York Times*, A23, October 24). She laments that "people keep dying" as we come to recognize that the Center for Disease Control is not "all-knowing." Dowd elaborates the layers of misinformation, misunderstanding, failures to act, inappropriate actions, and general confusion that followed the death of postal workers who had apparently handled the anthrax letter sent to Senator Tom Daschle, a Democrat, and frames the scene in terms of the public's right to know. Her most obvious complaint is that "officials kept telling us not to worry," when they still "don't know where the anthrax is from, who's sending it, how it spreads, how potent it is—or will not tell us."

Dowd offers a peek into our social class system and its disparities, looking at federal ineptitude (which might also be framed as negligence, disregard, or outright abandon) in contrast with the postal workers' loyal response, which was that "they were mad that Capitol Police dogs got tested before they did," but "they were going to keep working to defy the terrorists." Their complaints reflect a loss of confidence in the ability of government to protect them, yet their defensive stance against a perceived though imperceptible enemy remains firm.

Returning to her concern for the public's right to know, and the government's dubious ability to handle and disperse information, Dowd offers up her (our?) frustration with being told to stay alert when we are so completely in the dark, and voices the greater fear, which is that "they are themselves in the dark." "The only alternative to paranoia and prejudice is solid information," she tells us, so the government "should start telling us how much they don't know." Ultimately, her prescription is that the government should "get its scientific and political and rhetorical act together" as she asks "where is Robert Shaw to tell us how we're going to 'get the head, the tail, the whole damn thing'?"

In Dowd's vista, America is uneasy, losing public confidence in the government's handling of essential information as the people are told not to worry, to go about their normal lives, even in the face of extreme fear and anxiety due to terrorism and anthrax attacks. While the people "understand that we are at war," and that "we're unprepared for this sort of war," governmental authorities must do better, they must be open about what they do not know, even if it scares us. (This reflects the premise that authorities held back information for our protection.) Ultimately, what is most needed is the Hollywood ending, where Shaw, the shark-hunter, gets "the head, the tail, the whole damn thing." Again, the easy solution, or happy ending—Hollywood's specialty—emerges.

Richard Ford (2001), in 'The Worry Trap,' looks at the changes suburbanites are facing as a result of September 11th, characterizing the anxious state of the nation as a condition spilling over into the calm of the suburbs, which were designed "to keep worry out" (*The New York* Times, November 1, A27). He reflects on terrorism as "the new global accompaniment to life's ordinary routines." Ford draws a distinction between the September 11th attacks and the unsettling effects of the anthrax mystery. Worry is his central theme as he elucidates the raison d'etre of suburban life, offering that this life is "nirvana for the urban neurosis, a crisp, peaceable frame of reference." Ford's main concern is the disintegration of this taken-for-granted frame of reference for living "in the shadow of mayhem," where "the precise character of all our choices and reliances is cast into high, discomforting relief" as we see that we are defenseless, faceless. The result is that "our frame of reference is sprung, our old coordinates lead back to worry."

Ford contends that worry is indeed a new landmark in the suburban terrain, and he questions "whom we can sympathize with as much as we sympathize with ourselves," but he presents possibility for hope as well. His prescription, interestingly, is that we begin a "puzzling" about the meaning(s) of our connectedness to and our disconnectedness from others, and about the meaning(s) of community. He offers the hope that the process may "teach us that the knowledge of what confronts us..." happens also to be the "knowledge we will need to imagine our strength."

In Ford's vista, America is living a 'new day' where our everyday lives include terrorism as 'the new global accompaniment,' where 'worry' is a major theme that can no longer be excluded, even for those who live in the suburbs. Our reponse, according to Ford, is that we are wondering who to sympathize with 'as much as we sympathize with ourselves,' but we can also question the meaning of community and 'imagine our strength.'

Michael Ryan (2001), in 'Outrage, Not Rage,' recalls the feeling he experienced on September 11th, a feeling that was eerily familiar to him. Ryan, a former correspondent and editor for *Time*, Inc., recalls gunfire in El Salvador, mortar attacks on refugees along the border between Thailand and Cambodia, the horrors of war zones, and tells us that he "stopped going" (tompaine.com, September 15). He speaks of being "diagnosed post-traumatic stress," which "responded well to hours of talk and... little pink pills." He offers his conviction that "we all have post-traumatic stress today" and urges us to "recognize the damage, and... deal with it."

Are 'little pink pills' and 'post-traumatic stress' all that Ryan has to offer us? No, his concerns include a warning that "trauma can do strange things," that "anger and rage well up and spew forth," which is "horrific in a nation." He calls for restraint, for "the decency and strength not to inflict" this trauma on others, particularly on those who are innocent, not to "inflict it on the world."

In Ryan's vista, America is suffering from post-traumatic stress and needs little pink pills. Americans will live with the images of this trauma in their hearts and minds for years, but must 'recognize the damage,' and 'deal with it.' In this America, caution and discretion are to be exercised. What we need, Ryan believes, is 'decency and strength.'

David Helvarg (2001), in 'Consume for Victory,' mocks the new push for consumerism as a patriotic mode. He plans, he tells us, on doing a lot of traveling and shopping, "now that bio-terrorism is a reality," but he's not convinced that makes him a patriot. He wishes that "the Treasury Department, the White House and the media would stop flacking for the financial sector in the name of patriotism" (tompaine.com, October 29). He reminds us how "we've been bombarded with demands" that we "get back to our main function as passive consumers."

Helvarg extends his critique of misplaced values by sharing insights from an annual conference of environmental journalists where "a panelist from the World Resources Institute talked about the 'B4B,'" which is how the speaker referred to the "Bottom Four Billion," the 4 billion people in the world without access to the Internet. He mocks Secretary of Interior Gail Norton, who claimed "that the War on Terrorism proves our need to drill" in Alaska's protected lands. He also mocks Christie Todd Whitman, head of the EPA, who "reassured us that terrorists are not in a position to poison" us through our own water systems, and then "renewed her commitment" to "reducing the high levels of arsenic in our dringing water." He sees this dissembling and the new push towards consumerism-as-patriotism as insulting. He complains that we are "all pushed to become headless consumers of limited natural resources instead of thoughtful citizens," and that makes him feel "disrespected." His response is that he "may not buy that computer."

In Helvarg's vista, America is a place where the Treasury Department, the White House and the media are 'flacking for the financial sector in the name of patriotism,' where the people are being 'bombarded' with demands that we return to 'our main function as passive consumers.' In this America, government disregard for citizens who are 'trying to understand our role in the world,' their disregard for us as 'thoughtful citizens engaged in the work of democracy,' is an insult.

In summary, these texts indicate a *voyeurist* sense of the nation, where the citizen is either a passive watcher of events as they unfold, or is urged to *become this passive observer, sanctioning control*:

In Bochner, the desire is for a Hollywood ending, even as the 'defiant' voice 'off screen' asks to see the script (and receives only *silence* in response);

In Dowd, the Hollywood ending reappears and the bottom line is that, even if it means scaring us, the government has to do better by providing information as it takes care of us;

In Ford, we are told that even in the suburbs (where 'worry' is ostensibly shut out), we are more sympathetic to *ourselves* than to anyone else, but we can ask what *community* means and imagine our strength;

In Ryan, 'hours of talk' and 'little pink pills' seem to be the answer as we face our trauma and try to deal with it while working to maintain our 'decency and strength';

Finally, in Helvarg, the push to consume 'for victory' is an insult; we are disrespected as 'thoughtful citizens engaged in the work of democracy.' Our reponse might be to consume less.

In each case, the foundation for citizenship is *Reason*, while the mode of civic engagement is (passive) *Control*. The effect is to project a *voyeurist* culture of citizenship.

Vigilant Discourse

Davydd J. Greenwood (2002), in 'Alone and Together: A Reflection for *Qualitative Inquiry* on the terror attack,' shares his experience of September 11th, which he admits left him "in a vulnerable emotional and intellectual state" (191). Finding himself "lurching through personal flashbacks" to other "cataclysmic events" in his life, he works to make sense of a desire for "aloneness" within a space where unity appears to be ubiquitously called for (191). He tells us that he "could barely watch the endless so-called 'news' programs," that he resented the media interfering with his need to own the experience himself, and felt that his "memory was being manipulated and programmed into collective reactions" (191). He also shares that he has always had "a gut aversion to the conformity of crowds and imperious demands for unity" (191).

Greenwood goes on, however, to look for the meaning behind those demands, and realizes "that building this collective response" is related to "putting a name and face on the unspeakable and incomprehensible," "reducing the chaos" (191). He makes peace with the idea that a "shared sense may well be preferable to having a world that makes no sense at all" (191). His sense of this moment is compelling as he looks behind this 'shared sense' to uncover another layer of meaning, however. Rejecting the "commonplace that Americans have 'come together' because of the tragedy," he sees "the marathon reporting and image repetition" as a way "to nullify the searing nonsensical reality" of the moment, even if the narrative put forth was "malign and satanic" (192). This was, after all, a reality "that we momentarily and dangerously experienced uniquely and individually" (192). Experiencing it in this way, he argues, "threatened... our grip on the world" (192).

Greenwood finds himself "anxious to reestablish daily routines and to move my feet (and... my heart) back onto some kind of solid ground" (192). This, for him, is political in a way "that is deeper than flags and pep talks," and he assures us that "insisting that life goes on is a meaningful weapon against terrorists" (192). He asserts that "there is a kind of heroism and patriotism in going on with daily life against pulls of meaninglessness, blame, and revenge" (192).

In Greenwood's vista, America was 'manipulated and programmed' into 'collective reactions' by the media, was subjected to 'imperious demands for unity,' was willing to employ a narrative that is 'malign and satanic' in the name of 'putting a name and face on the unspeakable and incomprehensible.'

In this America, the features of daily life that really bring us together are: 'triviality,' 'vulnerability,' and 'meaninglessness.'

Frank Rich (2001), in 'No News Is Good News,' writes about the banning of bin Laden's videos from American television news reporting and characterizes the events and their implications for our society in general. He begins with a slap at the modus operandi of the Bush administration, who sought to "kick" bin Laden "off network television" (*The New York Times*, October 13, A23). In a conference call to television executives, Condoleeza Rice argued "that Americans must be shieded from his propaganda," and that he should not "appear unexpurgated in video again." Rich claims that this effort reflected both the fact that "the administration's ambitions to manage the news knows no bounds," and that "the White House was as spooked" as the rest of us by bin Laden's "almost instant rebuttal" to the President.

Rich attends to the mood of the nation and characterizes the inner workings of our leadership as they try "to tame an uncharted future into predictability by jamming it into a familiar historical paradigm," the cold war. After enumerating a number of ways in which this is *not* like the cold war, he gets down to the heart of the matter, which is that one characteristic within the nation looks *very much* like a cold war accompaniment: "a will to stifle dissent," which Rich sees as "one of the cold war's most self-destructive national maladies."

Rich looks at the 'Right' and their "knee-jerk refighting of yesterday's cold war culture wars," noting that they, too, are "unhinged by fear," and that some are even "eager to manufacture traitors." He critiques other actions taken by those in power: the administration's "determination to keep us in the dark and to stifle any criticism" by managing the news, "Ms. Rice's effort to browbeat the networks," to "replace honest journalism with propaganda," "to cut Congress out of the military and intelligence loop," and Karl Rove's leaning on an "historian he'd never met, Robert Dallek, ...after Mr. Dallek criticized the president in USA Today."

Rich enumerates incidents where the White House has produced misleading, and sometimes patently false, information. He concludes by assuming that the control being exercised, however, is *for our protection*, and he claims that the "point" of "this dissembling... is simple enough: what we don't know won't hurt us." He makes the point as well that we might question our sense of safety when "all the news is good news."

In Rich's vista, America is caught up in surreal and complex subterfuges, lost for want of an appropriate paradigm, its leadership therefore practicing legerdemain to keep control. The citizen is supposed to seek information, which is being withheld—not just from the public, but from Congress and the media as well. This hearkens back to a cold war paradigm whose central feature is the stifling of debate and the silencing of dissent. The administration's 'hidden' assumption is equally troubling to Rich: that no one is to be trusted except those in power at the White House.

Mark Danner (2001), in 'The Battlefield in the American Mind,' writes about 'the new war' in terms of the public sphere, reframing the battleground to explain how terrorists capitalize on the fact that "American power has coexisted with American inconstancy and capriciousness" (*The New York Times*, A23, October 16). Danner rehearses for us a litany of debacles and scenes of humiliation, but he is quick to point out that this isn't due "to any lack of American courage but to a lack of political grounding that has haunted the country's foreign policy for a half-century." Given our history in this regard, Danner recognizes that Al Quaeda's "terrorist operatives," exercising their unique ability of finding their "victims' points of vulnerability," "chose to attack America at its weakest point: its political psyche."

Danner fashions his own unique account of the terror of September 11th, focusing on the use of television as both "primary weapon" and "delivery vehicle" for the attack. He speaks as well of how "the Spectacular altered the terms of debate," bringing us face-to-face with our own "pervasive and unprecedented vulnerability." His analysis of the attacks resonates with my own recollection of my response to the repetitive visual images, followed by the (still) mysterious anthrax incident, and all the psychodramas, large and small, that followed on its heels.

Danner moves to an analysis of what 'they' want, depicting our dilemma as a nation condemning itself "to the role that its enemies have chosen for it." He articulates the underlying tactic, which is "psychological and political," and laments the choices our leadership made. They chose "a barrage of rhetoric" about the reason for the attack (positioning it as an attack on freedom), and framed it as "the fight between good and evil," which Danner sees as "stock ideology." He notes that "our presidents have habitually turned to ideology to rally the citizenry." He then considers realistically the prospects for the citizenry remaining rallied, cautioning that "political support thus purchased tends to be brittle and weak, having been built on emotion."

In Danner's vista, America is inconstant and capricious and suffers from a lack of political grounding while it trots out a 'triumphant cold war narrative' for purposes of self-aggrandizement and control. In this America, our leadership habitually turns to ideology to rally citizens on the basis of emotion, and in this moment, that means "a barrage of rhetoric about 'attacks on freedom' and the fight between good and evil." In this moment, it also means a president proclaiming our nation 'a city on a hill,' encouraging us to battle 'an enemy of apocalyptic proportions.'

William Safire (2001), in 'Seizing Dictatorial Power,' castigates recent moves by this administration to move away from the rule of law, along with the implications of those moves for the nation itself. He sees the nation as one that is "intimidated by terrorists and inflamed by a passion for rough justice," and warns that we are letting the President "get away with the replacement of the American rule of law" via "his infamous emergency order." Safire's complaint is that President Bush "seizes the power to circumvent the courts and set up his own drumhead tribunals" (*The New York Times*, A21, November 15).

Safire documents the grievances against this approach to apprehending the alleged 'enemy' within. Drawing on a cold war analogy, he contends that "no longer does the judicial branch and an independent jury stand between the government and the accused," and that what has displaced checks and balances is "an executive that is now investigator, prosecutor, judge, jury and jailer or executioner." Safire sees this as "an Orwellian twist," and condemns it as a "Soviet-style abomination." Considering this series of executive decisions in terms of partisan division, he admonishes conservatives to defend American principles, not to succumb to the "arguments of the phony-tough." Bush's proponents, he tells us, call those who question this policy, "soft-on-terror," but his answer is that "it's time for conservative iconoclasts and card-carrying hard-liners to stand up for American values."

In Safire's vista, America's president is 'seizing dictatorial power.' This is an America that is so intimidated by terrorism and 'inflamed by a passion for rough justice' that we are letting our leadership 'get away with the replacement of the American rule of law.' In this America, a 'Soviet-style abomination' is taking the place of cherished principles, while those who speak out against these measures are accused of being 'soft-on-terror.'

Paul Krugman (2001), in 'An Alternate Reality,' writes about behind-the-scene realities not shown on television that are a definitive part of what happened in America after September 11th. While he concedes that the good behavior of the citizenry is shown on television and is "heartwarming," that "the vast majority of Americans have been both resolute and generous," he also warns that "that's not the whole story," that "the images TV doesn't show are anything but heartwarming." In his narrative, a "full picture would show politicians and businessmen behaving badly," due in part to "the fact that these days selfishness comes tightly wrapped in the flag." He encourages us to look at the bigger picture, and claims that if we do, we will see that we "are living in a different reality from the one on TV" (*The New York Times*, November 25).

Krugman's 'different reality' revolves around economics, and his major complaint is "politicians' fondness" for "lump-sum transfers," which he claims are a truer indicator of what's going on than television coverage. He explains this term as "economese for payments that aren't contingent on the recipient's actions," and he objects to the $15 billion Congress voted to give as "aid and loan guarantees for airline companies" and a "'stimulus bill' that contains almost nothing for the unemployed but includes $25 billion in *retroactive* corporate tax cuts." He looks at a change in the economic terrain after September 11th, and the secret and mysterious 'giveaways' to those who were already affluent, noting that this information is available, if one knows where to look and how to think about what one is looking at. "The alternate reality isn't deeply hidden," Krugman claims, and is "available to anybody with a modem," but "political reporting about the stimulus debate describes it as a conflict of ideologies." For Krugman, "ideology has nothing to do with it," since he's not aware of any "economic doctrine" that says that, for instance, "an $800 million lump-sum transfer to General Motors will lead to more investment" when General Motors "is already sitting on $8 billion in cash."

For Krugman, this unfortunate agenda colors the state of the nation in unseemly hues. He recalls other moments when similar scandals rocked the nation, and asserts that "for 99.9 percent of Americans this war... is a spectator event." Further, while on television this "looks like World War II," here at home it looks "like a postwar aftermath, in which the normal instincts of a nation at war... are all too easily exploited." He evokes the image of the post-World War I Palmer raids, "which swept up thousand of immigrants suspected of radicalism," some of whom "turned out to be U.S. citizens," and "the vast majority" of whom "turned out to be innocent of any wrongdoing."

Finally, he calls for greater government accountability, proclaiming that what we really need "is a return to normalcy," but not "the selective normalcy the Bush administration wants, in which everyone goes shopping but the media continue to report only inspiring stories and war news." For Krugman, the time has come "to give the American people the whole picture."

In Krugman's vista, America is suffering from a dual reality. On the one hand, Americans themselves are 'behaving well in a time of crisis,' showing themselves to be 'both resolute and generous.' On the other hand, America's elite—businessmen and politicians—are 'behaving badly,' and their 'selfishness comes tightly wrapped in the flag.' This second reality, however, is not accessible to everyone because TV only shows the issues behind this bad behavior as 'a conflict of ideologies.'

John Rieger (2001), in 'What Does Retaliation Mean in a Media War?' reframes the attacks of September 11th in symbolic terms, as "a war of symbols, impressions and ideas in which acts of mass murder jocky for mind share in the global media." In such a scenario, he tells us, "everyone with a television set, the world over, reacts viscerally" (tompaine.com, September 12). Rieger takes a closer look at what the terrorists really won by attacking civilians in the World Trade Center, reasoning that "from a military standpoint, this brutal attack was a pin prick." So what, Rieger asks, was the goal? He sees terrorism as a kind of warfare that is "tailor-made for the Information Age," where "terror spreads with the news." What the world saw was that "a handful of fanatics, intoxicated by their own sense of justice, could knock out the front teeth of the world's only superpower."

He points his savvy finger at our leadership, which in his words, "stumbled" as President Bush "addressed the nation on video tape from a safe location" and announced that "there were technical difficulties." Their error, he claims, was all the more important because they were responding to "powerful ideas," and he works to reframe our understanding about the intended logic of the attacks. He acknowledges that "in many parts of the world, the terrorists "are clearly viewed as courageous" because they "deliberately sacrifice their lives in an act of war," despite the President's proclamation of their cowardice. The important point for Rieger is that "these symbols are in play in the global mediascape," that they are "part of a war between us and our terrorist enemies," a war "for the hearts and minds of those who would become the next generation to spread terror." He questions how we can "fight this battle of symbols." He offers a prescription based on America's many vulnerabilities in such a "war of symbols," even as he acknowledges that "we are wealthy, powerful, and proud," that "our nation is filled with symbolic targets, although "for American vengeance, there are no hard targets." He reminds us that "our weapons are ideas, like Freedom, and Justice, ideas that are often best exemplified by what we do not do." He advocates that these are our best weapons, but that we need to live up to these ideas.

In Rieger's vista, America is in a war of symbols being fought in the Information Age on a global electronic terrain. In this America, the nation is vulnerable because 'we are wealthy, powerful, and proud,' because 'our nation is filled with symbolic targets,' and because 'our weapons are ideas, like Freedom and Justice,' ideas we *don't* live up to.

David Corn (2001), in 'The Loyal Opposition: Far from Normal,' writes of his obsession with nuclear attack, a concern that re-emerges in post-9/11 America as he speculates that "our national leaders have not quite grasped the profound change that has been wrought" (tompaine.com, October 5). He cites Health and Human Services Secretary Tommy Thompson, who contradicted his statement on *60 Minutes*, where he had assured us that we were "prepared" for "any kind of bioterrorism attack," but then, "later acknowledged that, um, we're not." Pointing out that in another hearing, when a "terrorism expert was asked if the medical establishment was equipped to deal with a biological attack," he responded that "half the public health officials in this country don't have computers on their desks" (tompaine.lcom, October 5).

What Corn attacks here is a 'new normal,' finding its surreal side less than amusing as we are told to "head to the malls" and "get back on those airliners, too." Reflecting on the notion that the terrorists probably "put the second wave into place before" September 11th, he quotes a number of inner-circle sources showing this distinct possibility, but also points out that "White House press secretary Ari Fleischer declared there are increasing signs that life in America is getting back to normal." While we wait to find out when the next attack will come, Corn tells us, each of us will hope "the next tragedy occurs in another town and penetrates our own world only via the television screen." This, he asserts, is our welcome message from those who brought us globalization. Questioning "how best to proceed within this new world disorder," he offers two choices: 'Should we join the rush to normalcy?" or, he asks, "Should we be screaming: *this is so god-damn crazy?*

But Corn also acknowledges an alternative approach to terrorism, noting Tony Blair's assertion "that the war on terrorism ought to be tied to a global campaign for social justice." He sees this option as "the best chance the West has to free itself from the madness of terrorism." His complaint, however, is that our "present leadership... shows little interest in a holistic strategy that gazes beyond the us-and-them perspective of the commander-in-chief."

This complaint goes to the root of our new position in this world as reflected in our failed leadership, and Corn asks: "So what, then? Get used to it? Life has risks—and now there are more?" He claims that that is precisely what the President and his entourage are telling us—"Don't ask too many hard questions," and "shop while you fret," answers that are provided because "they're lost, too." His irritation surfaces as "Bush keeps insisting he is waging a campaign for freedom, as he makes military alliances with repressive, non-democratic or autocratic regimes that care not a whit for freedom." Corn also notes that a senior official "traveling with Deputy Defense Secretary Paul Wolfowitz told a reporter, 'It is difficult... to overestimate how much we don't know."

His parting thoughts essentially echo the fears of many in this moment, and for those not wanting to "repress reasonable fears," he advises that "we ought to demand more from our leaders—even if we do not know precisely what that entails." Having "failed us in imagination, preparation, and protection," he argues, "they should be pressed to talk straight about the threat and the possibilities for achieving a secure world," they should be made to "acknowledge" that "we're far from what we once believed was normal," and that we're not "likely to be in that territory for a long time."

In Corn's vista, America's leaders are prematurely urging the people to return to normalcy, and this leadership has 'failed us in imagination, preparation, and protection.' In this America, the leadership hasn't 'grasped the profound change that has been wrought,' and even the opposition 'shows no signs of being able to address the disturbing fundamentals of life after 9/11.'

In summary, these texts indicate a *vigilant* sense of the nation, where the citizen becomes an active 'watcher,' not only of events, but of government actions and responses as well, although sanction of governmental authority remains a factor:

In Greenwood, media interference and manipulation evoke in him an aversion to 'imperious demands for unity.' Seeing the 'marathon reporting' and 'image repetition' as malign attempts to 'nullify' the terrifying reality, he resolves that 'going on with daily life' against the 'pulls of meaninglessness, blame, and revenge' is both heroic and patriotic.

In Rich, the administration is working to displace the anxieties of an 'uncharted future' by forcing events into a cold war paradigm. The dangers in this scenario are: a gaping hole in government accountability, 'a determination to keep us in the dark,' and an 'alarming' lack of (visible) dissent. We should keep watching, even if it scares us.

In Danner, our vulnerabilities as a nation derive from inconstancy, a lack of political grounding, and our government's tendency to rely on ideology to rally citizens. We should resist such ideology and demand that the government provide 'a clear and honest defense of our interests and commitments.'

In Safire, the President has 'assumed... dictatorial power,' replacing the rule of law with his own devices. Safire sees this as a 'Soviet-style abomination' and advocates that conservatives stand up for 'American values.'

In Krugman, TV is showing us 'a picture of the nation behaving well in a time of crisis,' but behind the scenes, elites 'are behaving badly.' Writing about 'the stimulus debate,' depicted by the media 'as a conflict of ideologies,' he sees that 'the normal instincts of a nation at war' are being exploited. The answer is to give the American people 'the whole picture.'

In Rieger, the events of September 11th constituted a symbolic victory for the terrorists—a victory that was viewed around the world via global media. In this symbolic war, America is highly vulnerable, because our best weapons are ideas like Freedom and Justice, but we don't live up to them. The answer is to begin living up to them, starting with Justice.

Finally, in Corn, we have experienced 'a profound change,' one that our leaders 'have not quite grasped.' We are unprepared for the threats we are facing, and we must 'confront inequity and deploy compassion.' The current administration has failed us 'in imagination, preparation, and protection.' The answer is to 'press them' for 'straight talk' about our new 'normal.'

In each case, the foundation for citizenship is *Reason*, while the mode of civic engagement is (engaged) *Control*. The effect is to advocate a *vigilant* culture of citizenship.

Pluralist Discourse

Carolyn Ellis (2002), in 'Take no chances,' shares a tale of her inner wrestling as she tries to heed her husband's advice while confronting her fear of the 'other' during a ride in a Muslim driver's taxi. She acknowledges that "the word *Muslim*" makes her "flinch, slightly," that her "feelings are jumbled," that she is "slightly apprehensive," "numb still and fatalistic" (171). Still, she expresses a "strong desire to communicate with him" (171). In Ellis' recounting of thoughts and feelings during her conversation with this Middle Eastern cab driver one week after September 11th, we are invited to listen in and to explore with her dimensions of mutual grief as she confronts her own fear and distrust. She asks whether Americans have treated him badly, and he responds that "they haven't," that, in fact, his "American friends... are worried," that he and his Muslim friends cry together (171-172).

Ellis' narrative explores the inner workings of her own mind as she seeks closure on her experience of September 11th, admitting that "the revenge talk resonated with me... momentarily" (172). While this moment "didn't last long," she confesses, it "was strong and interrupted briefly the void of hopelessness, fear, and vulnerability" that overcame her (172).

Having personally experienced rage and the desire for revenge, however momentarily, she draws a parallel between these 'new' others—Middle Eastern men—and African-Americans, who "often have had to pretend to ignore prejudice" (173). She reflects on how "the category 'us' suddenly has gotten bigger and more diverse," but notes that "the line between this 'us' and 'them' feels ominous and sinister" (173). She tells the driver that he shouldn't take people yelling at him personally, that they are, in fact, "yelling at a symbol," and she wonders whether that makes him "feel better or worse" (173).

In Ellis' vista, America is home to fear and distrust, a place where we separate 'us' from 'them,' not just in the face of terror, but consistently and to our shame, a condition that we must work to overcome.

William G. Tierney (2002), in 'A walk in the olive grove,' begins with a pertinent excerpt from Pericles' *The Funeral Oration*, which proclaims that "the freedom which we enjoy in our democratic government extends also to our ordinary life," that "we throw open our city to the world, and never by alien acts exclude foreigners from an opportunity of learning or observing," even when "the eyes of an enemy may occasionally profit by our liberality" (183).

Tierney shares a tale from his days as a Peace Corps worker in Morocco, inviting us inside his experience of the Arab world in a way that draws on both his experience of being different and his learning from that experience. He explains how different it is, and how difficult, "on an individual level when I must live in the foreign culture," as opposed to "reflexive responses" of the kind being used in this moment (184). He shares with us some of the reflexive responses he felt in Morocco as a result of his being both foreign and American, where "relations between men and women were topsy-turvy, making a mockery" of what he had learned in his college classes; where "the pacifism" he had "articulated so clearly in working against the Vietnam War seemed out of place in a society where everyone seemed to shout at one another"; where his "definition of... 'fair' was challenged in a society where one had to bargain for everything" (184).

Tierney's experience of Morocco (and of his difference) was aided, however, by having a teacher, Nezmi, who taught him Arabic and another, equally important lesson, namely, that "evil occurs when we forget," and that "the suffering of the world is from those who neither remember nor learn" (185) Tierney voices the dilemma that plagues us all as a result of September 11th, "the dangers that exist when we throw open our city to the world," but looks also at the "joys that arise when I am able to avail my selves to opportunities of learning and observing that same world" (185).

In Tierney's vista, America is a 'city' thrown open to the world and therefore vulnerable. This America doesn't 'exclude foreigners,' although 'the eyes of an enemy may occasionally profit' from such openness. There is a deep understanding of difference expressed here (and of how it complicates the nationalist narrative and its 'reflexive responses').

Kathy Charmaz (2002), in 'Tenets of terror,' shares her thoughts on the events of September 11th through images reflecting the horror of that day. She offers that like the towers, which "ripped open and disintegrated—in instants," her "assumptions about the world dissolved" (189). Charmaz proceeds from a scene strewn with images of destruction to the flattening of social myths and the illusions they supported, as "a North American way of life became undependable, unpredictable" (189). She speaks of "the dream of reason—*American reason*" as experiencing a crash, offering that "myths of safety, security, personal invulnerability, and collective invincibility disintegrated with the falling of the Towers" (189). For her, the American dream meant that "our reasoning reigned throughout the world and guided the course of history" (189).

Charmaz resonates with the "stifled fears" of her students, but moves the focus of her thoughts to interpretive inquiry itself, conjecturing that, like her students, "many of us stand between speech and silence on collective grief and loss," that "we too speak of palpable uncertainty and take silent refuge in routine realities" (190). "Yet as interpretive social scientists," she urges, "we can contribute to the shape of the world to come," as we respond to the call to come out of our universities "and into the world" (190). Charmaz calls for a new attention "to how cultural context, historical location, and social position are played out" within individual lives (190). Arguing that "we can move back through centuries and forward into unanticipated futures," she sees "the possibility" of "transcending the boundaries of culture, place, and time to bring new understandings of and to the world" (190). Further, arguing that interpretivists have "special tools to study processes that shape social life," she offers avenues for exploration that might serve to spark thinking about the curriculum of this moment. She offers a number of avenues for inquiry, among them "the battle of words for controlling images in the media" and "the development and change of meanings and actions—of nations, leaders, and ordinary citizens" to see what kinds of acts and speech-acts (Barthes, 1989) "give rise to escalated reactions" (190).

Charmaz' final thought is about what interpretive social science has to offer social policy—namely, "understandings"—as she calls for interpretivists to "work to make our dream of reason a reality" (190).

In Charmaz' vista, America's sense of reason and order has vanished, become 'undependable, unpredictable.' This America finds itself at the end of 'the American century,' and it is crucial to explore 'the battle of words for controlling images' and to work 'to make our dreams of reason a reality' that can inform social policy.

Gerardo Lopez (2002), in 'From Sea to Shining Sea: Stories, Counterstories, and the Discourse of Patriotism,' addresses the messages of patriotism. He looks most specifically at the media and their symbolic imagery, sharing that he has witnessed "an enormous outpouring of American patriotism, national goodwill, and public spirit from all corners of the globe" (196). He notes that "the American flag has taken on new and significant meaning in the public discourse" as "Americans search for a common symbol of allegiance to bring them together," which they find in the flag (196). Even at present, this 'unity' is problematic, however, and Lopez points out that "the construction of an American 'national identity' has been built on the evilization of the... Other."

(196) He contends that "acts of hate, racism, rancor, scorn, and admonition... have paralleled this rise in American nationalism" (196).

For him, this 'evilization' is truly troubling, and he offers that these two proclivities intertwine more fully than we realize. "As the national media delivers images of an America 'under attack,' messages are delivered into homes" telling us that "'they' hate 'us' because of what America stands for, namely, our freedoms. Lopez reminds us that "America has many enemies, and common sense should tell us there is more to this story than a mere hatred of American democracy" (196). This "evilization" of the "Other," coupled with the dualism of good versus evil, effectively mis-shapes the people's consciousness, according to Lopez, who argues that "the messages we receive in the media, the stock stories... are constantly filtered into our daily consciousness," and he worries about the effects when "stock stories... are universally accepted as truths" (197). This raises the question, in Lopez, of "what message is sinking in and whether this discourse serves to 'bring us together' or to solidify and reinforce subliminal fears of the Muslim and/or Middle Eastern Other" (197). He makes the case that "what are not circulated are the counterstories (Delgado, 1995) that undergird these same incidents: stories that are not told, stories that rub up against our most fundamental understanding of reality, stories that reveal the underbelly of American society—the hate crimes, the scapegoating, the vilification and denigration of anything 'un-American.'" (197-198)

Lopez notes that "the national sentiment expressed toward Arabs and Muslims under the guise of 'American patriotism' isn't anything new" (197-198). Reminding us of how it was applied towards the Irish, the Germans, the Japanese, the Mexicans, and the Russians at different times throughout our national history, he concludes that we are indeed a "wounded" nation, but our wounds "are far deeper and more pervasive than the physical and emotional wounds made by terrorists" (198). He offers, finally, that it might be "better for us to do some introspection and ask ourselves what is an American and who is (and who is not) included when we wave the American flag and sing songs of what makes America so beautiful" (198).

In Lopez' vista, America is in search of 'a common symbol of allegiance' to bring us together. In this America, 'the construction of an American national identity' is 'built on the evilization of' the "Other," while the president 'suggests "they" hate "us" because of what America stands for—those ideals, values and principles that center on freedom. In this America, 'stock stories' are 'universally accepted as truths, and are constantly filtered into our daily consciousness.'

Nina Burleigh (2001), in 'Op-Ed Pages Trot Out the White Hawks,' bemoans the representation of wisdom following September 11th. She accuses "the nations' [sic] great editorial page editors" of proffering "the wisdom of a group of middle-aged white men whose claim to fame is that they lost the Vietnam War" (tompaine.com, September 12). She laments that the *Washington Post* "solicited the wisdom of a pair of Nixon administration chicken hawks," and that *The New York Times* allotted space for "the advice of its resident ex-Nixon speechwriter." And this occurred, further, "on a day when every television and newspaper hack around the country was proclaiming 'a new era' in national defense needs."

Burleigh casts her gaze on the public sphere and her assessment of its representational mode. She does so by pointing out other possibilities, particularly alternative resources. She is seeking "smart people" and "new ideas," and she is addressing the failure of imagination, not just the question of who gets to represent the voice of wisdom and experience in mainstream media. She decries the extent to which these editors "are apparently time-warped by the soothing sounds" of those patriarchs, who failed us in the past, especially Donald Rumsfeld and Dick Cheney, "our vice president 'in charge of the government,' as network television reassuringly put it, while President Bush officially went missing" as the twin towers came crashing down.

Burleigh's complaint is not just that women weren't represented, but that no 'new ideas' were, either. Her complaint goes beyond who does and doesn't get represented as she advocates making space for new social imaginaries. She critiques the "conventional wisdom" associated with this selection of voices to be heard, drawing parallels between the situation our troops faced in Vietnam and what they might face now in a search for bin Laden, namely, "precisely the same breed of committed, angry brown men capable of living in deprivation." "Their conventional wisdom then, as now," she reminds us, "was to attack the state that harbored the network, with American boys sent in to fight a jungle war against an invisible, committed enemy." What really chafes, however, is the "profound reliance on outworn thinking to address dangerous new territory."

In Burleigh's vista, America is suffering from a lack of imaginative and informed leadership, the effect of which is to ignore 'the ideas of young, and possibly female, experts,' as leaders continue to trust the ideas of 'the failed patriarchs of the past.' In this America, there is a 'profound reliance on outworn thinking to address dangerous new territory.'

In summary, these texts indicate a *pluralist* sense of the nation, where the citizen is awake to and mindful of difference *and* of how that difference is represented (or not):

In Ellis, deep reflection on the dynamics of difference is needed, as well as confronting ourselves through 'self-critique, self-knowledge and the exploration of our differences,' which should help us to 'work out categories of fear and distrust' in order to overcome them.

In Tierney, 'reflexive responses' should be replaced by a deep understanding of differences in the world and developing sensitivity towards what is 'foreign.'

In Charmaz, America's sense of reason and order has vanished. Civic courage means contributing 'to the shape of the world to come' by 'transcending the boundaries of culture, place and time to bring new understandings of and to the world.'

In Lopez, Americans and others around the globe receive messages that 'position American values and mores as neutral,' while 'the law and other juridical apparatuses normalize racism' by 'circulating stock stories and sanitized understandings of events.' This America is as wounded by its own racism as it is by the terrorism inflicted on it on September 11th, and we need to address 'who is (and who is not) included when we wave the American flag and sing songs of what makes America so beautiful.'

Finally, in Burleigh, this America should find a greater diversity of ideas and people to address 'a new era' in national defense needs, and issues of difference therefore underscore the legitimacy (or lack thereof) of those who represent 'conventional wisdom.'

In each case, the foundation for citizenship is *Perspective*; the preferred mode of civic engagement is *Representation*. The culture of citizenship advocated for the nation is *pluralist*.

6

A Post-9/11 American Autobiography

PART II

In this chapter, vistas reflecting alternatives to control (that is, reflecting active resistance to, or re-appropriation of, the message(s) of control) (*communitarian*, *globalist*, and *reparationist*) produce new convergences. These texts speak in a more active voice, displaying vistas where the actor(s) maintain their claim to agency, i.e., to difference from the enunciated visions of authority, and protect that claim against all incursions. They 'hold the fort,' if you will, on social, cultural, political, and moral autonomy.

Communitarian Discourse

Michelle Fine (2002), in 'The Mourning After,' relates her local experience as she attempts to make sense of the moment, bewailing the "creeping nationalism" she sees as "a flood of flags, talk of God, military, and patriotism chase us all" (137). What may have been comforting for some does not comfort her: "the flag worries, it feels like draperies for war" and "the globe doubles as globalization" (137). As her thoughts move to our 'positioning' in the world, Fine observes that we have "learned the vulnerability of isolation" and that isolation and privilege make for "a dangerous combination" (137). She invokes "the Fantasy of Invulnerability," pronouncing that it lies "in ruins" (137).

Turning her attention to the dilemma of the academy and its freedom in the midst of the madness, she notes that we seem to be in a moment where "to raise questions about the horrors of terrorism and U.S. imperialism" somehow "morphs into a betrayal of patriotism, a disregard for" the thousands of lives lost on September 11th (137-138). It seems odd to her that there is a separation between "grief and critique," that "what counts as dissent has swollen beyond recognition" (138). Haunted by a past history that includes "Japanese interment, McCarthy, and Vietnam," she is concerned with a censorship "that spawns mild and bold" (138). She recounts efforts to call attention to the situation in critical ways: a "brilliant and powerful" e-mail from the Black Radical Congress that "provoked a protest," and was followed by "complaints to the Provost, followed by more e-mails about academic freedom," and "a speak out at City College of New York," which resulted in "nasty newspaper coverage, followed by pressure for us all to rally around America" (138).

She articulates her "worry that a suffocating 'consensus' is choking democracy" and offers as well her hope that "critical social scientists can carve out spaces before the narrative of war freezes solid as the only acceptable position to assert" (139). For Fine, what is needed is a "fan dispersing democratic contradictory consciousness; a strategy to keep the oxygen circulating" (139). She asserts that in light of "the shrinking community of people who are allowed to speak, the scripts for public intellectuals must grow correspondingly bold," and she insists that "we ask the hard questions," offering that "the stretchy capillaries of surveillance surrounding public talk require that intellectuals dare to speak, dare to frame, and dare to analyze critically when so few will—or can" (140).

In Fine's vista, America is suffering from: the loss of identity as a land of difference; a loss of social space for dissent and for academic freedom; and a suffocating and false 'consensus' that would choke and kill democracy. Exercising civic courage means acting: to disperse 'democratic contradictory consciousness'; to avoid becoming part of the emerging false 'consensus'; to affirm the role of dissent; to save young lives from being lost in war; to confront false, reductionist notions of 'normalcy'; and to prevent surrender to apocalypse.

Jeff Faux (2001), in 'Three Things We Learned,' turns his post-9/11 gaze towards America's political economy, acknowledging "that it is unseemly to begin thinking about the economic consequences" of this moment (tompaine-com, September 20). Pointing out that "investors are selling the stocks of insurance companies and airlines, buying those of military contractors and companies that will benefit from the new security-conscious society," he calls for those returning to business matters to accept the "obligation... to reflect on what we have seen." For Faux, September 11th "revealed some truths... that have been obscured in recent years," and he frames his discussion to highlight two essential revelations. The first relates to us as a nation of workers as he considers "just how much of our economy is made up of... the 'working class.'" He points out that the media looks at economic trends "through the eyes of the glamorous, globe-trotting, business executive." He notes, additionally, that "one could hardly find a more fitting symbol of the new global economy than the World Trade Center—surrounded in the evening with a herd of sleek limousines waiting to serve the masters of the universe at the end of the day."

Faux points out that September 11th affected the lives of *real* workers, not just those 'masters of the universe,' as he takes into account the "thousands of data clerks and secretaries, waiters and dishwashers, janitors and telecommunication repair people," not to mention "firefighters, hotel and restaurant employees, police, communication workers, service employees, teachers, federal employees, pilots and flight attendants," and so forth. Faux turns his focus to the nature of an American ideology of self-interest that has prevailed in recent years, which is his second revelation, namely, "how ill-served we have been by a politics that perpetuates the illusion that we are all on our own" and that "holds the institutions of public service in contempt." The problem for Faux is that our politics celebrates "the pursuit of private gain over public service," that our politicians are preoccupied with the idea of "shrinking government... through deregulation, privatization, and cuts in public service."

What this means for Faux is that the first revelation—namely, that we are a working nation, even if we are working with very little visibility—profoundly influences our national character. Asking where we turn "when the chips are down," his answer is that we turn to our government, to our public service sectors, and to nonprofit sectors for help. He highlights how investors, despite being asked to" exercise patriotic restraint," responded by producing "an avalanche of sell orders," and he concludes that "the market is about prices, not values." This, he claims, is something we might have learned about our "national identity."

Faux shares additional insights into America's national identity as it was enunciated by the triumphal narrative, and about the foundations of this identity. He outlines some basic understandings of America's 'exceptionalism,' which has various meanings: for some, it means "that it is the best place to get rich"; for others, "it is our unique set of laws"; and for yet others, it is "a patchwork of ethnic groups and regional interests." "Those who risked and gave their lives," he notes, "acted as human beings responding to the agony of other human beings, or trying... to spare their country more damage... because it is their country."

Finally, he draws a scene for us of our common humanity and decency, asserting that America is great not because "we as individuals are exceptional and different from the rest of the world," but rather "because we are much the same," and he offers that "America's strength, like the strength of any other society, is our ability to be there for each other."

In Faux's vista, America is 'ill-served' by a 'politics that perpetuates the illusion that we are all on our own,' where politicians 'have celebrated the pursuit of private gain over public service.' This America has, as a result of September 11th, perhaps 'learned something about our national identity'—that we are a working nation. Exercising civic courage, in Faux, means recognizing that 'simple patriotism' is a common thread of 'humanity and decency found in all people,' and that America's real strength is in our 'ability to be there for each other.'

Betsy Taylor (2001), in 'Heed Not the Calls of the Consumers-in-Chief,' looks at how Americans are being called upon to address the current crisis, and critiques the new push to consume as a patriotic motif. Calling September 11th a "gut check for Americans," she observes that "our priorities snapped into focus" (tompaine.com, October 24). She portrays Americans as performing "acts of astonishing charity, kindness and heroism" in this moment, but turns her attention to the call to "shop till we drop" as an expression of patriotism. Citing the fact that President Bush, Mayor Guliani, and former President Clinton "have morphed into consumers-in-chief," her response is that it is "very unsettling" to be "asked to stuff ourselves to keep the economy humming and help fight terrorism."

Taylor points out that "the American people are simply in no position to do what's being asked of them," and highlights how "painfully ironic" this demand is as she questions what a "loyal citizen" *can* do. She outlines a four-point program, which includes "focusing on our true priorities, living within our means, targeting our spending wisely and weaning ourselves from oil." Her expectation is that by following these principles, "we can show our neighbors, our leaders and the rest of the world a level of patriotism and humanity we can all agree on."

In Taylor's vista, America has had a 'gut-check' that made us rethink priorities as 'we resolved to try to make things better.' In this America, however, our patriotic duty is being newly defined for us in terms of buying "something, anything, to aid the economic recovery." Exercising civic courage, in Taylor, means new priorities, such as "living within our means, targeting our spending wisely and weaning ourselves from oil."

Joseph A. Palermo (2001), in 'A New Deal for Our New Era,' also critiques a failure of leadership in the crisis following September 11th, which he thinks "should have ushered in a time of national leadership—self-reflection, and the setting of new priorities and long-term goals" (tompaine.com, October 30). What we've witnessed instead, he asserts, is "corporate America... take cynical advantage of this crime." This was accomplished as they "rammed through a cornucopia of tax breaks, bailouts, and deregulation benefiting the wealthiest corporations." He sees President Bush's "so-called 'economic stimulus' package" as "the granting of a corporate wish list" that was "years in the making" and laments that it "will limit our ability in the future to provide... health care, education, and security in old age."

For Palermo, this failure of leadership is the crucial and central issue, and he asks where our leadership is, and who might be "articulating a vision for national renewal that embraces the interests and aspirations of all our citizens, not just those who fund campaigsn." Pointing out that in past crises, "our leaders in Washington responded to a national emergency with bold initiatives," he offers that "big ideas... could rally all Americans, and give us a shared sense of solidarity, solace, and security."

After rehearsing a number of such 'initiatives,' revisiting presidents who provided us with this 'shared sense of solidarity' at other times, in other crises, he ultimately returns to the present administration's focus, which "entails little more than calling upon Americans to break out their credit cards and go shopping" at a time when we should be reevaluating national priorities. For Palermo, this means we should "reconfigure our energy infrastructure toward renewable fuel sources; create a more balanced transportation system; decentralize our energy production; advocate conservation and greater fuel efficiency standards; and lend a helping hand to the newly unemployed." Instead, he asserts, our leadership has elected to "shove through yet another corporate give-away that will further enrich the already wealthy." The outcome, he suspects, will be to "divide Americans in the long run more than unite them." Ultimately, Palermo declares that "our leaders have failed to offer us an overarching vision to pull us through the current crisis," a failure that will ultimately divide us even more deeply, and he believes that "could be worse for the nation than the attacks of September 11th."

In Palermo's vista, 'the events of September 11th should have ushered in a time of national leadership' that would have included 'self-reflection and the setting of new priorities and long-term goals.' Instead, this 'corporate America' has taken 'cynical advantage' of this moment. The 'so-called 'economic stimulus package,' nothing more than a 'give-away' according to Palermo, 'will further enrich the already wealthy' while degrading our future ability to provide health care, education, and social security for the elderly. Exercising civic courage, in Palermo, means making serious changes in the way we live, making sacrifices that will contribute to the greater good of the nation as we work to protect our citizens from a rapacious system based on greed.

In summary, these texts indicate a *communitarian* vision of the nation, where the citizen is a member of a community of solidarity whose primary concern is for the collective good:

In Fine, grief and critique must work together to produce a 'democratic contradictory consciousness' to protect both dissent and resistance to the aims of power;

In Faux, our national identity is defined by two understandings: first, that we are a nation of workers; and second, that we must denounce the illusion fostered by our politics that an ideology of self-interested anarchy is desirable. Our strength lies in solidarity, in 'our ability to be there for each other';

In Taylor, we are suffering an ironic push to consume in the name of patriotic duty, but solidarity of consumerist conscience could demonstrate 'a level of patriotism and humanity' not based on the false consciousness of our leaders, but rather on the greater good of *all*;

Finally, in Palermo, a failure of leadership has occurred in our corporatist state, which has taken 'cynical advantage' of this moment, producing economic effects that promise to divide us even more deeply in the future. Our answer should be to make serious sacrifices for the greater good.

In each case, the foundation for citizenship is *Reason*; the mode of civic engagement is (collective) *Activism*. The effect is advocacy for a *communitarian* culture of citizenship for the nation.

Reparationist Discourse

Lois Weis (2002), in 'Thoughts beyond Fear,' captures her experience of the moment by disclosing her fear for her brother, who was in the World Trade Center when it came under attack, and expresses feeling powerless and "deeply scared" (153). Weis raises the ubiquitous question of this moment: how could this happen? She shares her fear—"fear for all of us"—and her grieving, in which she feels especially for the young—"for their loss of innocence, for the moment that will never go away in the lives of so many" (154). For Weis, this is a moment that ought to spur serious reflection in a field that prides itself on its close connections with real people experiencing loss, a field that connects intimately with the pain and suffering of those who are marginalized in our own society. "We get so close... we cry," she shares, as she speaks from "our space as social activists" (154). She asks that we "not be blind to atrocities in our own country," that we should "look inward as well as outward," that we should begin by looking at "the tragic lives of those who daily survive at the margins in the United States" (154).

Weis reflects on the interconnectedness between research and the people whose lives inform it. For her, the interpretivist stance is not one of distancing, of abstraction, of removal from the real world, but instead she responds, from an intimacy of knowing, through an agenda of social activism. She urges us to "hold on to our responsibilities," to speak critically "as we represent ourselves and others in our work," and she warns against explaining away "that which can have no explanation or excuse" (154). Weis argues that we "cannot and should not be lulled by the drug of objectivity or deconstructionism," that we should be "politically engaged," and tells us that the closeness activists experience "touches chords within our heart and our soul that match those of the people with whom we work" (154). The positioning of interpretivist intellectuals within society is highlighted in Weis. There is a mandate—for dialogue followed by action—that reveals her vision for the future, however deeply troubled that future may become. This moment of national tragedy, she tells us, "should make us remember that we have our part to play in hearing those who speak to us and that we must continue to engage in conversation and action around leaving the world a better place than when we first met it" (154).

In Weis' vista, America ignores those who live at its own margins, and also ignores 'the powerlessness that so many experience on a daily basis all over the world.'

William L. Miller (2002) in 'A Time for Butterflies and Salmon,' shares his unique experience of September 11th as a physician waiting, along with many other medical professionals, "for burned and wounded bodies," but they didn't come: "we heard only the silent screams of thousands of souls lost in the rubble" (156). Miller's reflection uses metaphors from nature that offered him hope in the midst of terror: the butterfly and salmon. For Miller, the butterfly is "a metaphor of vulnerable knowing and of fragile, awesome power for change" (156). He draws a parallel between the butterfly as metaphor and "a radicalized, interpretivist social science" that is at once "participatory, emerging, dependent, constituted by cycles, migrations, place, development, and spurts of confused flight" (156). This is a social science that "is deeply committed to the many contingent truths moving toward better life together" (156).

Seeing the butterfly as a metaphor of the air for vulnerability, Miller also looks to the water and imagines "salmon vigorously swimming upstream," although the salmon are gone (157). He finds hope in the possibility that "salmon are still out there that remember the way," expressing his belief that there exists "a hidden tide of history that swims upstream and keeps returning" (157).

Miller brings the two metaphors together to make his own sense of the work of interpretive inquiry within this moment, offering that "we are about deep meaning and memory, like the salmon, and about resilience and diversity and faith in emergence, like the butterfly" (157). He asserts that our "strength is in the many connections between and among the migratory routes and passages" (157). Addressing the conceptualization of evil, Miller declares that "evil is the arrogant poison that spews from the smokestacks and sewers of certainty and superficiality" (156). He offers an alternative to the 'us and them' logic: "it is up to each of us to deconstruct the myth of evil as other and as stereotype" (156).

In the end, Miller returns to the lessons of nature, which offer him hope for change, and he appeals for us to "answer the quiet call to keep growing connections and complications, to help Love grow" (157).

In Miller's vista, America's national response adds to the terror because of its 'false dualisms.' This is an America that needs a wisdom based on local and patterned ways of knowing and on respect for the 'mystery and abundance of life.'

Howard Zinn (2001), in 'Not Vengeance, but Compassion,' shares his double experiencing of revulsion as a result of September 11th, the first, the scenes on television, which Zinn acknowledges "horrified and sickened" him; the second, when our leaders came on and "spoke of retaliation, of vengeance, of punishment" (tompaine.com, September 13). Zinn laments that "they have learned nothing... from the history of the twentieth century," nothing "from a hundred years" of "violence met with violence in an unending cycle of stupidity." For Zinn, the revulsion comes not just from the lack of wisdom in our leaders, but also from the failure of imagination. Questioning "the old way of thinking," which "has never worked," Zinn calls us to "imagine that the awful scenes of death and suffering we are now witnessing on our television screens have been going on in other parts of the world for a long time," "often as a result of our policies." He calls us to "rethink our position in the world," "to stop sending weapons to countries that oppress other people or their own people." "War," Zinn tells us, "is terrorism, magnified a hundred times."

Does Zinn have a prescription for change that might strengthen us in the face of terrorism? He offers that for real security, we need to use "our national wealth... for the health and welfare of our perople." He prefers that we "take our example" from those—doctors, nurses, firemen, policemen "saving lives in the midst of mayhem"—"whose first thoughts are not violence, but healing, not vengeance, but compassion."

In Zinn's vista, America has been traumatized twice: first by the terrorist attacks, and second, by the proclamations of a vengeful leadership. In this America, we are suffering from a lack of genuine vision, as our leaders rehearse and repeat 'the old way of thinking, the old way of acting,' a way 'that has never worked.' In this America, 'we need to rethink our position in the world' so that our wealth is used to strengthen our own hand by improving 'the health and welfare of our people.'

In summary, these texts indicate a *reparationist* sense of the nation, where the citizen understands the need to rectify past (and present) wrongs against persons and peoples in order to claim our place in the world:

In Weis, we need to learn about 'touching other people's lives,' about crying with 'those whose humanity and dignity have been stripped and robbed,' about holding on 'to our responsibilities.' This America is about remembering to play a part, to listen to those who suffer, and to act to 'leave the world a better place than when we first met it.'

In Miller, our central focus should be on 'restoring and preserving ecological health and social justice,' 'deconstructing the myth of evil as other and stereotype,' complicating 'certainty and superficiality' and growing 'connections' that can 'help Love grow.'

In Zinn, we need to find a new kind of leadership in new places, a leadership that has greater legitimacy, 'whose first thoughts are not violence, but healing, not vengeance but compassion,' where healing is the primary focus.

In each case, the foundation for citizenship is *Perspective*; the mode of preferred civic engagement is (healing) *Activism*. The culture of citizenship advanced for the nation is *reparationist*.

Globalist Discourse

Mary Gergen (2002), in 'September 11, 2001: Changing the Ways of the World,' begins with her initial response to the moment, which is that she resents the way the events were reported, resents "the same old words and pictures" (150). She follows this with a plea for 'sense making' and considers the possibility that "we all keep on talking because we cannot rein in the tumult to make some sense," and notes that "the absurdity is almost palpable" (150).

Attending to America's 'new climate,' she looks to her own field, raising questions that center on social justice while highlighting the new dualism dividing the world now. She questions where the "leverage points" are for balancing extremes, to "survive this onslaught of 'Terror INC.' on one side and Modernist military experts and their supporters on the other" (152). She questions how we are to "understand the dynamics of the development of a new world order discourse" (152). She offers that this is perhaps "a time of reflection and reflexivity," that we should intervene "with new and refashioned languages that can incorporate the desires of the people" for safety "while averting... calls for eradicating and destroying many other people and places" (152).

Gergen makes a claim for the times that gives one pause for thought, as she speaks of patience, insight, reconciliation, and respect for difference. She would like "to insert into public dialogue alternative forms of sense making" and believes that we must try "to bring together in a new space those who have the influence and wisdom to allow for the marginalized voices to be heard" (152). Gergen's civic courage and her vision entwine as she looks to a positive future, voicing her conviction that "alternative voices" can "be silenced in a democracy" for "only so long" (152). "We must not lose courage or the faith that there are better ways of living together," she pleads, and "we must discover and support those who would go with us on this adventuresome trek" (152). Finally, she shares with us her belief that "only an optimism born of our capacity to leap into a fateful future is potent" (152).

In M. Gergen's vista, America is constricted by a "seemingly unified stance," too close, too quiet, an America caught between two forces, Terror INC. and the Modernist military, neither of them addressing the "deeper issues," which are global in nature (151).

Ivan Brady (2002), in 'Show Me a Sign,' looks at the human condition, offering that "there is hope in believing that... human nature is ultimately one of sociability, not social pathology" (176). He acknowledges that "resource sharing contracts in scope with prolonged deprivation," and sees that this is partly "a reaction to changing environmental circumstances that seeks to expand against cultural difference in wars of ideological and territorial aggrandizement, all... fueled by intolerance" (176). His concern is with what this means for us as "species beings" (176).

Brady seeks to characterize the interplay of deprivation with human nature, drawing uniquely positive conclusions. He declaims the notion that humans, "when all the strategic resource chips are down," wind up in a 'Hobbesian war,' and instead proclaims his faith in us as "social animals" (176). Brady makes his case by examining closely "the grisly facts revealed to the liberators of Auschwitz and other concentration camps at the end of World War II," where there came a point in which "a sign emerged, ...a symbol of triumph of the human spirit drawn out of the psyche in desperation and left for us like a text to be read in a twisted pile of dead men, women, and children" (176-177). The sign was this: that "many chose to die in a final physical embrace, entwining family and strangers alike." For Brady, this is "poignant and enduring evidence that we *can* matter to each other, irrespective of who we are, even (or especially) under the direst of circumstances" (177).

In Brady, this is the primary feature of humanity for us to consider. He explains that "the ultimate concerns of life transcend what separates us as cultures," and that, in fact, these concerns "combine us in one big mirror image as a species" (177).

For Brady, the question that emerges is how to operate from a perspective based on "this larger sense of humanity," especially where it is "lost to consciousness in the ordinary run of cultures and competitions for space, food, and the certainties that meaningful and satisfying lives must conform to the values of your own cultural beliefs" (177). Brady looks at this lost consciousness in terms of cultural dependency and reports that nothing exists "in our current global repertoire of behaviors and persuasions to keep that pattern from devolving into dangerously competitive relationships," as September 11th demonstrated (177). Does this mean that there is no hope left for this lost consciousness, that we are destined to continue to operate from culture-bound perspectives? Brady takes a unique view of this as he speaks of America's other side, which shone forth "as it moved to embrace its own... and began to build a levee of heroic strength, high-risk relief, and soothing words to stem the tide of outrage and tears" (177). He points out that in that scenario, "the prospect for global humanity known and cherished was insinuated in that resurrected solidarity" (177). For Brady, these were moments of hope and of healing, not just for the nation, but for the world, as "the pain was human, not just American" (177).

Brady raises the most poignant of images of the day to the foreground, the sight of those who "chose to jump to a certain death rather than face a terrifying immolation," and that is where he finds a sign of "hope for the species": "some of the jumpers were holding hands" (177).

In Brady's vista, America showed solidarity in this moment 'as it moved to embrace its own' and 'to build a levee of heroic strength,' demonstrating to the world what humans as species-beings can become in the face of 'wrenching national pain.' For him, despite the tragedy, in this moment 'the prospect for global humanity' shone brightly.

Kenneth J. Gergen (2002), in 'September 11 and the global implications of interpretive inquiry,' looks for "more positive possibilities" as he considers "beliefs that for many of us drive our efforts" (187) within the field of interpretive inquiry. He catalogues these beliefs, attesting to the importance of each, and these are worth noting. First, he points out that for us, "the point of inquiry" is to establish "interpretive intelligibility," rather than "Truth," which is "oppressive" because "if we fail to agree... we are maligned, disparaged, barred from conversation, or eliminated" (187). Our goal is different; we provide "lenses of understanding" to "broaden the possibilities of dialogue and action" (187). Second, we "attempt to give voice" to those we research, "to enable them to speak in their own ways" about what is important to them (187). This works, he tells us, to open access for them "to legitimate their modes of being" within the larger society (187). Third, our approach to inquiry also has merit because we recognize "the intelligibility of multiple realities and sense of the good," so that we see "the necessity of 'cross talk,' the unfolding conversations" that bring "antagonistic parties" into dialogue together, making space for "mutual enrichment" (187). Finally, our approach "emphasizes the importance of relationship," providing "illumination" for the purpose of enhancing relationships (187). He offers that "the willingness of interpretivists to experiment with multiple forms of representation" also shows that we value relationships (187).

Gergen's synopsis is meant to reveal the characteristics and dimensions of a field that offers 'positive possibilities,' leading him to look to the global implications. He sees that this kind of scholarship "is itself an action in the world," and argues that "if such actions can be extended," we may create other ways of seeing and responding to crisis, alternatives to war. Offering his hope, he declares that we "may now represent only a candle in a vast darkness," but as we gather more candles and "rekindled energies" to us, "we move toward the light" (187).

In K. Gergen's vista, America can benefit from abandoning its sense of Truth with a capital "T" to broaden 'the possibilities of dialogue and action.' This America needs to understand "the Other" and the invitation to dialogue, needs to appreciate relationship.

Norman K. Denzin (2002), in 'Week Four,' shares his appraisal of the war against terrorism in Afghanistan, along with his personal response, through a synopsis of newspaper headlines. His appraisal begins with "Week Four of the War," in which our planes attack Taliban artillery, but a lack of coordination "between American air strikes and the battlefield remains problematic" (199). He tells us that while "American bombs were dropped on Red Cross headquarters" in two separate accidental incidents, attempts "to calm the nation's fears over the anthrax threat spin out of control," but our leadership assures us that "God is on our side" (199). On October 28, a Sunday morning, there was a shooting in a Catholic Church in Pakistan, and sixteen are dead. An interview with a nurse and her husband revealed that they believe "the trouble started when President Bush called America's war on terrorism a crusade," which for them means "the revival of history," "Muslims against Christians" (199). Also in Week Four, Denzin sizes up what "America on Alert" means (199). "The FBI," he announces, "has arrested 900 suspects," but none have been "criminally charged" (199). Following the administration's instructions, "the major networks now censor the news about the war," and while a peace movement is growing across the nation, it "is barely reported on by the media" (199-200). "Patriotism," he observes, "is the national watchword," and "the American flag waves everywhere" (200).

Denzin segues into Game 2 of the World Series, where Ray Charles is singing our anthem "like only he can sing the blues," "slow and painful, drawn out, like a funeral march" (200). Denzin hears "pain, sorrow, and suffering" in his voice, and concludes that it was like "he felt the blues for American, as if he were singing at America's funeral" (200).

The sounds of the blues get Denzin thinking about Wendell Berry's (1981) poem, 'The Peace of Wild Things,' where the poet says that even as "despair for the world" grows stronger, "I come into the peace of the wild things," "I rest in the grace of the world and am free" (200). He seeks to resolve what he is seeing and feeling by going to the place where wild things dwell, to "accept a power that is unfathomably secret and holy and fleet," "a serenity that allows me to rest in the grace of the world" (200).

In Denzin's vista, America believes that 'God is on our side,' and is being led by a president who calls the war on terrorism 'a crusade,' evoking historic civilizational clashes between Christianity and Islam. This is an America for which Denzin has 'the blues.' In this America, news about the war is censored, the peace movement is treated by the media as though it doesn't exist, and 'patriotism is the national watchword.' In this text, there is acknowledgment, acceptance, and gratitude toward a greater power—the power of resting 'in the grace of the world,' where 'the peace of the wild things' may be found. This peace does not claim that there is a god who is on our side when we go to war. If there is hope to be had, it lies in a deep and profound belief in the secret and unfathomable holiness of the universe.

H. L. Goodall, Jr. (2002), in 'Fieldnotes from Our War Zone: Living in America during the Aftermath of September Eleventh,' shares with us his own reactions, "the sheer hopeless reality of this full, silent deadening of the spirit," "this quick eclipse of the human soul, this all-powerful evil awfulness" (206). He turns from September 11th to a personal recollection, using his father's story to tell a narrative of America. He tells us that his "father was very much like his country," and he rehearses for us the lessons he learned from his father: respecting our flag, obeying his parents, honoring our servicemen and women, getting a good education, reading the Bible, and preparing for world war. Acknowledging that neither he nor his father saw "the complicitness of those values in the political construction of the world," he highlights America's weakness, which is "deep self-deception" (208). He speaks of "our international arrogance and ignorance" and voices the thought that "we *are* a careless people" [emphasis in original] (208).

Goodall explores the symbolism involved in the attack on the towers, to assess what the war is *really* about, and concludes that it is, after all, "about people" (209). He counts the deaths resulting from the attacks, but includes as well "the untold millions of people who have died of starvation, poor health care, political violence, and of... having been born to a lifetime of poverty and despair" in places that are either unseen or unnoticed by those not sharing their fate (209). Goodall raises the question of what we should do. How we answer this question, he indicates, varies with our understandings of "what we think has been done and should be done," and there are, of course, diverse answers. This consideration returns him to thinking about symbols, which "give us something to rally around" (209). Noting that "our flag is a symbol of unspeakable unity with the ideas of the ideas of freedom, of democracy, and... of capitalism," and the act of wearing or displaying the flag communicates "a commonality of agreement about large ideas," he also points out that these symbols are normally "used as resources for articulating alternative perspectives" of America as a "national experiment," but "not right now" (209). Appreciating the symbolic value of the flag under these circumstances requires, then, an awareness as well of the dark side of that symbolism, since this symbolism can be "abused by those in power; used for questionable and unlawful political ends; claimed by racists, sexists, and the always heavily armed ignorant as theor own" (209).

While Goodall takes many twists and turns as he moves through the calamities and resulting fears of the moment, ultimately he turns his focus to war, which he describes as "explosions of raw emotions, this new American life of ours under the mediated watch of unfolding ambiguous uncertainties," and he offers that "war is incoherence," that it is "what happens when we stop making sense," as he admits he, too, lacks answers about what to do (211).

Goodall's sense of the power of narrative—which is, after all, the power of the *imaginary*—has something to teach us. He tells us that part of what we should learn is "the power of stories in the world," since this is "certainly part of the challenge we are facing as civilized people" (215). "Terrorism," he explains, "is an attack on our story ...the story we offer to the world" (215). Our interpretation is, however, not universal, and "our freedoms are read as signs of irresponsibility, our democracy and equality viewed as arrogant insults, our individuality evil, and our wealth the rotten core of the apple that spoils the rest of the world's harvest" (215). He argues that such an interpretation of our story, "as an American contradiction that is dangerous when loosed upon the world," not only makes terrorism possible, but "it constructs an oppositional storyline" that also makes terrorism "inevitable" (215).

Terrorism, after all, has its own storyline, he reminds us, and it is "a powerful one" about "righting the wrongs of the world," surrendering to a "cause greater than one's self," and "answering a call to duty" that might mean "sacrificing one's life" (215). In short, he points out, it is "the story of all revolutions... and... the plot common to heroic epics" (215). It is the reason we send our sons and daughters to war. Goodall has an answer to the world gone mad, to the stories and the antistory in our midst, but it depends on us responding to this story "with our lifetimes," because how we respond "will become part of the unfolding story of history," and it is "about the direction and moral content of that American story," our "great contribution to the epic story of life on this blue earth" (217-218).

In Goodall's vista, America is enveloped in an 'all-powerful evil awfulness,' as a nation complicit 'in the political construction of the world' and is suffering from self-deception. In this America, 'international arrogance and ignorance' come from our 'privileged carelessness,' and this war is about people: those lost in the attacks on America and those lost elsewhere as well, 'the untold millions' who die 'of starvation, poor health care, political violence,' and who suffer poverty and despair while we fail to see, fail to help.

George McGovern (2002), in 'The Healing in Helping the World's Poor,' articulates a global outreach program that could "produce less hate and more love," and frames the healing of America in those terms by asking whether any good can come from such a tragedy. His answer begins with the thought that "perhaps a more enduring and constructive change" is that we are finally asking "meaningful questions" about our world, and "looking at the hatreds directed at our commercial and military power" (*The New York Times* OpEd, A23, January 1). Asserting that his insights come from forty years spent working with "the world's poor," McGovern claims to "have learned something about the sense of powerlessness that millions feel" and assures us that "the stubborn realities of global hunger and poverty that help fuel hatred exist." In his analysis, the public sphere has a role to play, since it is through global electronic media that the word has spread "that the privileged few who rule them are living in luxury," that "the poor observe others with wealth, military might, comfort and pleasure that overwhelm the imagination." In light of this extraordinary fact, he raise the possibility that many see these "cruel and fanatical upstarts" as "downtrodden," that these "desperate young men rebelling against their powerlessness" saw in these attacks "a sign that they are not wholly powerless."

Still, McGovern brings the focus back to us, back to America, where "thoughtful citizens" have been telling us for a very long time that "the world's poor would one day explode out of their misery," and the revolutions in technology and communications "will aid that explosion," and offers that one answer—an answer that is reachable in our times—is that "we can end the world's hunger." Moving through details about proposed programs and projects, McGovern concludes with the notion that ending world hunger "can reduce the power of those who appeal to desperation and hopelessness," and that by doing so "we'll produce less hate and more love."

In McGovern's vista, America is a place where the people are 'united in our patriotism and in support for our government's efforts,' an America where the people are 'asking more meaningful questions' and 'looking at the hatreds directed at our commercial and military power.' In this America, we have 'wealth, military might, comfort and pleasure that overwhelm the imagination,' and we need to be aware that 'modern communications have spread the word' to those who suffer from 'the stubborn realities of global hunger and poverty that help fuel hatred.'

Tom Vellenga (2001), in 'Now, Engage the World,' takes on "the Bush administration's unilateral and increasingly imperial approach to global strategy," and that the events of September 11th require "a comprehensive examination of all of our assumptions and strategies." He offers that now is the time for us "to come together as one." For some, he acknowledges, "their impulse is to take on foes" (tompaine.com, October 1). Vellenga, however, critiques the administration's approach. His stance reflects his vision of America's place in the world, and McGovern argues that "this moment requires historical perspective," that "in the short term, we must heal, and we must seek justice."

He has a prescription for America's response, and, less explicitly, for a view of America's positioning in the world. "In the long run," he asserts "we should reflect on the... wisdom of a more multilateral approach," and that the events of September 11th have "given us the chance to set about fashioning a foundation for an international alliance against terrorism," rather than "going it alone." Vellenga goes on to argue that we should "send clear, systematic signals that we shall... adopt our mantle of responsibility and lead nations in a multilateral approach"—not just in the 'war against terrorism,' but "in every international sphere." He paints a broad picture of the kind of multilateralism America ought to—and might need to—pursue, which includes expanding how we define "the national interest," which would have to include issues of mass migrations of refugees due to "natural and man-made catastrophes" that spread both conflict and disease.

For Vellenga, the dimensions of the problem are global, and therefore the approach America takes also ought to be global and take into account the "root causes" of terrorism: "ignorance, inequity, hunger, impoverishment, and disenfranchisement."

In Vellenga's vista, America needs to re-examine 'all of our assumptions and strategies,' needs to 'come together as one,' needs to 'set about a national dialogue to construct a unified response.' In this America, 'we must heal, and seek justice,' while we encourage our leadership to 'awaken' to 'the utility of multilateralism' on all issues facing the world's citizens.

Reverend Graylan Scott Hagler (2001), in 'A Worldview on Peace and Restraint,' comes to terms with the implications of our response to September 11th and of President Bush's attempts "to suppress debate in our nation" (*The New York Times*, October 25). He asserts that he is "not with the President, his war, or mindless patriotism," and that he is not "with the terrorists," either. "I have spoken out for peace," he tells us, and as a result has received "dozens of hate calls and some death threats." He declares, however, that he chooses "not to be silenced because a true democracy needs voices that will test and challenge." For Hagler, the issues of belief and perception are complicated by different experiences of the nation based on race, and he speaks to "divergent worldviews from within white mainstream America and that of black Americans." When he preaches in black churches, he discloses, he teachers that Christianity "calls for us to seek alternative and less violent ways to solve crises." While "black audiences have reacted with enthusiasm," he offers, "mainstream white audiences" react "with great hostility," and he asks why this should be so. He characterizes this difference between black and white audiences in terms of a different awareness of the character and behaviors of the nation, arguing that "blacks are more familiar with the historical dirty deeds" of our government; that they "have seen U.S. foreign policy favor colonial and neo-colonial powers"; that they "know what it is to be insecure." They know "racial profiling and have never lived with the same degree of safety and well being most white Americans take for granted." In the present crisis, he indicates that their "insecurity is largely unchanged," that "Black Americans have reason t believe their government does abroad just as it has done at home," that its actions "are neither fair, just, nor righteous."

He reads the situation from his positioning within a right to civic-cultural difference, and offers a prescription, which is that we "must address the grievances of the world's struggling, poor and oppressed populations." "When we fail to do that," he cautions, "extreme and charismatic voices find fertile ground to organize." He rejects the idea that the events of September 11th should have resulted in "a cry for war." He prefers that we "pursue means that will bring safety and security," that what we need are "peaceful solutions developed in sane and reasoned ways."

In Hagler's vista, America's president seeks 'to suppress debate in our nation,' so that being 'with him' means being for 'his war, or mindless patriotism.' In this America, there is a difference between blacks and whites that emerges because blacks and whites know America differently: blacks know 'the historical dirty deeds of the United States at home and abroad' and 'what it is to be insecure,' but they do not know 'the same degree of safety and well being that most white Americans take for granted.'

In summary, these texts indicate a *globalist* sense of the nation, where the concerns of citizens here at home reflect the following:

In M. Gergen's vista, civic courage is about resistance and dissident voices, reflection and reflexivity based on patience, pragmatic insights, reconciliation, and respect for differences. In this America, if we are 'to live safely and peaceably in this world,' we need 'a new space' for those with influence and wisdom to ensure that 'the marginalized voices' get heard. We need courage and faith that we can live together in this global world in better ways, ways that we have not yet tried.

In Brady's vista, exercising civic courage is about 'sociability' and is universal: beyond the cultural conflicts and the competition for resources, we are all species beings, and our social nature brings out the best in humans everywhere, especially in adversity, 'when all the strategic resource chips are down.'

In K. Gergen's vista, scholarship based on principles can serve as 'an action in the world,' creating alternatives to 'the wars on Westernism, on terrorism, or alterity of any kind.' Such scholarship can show how 'lenses of understanding' can be used as points of light to take part in the bettering of the world. Exercising civic courage means acknowledging a global interconnectedness and equates open, respectful dialogue with action.

In Denzin's vista, exercising civic courage is personal, and in this text, there is acknowledgment, acceptance, and gratitude toward a greater power—the power of resting 'in the grace of the world,' where 'the peace of the wild things' may be found. This peace does not claim that there is a god who is on our side when we go to war. If there is hope to be had, it lies in a deep and profound belief in the secret and unfathomable holiness of the universe.

In Goodall's vista, exercising civic courage is about 'a commonality of agreement about large ideas—philosophical principles—that may be used as resources for articulating alternative perspectives.' Exercising civic courage is also about being aware of the dark side of our symbolic imagery—what it can be used to conceal, how it may be abused for unjust purposes, 'used wrongfully, hatefully, coercively.' Hope is to be found in 'the power of stories in the world.' War is what happens when we 'stop making sense'; it is incoherence. The answer to war, then, and to terrorism as well, is to invent 'new possibilities' for the storylines of our own lives, the life of our nation, and the life of tomorrow's world. The 'epic story of life on this blue earth' is a storyline we all construct in, through and for 'our lifetimes.'

In McGovern's vista, we have 'wealth, military might, comfort and pleasure that overwhelm the imagination,' and we need to be aware that 'modern communications have spread the word' to those who suffer from 'the stubborn realities of global hunger and poverty that help fuel hatred.' Exercising civic courage means ending world hunger to 'reduce the power of those who appeal to desperation and hopelessness,' it means producing 'less hate and more love' worldwide.

In Vellenga's vista, we should send out the word that we will 'adopt our mantle of responsibility' 'in every international sphere.' In this America, our definition of 'national interest' must be expanded to include the 'root causes' of terrorism: 'ignorance, inequity, hunger, impoverishment, and disenfranchisement' throughout the world. Exercising civic courage in this America means becoming better world partners with other nations in 'sowing the seeds of peace.'

In Hagler's vista, exercising civic courage in this America means addressing 'the grievances of the world's struggling, poor and oppressed populations,' and pursuing means to safety and security through 'peaceful solutions developed in sane and reasoned ways.'

In each case, the foundation for citizenship is *Perspective*; the mode of civic engagement is *Representation*. The culture of citizenship advanced for the nation is *globalist*.

7

Mapping Autobiographic Terrain

CULTURES OF CITIZENSHIP

Today, we are challenged to map out a new poststructural order of things—its immanent logic and ironic form. In a time of pervasive deconstruction when electronic media generate hyperreal models seemingly without origin or reality, the territory may no longer precede the map. Now it may be the map that engenders the territory. With the world of human culture constituted through the work of signifying practices, our task today is to de-code and pattern this new reality of information networks and electronic communication without naïve essentialism or undue nostalgia for the world we have lost. (Paulston, 2005, 12)

Somewhere between progress and retrogress, construction and deconstruction, lie places where both notions take on some new, transcendent meaning when considered not as polar opposites but as complements. That place might aptly be characterized as the postmodern condition.

Standing at the edge of the twentieth century's final decade, curriculum workers prone to reflection acknowledge that dichotomies have imploded, for the most part, as curriculum scholarship strives to reconcile not only its binaries... but also the numerous unexplored and unnamed territories between them. (Marshall, Sears, and Schubert, 2000, 225)

...the source of light, like human knowledge, is always situated, here or there, rising or setting, or just breaking through as the clouds pass. The figure is never fully illuminated. Light moves through time as well as space, and so clear seeing is burdened with all the limitations of human consciousness, always situated in spatial perspectives and temporal phases. Furthermore, our work, no matter what its form, is not the seeing itself but *a picture of the seeing*. [Emphasis mine] (Grumet, 1988, 61)

Orientation to the Space from which I Speak

The three passages above are meant to indicate the spirit in which this work is offered for consideration, and also to disclose the space from which I speak. First, Paulston's 'invention' (2005) and cultivation of a research approach he named 'social cartography' (1996) has its limitations and constitutes a 'complicated conversation' (Pinar, 2004) in its own right, but a failure to attempt to address the growing diversity of perspective(s) across a wide array of intellectual battlefronts, and an awareness of the unraveling of an ethic based on a fixed notion of progress and the belief that certainty is attainable in human affairs, an unraveling that signals the advent of the postmodern condition, was *not* among those limitations.

At the University of Pittsburgh, in the Department of Administrative and Policy Studies (APS) in the School of Education, Rolland G. Paulston,[1] Professor Emeritus of Comparative Education and past president and Honorary Fellow of the Comparative and International Education Society in the United States, engaged some of his doctoral students in The Social Cartography Project as he called for a critical postmodern cartography (1993) and mapped what he saw as a 'perspectivist turn' in comparative education (1997). He would later map what he called 'reality turns,' or 'ontological eras' in Western thinking in general, and in the field more specifically (2005).

His thesis is formally stated as follows:

> It is our thesis that when scholars address the cultural values and differences revealed by different and often competing knowledge claims, they can enhance their research by developing and including in their findings a cognitive map showing their perceptions of how these multiple knowledge claims interrelate. Social cartography rejects no narrative, whether it is a metanarrative or that of a localized culture. Although metanarratives are accepted and mapped, they are neither privileged nor accepted in their previous role of dominating other narratives. Rather than legitimizing metanarratives—and their ideologies in their modernist form—our mapping project introduces the concept of the mininarrativization of the metanarrative. Thus the breadth of research possibilities and understanding that social cartography envisions recognizes...all points-of-view. (Paulston, 1996, 22)

Some members of this project, many of whom were international students, mapped organizational, institutional, or programmatic disputes—for instance, debates over decentralization in Latin American educational contexts (Gostoriaga and Paulston, 1999) and in Argentina specifically (Gostoriaga and Paulston, 2004), or entrepreneurial debates in the U.S., the U.K., and Finland (Erkilla, 2001). Ahmed (2000) used this perspectivist lens to map women's responses to the lack of feminist conscientization in non-formal education programs in rural Bangladesh. I saw the mapping project as an opportunity to ponder changes in social thinking, envisioning this approach as a contemplative mode of inquiry for studying ways of seeing expressed in discursive activity. I initially explored environmental discourse as conflicted, or eclipsed, social thinking about human-nature relations (Nicholson-Goodman, 2000; Nicholson-Goodman and Paulston, 1996).[2] Later, mentor and friend Noreen Garman[3] and I would map teachers' narratives of their perceptions of the dictum, "It's research-based," to reflect on what such perceptions meant in terms of teachers' ways of seeing and appropriating research (Nicholson-Goodman and Garman, 2007).

Mapping Autobiographic Terrain 153

A comparative educator of some acclaim, Paulston was an early mentor, as well as a beloved figure, in my doctoral program. His writing in the excerpt above reaches to articulate what he proposed as a post-foundational non-paradigmatic method for mapping the intertextual field of comparative education discourse. Paulston, despite the acclaim his work had earned him, understood the hubris of taking himself too seriously, and was open to transformation, particularly as he came to acknowledge and embrace, *inter alia*, feminist, post-structural, postmodern, and post-colonial discourses, which were catalysts in his thinking about comparative education discourse as a matter of perspective.

The 'line of flight' taken by members of the Project, however, found a mixed reception in the field. On the one hand, our attention to representing diversity was duly acknowledged, and some properly understood that the mapping approach we were taking "pointed to the difficulties of undertaking comparative studies in a post-modern, global world" (Watson, 1998, 9), and that mapping as we undertook it was, in fact, a form of disruption, which Fischman (2004) described—acknowledging Foucault's notion that "analyzing social event-spaces requires seeing them as a set of heterogeneous relations saturated with characteristics, qualities and temporalities" (114)—this way:

> Rolland Paulston acknowledges that his perspective about social cartography is not located outside power relations, arguing that it is another strategic movement in the field of comparative education. Therefore, whether these mapping strategies are going to be incorporated into the repertory of our scholarly production or not will depend ...on the conflictive epistemological struggles of the field... (114)

Fischman, further, asserted that "A good map needs to simplify the intricacy of the territory so the traveler can understand the information," and that in a "very concrete way, to create maps is to disrespect the territory mapped" (114), which is, of course, congruent with the nature of unmasking. We were, alternatively, accused of taking this perspectivist turn "too far" (Watson, 1998), and even of leading the field astray, of "abusing ancestors," as we ventured into 'dangerous' postmodern territories, transgressing as we had against the canon and the (now to be enforced?) boundaries of the disciplines and methods informing the field (Epstein and Carroll, 2005).

Webber's complaint (Reynolds and Webber, 2004) that such responses may be seen as "unproductive means used by senior university scholars to block the entrance of new scholars into the field" (6) therefore resonates vividly with my own experience as a doctoral student in the field of comparative education. No reconceptualization has been effected to date that I know of by 'senior university scholars' in that field, despite valiant efforts to 'reimagine' it (e.g., Ninnes and Mehta, 2004). Paulston therefore represents, for me, both an exceptional figure in senior scholarly work and a treasured anomaly.

Under Paulston's tutelage, the mapper within me found space to emerge, as I was provided with rich experiences in scholarship and study, in the struggle for conceptualization and reconceptualization, iteration and reiteration, and in the ongoing development of an aesthetic spatial sensibility as I worked toward illustration through a perspectivist lens. Having already violated the canon of comparative education, I turned, under Noreen Garman's tutelage, to the study of the reconceptualist movement in curriculum studies, a movement that seemed to clearly resonate with my own eclectic and postfoundational sensibilities. As I began to participate in annual meetings and conferences in the field of curriculum studies (Bergamo, Curriculum and Pedagogy, and the American Association for the Advancement of Curriculum Studies), I became familiar at last—in a personal-intellectual rather than a purely textual manner—with curricularists themselves and with some of their terrains of inquiry. The initial conceptualization of this curriculum inquiry project constituted my 'entrance' into the field. It is my hope that this effort has produced something of value and interest to other curricularists.

My discussion of social cartography here is therefore concerned with its appropriateness as a complement to autobiography, i.e., in producing a 'cultural portrait' drawn from analysis of the interrelations of truth- and value-claims expressed in discourse, claims that effect confrontation and contestation within a civic-cultural struggle, in this case, for a working sense of national identity, or selfhood, the nation's autobiography. The postmodern condition and the bodies of discourse theorizing its meanings for social life and social thought informs much of this study, albeit 'offstage.' While this 'condition' is not the focus of this work, it certainly feeds into many of the complications in our civic-cultural struggle, as well as contradictions of the dominant modernist view that has shaped and constrained both the curriculum of that struggle *and* the space of 'through education' in our times, and so deserves some attention. The question of representation emerges within this postmodern condition in new ways, but in order to understand their novelty, or 'newness,' one must understand how the question has been addressed by curricularists in the past. For this purpose, I provide in this chapter a fairly detailed review of Kemmis' (1986) attention to this problem, augmenting this with attention to Greene's (1978) 'landscapes of learning' and her (1986) 'search for a critical pedagogy' and Pinar's (2004) work on autobiography as a 'revolutionary act.' First, however, I want to speak very briefly to the relations between the advent of the postmodern condition and the approach undertaken here.

Marshall, Sears, and Schubert's (2000) depiction of the postmodern condition (above) echoes W. T. Anderson's (1990) notion that the postmodern moment would be a space of confusion, disintegration, and contestation, but also of hope. It is this space of hope that Marshall, Sears, and Schubert point to in the form of 'unexplored and unnamed territories' between imploded binaries above. In curriculum inquiry, this notion of the 'in-between' may be approached via interdisciplinary scholarship to explore and map new sociocultural, political-economic, historical, philosophical, aesthetic, literary, moral, and spiritual 'territories' criss-crossing multiple disciplinary 'boundaries.' The need for such eclectic scholarship may continue to expand in our times, particularly along 'lines of flight' (Reynolds and Webber, 2004), as we work to figure out just where we are in this new *predatory age*, how to survive in it, and where creative inroads may be found or made for the possibility of revived democratic aspiration (West, 2004).

To accomplish this, I believe that we should map the terrain, taking in the vistas from 'a thousand plateaus' (Deleuze and Guattari, 1987). We are all nomads now, although some of us have *always* operated in smooth space (life may dictate this to some extent, but for some, such a positioning is a matter of choice, and therefore expressive of agency.) But this requires some explanation:

> The classical image of thought, and the striating of mental space it effects, aspires to universality. It in effect operates with two "universals," the Whole as the final ground of being or all-encompassing horizon, and the Subject as the principle that converts being into being-for-us. *Imperium* and republic. Between the two, all of the varieties of the real and the true find their place in a striated mental space, from the double point of view of Being and the Subject, under the direction of a "universal method." It is now easy for us to characterize the nomad thought that rejects this image and does things differently. It does not ally itself with a universal thinking subject but, on the contrary, with a singular race; and it does not ground itself in an all-encompassing totality but is on the contrary deployed in a horizonless milieu that is a smooth space... An entirely different type of adequation is established here, between the race defined as "tribe" and smooth space defined as "milieu." [Emphasis in original] (Deleuze and Guattari, 1987, 379)

Some of us have left 'universal method' behind us in this postmodern moment, in part due to its deficiencies and limitations, in part because the Whole and the Subject have been fragmented and decentered. What, then, is the space in which, and through which, the nomad operates? Deleuze and Guattari explain the difference between striated, or sedentary, space and nomad, or smooth, space:

> The nomad has a territory; he [sic] follows customary paths; he goes from one point to another; he is not ignorant of points... even though the nomadic trajectory may follow trails or customary routes, it does not fulfill the function of the sedentary road, which is to *parcel out a closed space to people*, assigning each person a share and regulating the communication between shares. The nomadic trajectory does the opposite: *it distributes people... in an open space*, one that is indefinite and noncommunicating. ... there is a significant difference between the spaces: sedentary space is striated, by walls, enclosures, and roads between enclosures, while nomad space is smooth, marked only by "traits" that are effaced and displaced with the trajectory. ... The nomad distributes himself in a smooth space; he occupies, inhabits, holds that space; that is his territorial principle. ... Whereas the migrant leaves behind a milieu that has become amorphous or hostile, the nomad is one who does not depart, does not want to depart, who... invents nomadism as a response to this challenge. (Deleuze and Guattari, 1987, 381)

The images Deleuze and Guattari impart here speak to some of the same issues highlighted by Appadurai (1996) and Bhabha (1994) (see Chapter 4), to the notions of transnational and postnational space, to the dispersion of ideas as they embody "social and textual affiliation" (Bhabha, 1994, 201), and, most particularly, to the "diasporic public sphere" (Appadurai, 1996, 21). They inform the dynamics of social mapping as a mode of representation, and speak as well to my own autobiographic positioning within this postmodern moment. I take the opportunity here to briefly elaborate this positioning, since the occasion has presented itself.

I have lived my life in nomadic space, moving every few years with the constantly fluctuating circumstances of my parents' situating in the world and with the flow and flux of my father's artistic aspirations, across boundaries and across borders, from Toronto to Montreal to New York City. I was encouraged, as the child of artists, to explore and create, to direct my own learning, and to envision my own quest—in short, to grow as an autodidact and free thinker. The range of my intellectual efforts is always and in every way informed by the space I occupied as a child: the space of movement, of creation, of change, of instability, and of flexibility. I have stumbled, but I have not wavered in my conviction that the pathways I have traveled were worth the costs of the traveling. My 'territory' *is* this space. It comes with me wherever I wander, and I am no stranger to wandering. My center, therefore, is in the autobiographic self that has evolved through multiple passages, but this is an evolution that carries with it *remembrance* of past crossings and past transgressions, both my own and those of my parents, embodied in the narratives they passed down to me as much as in the lives I have lived. I am a nomad, and my eclecticism is authentic, perhaps the result of the multiple selves that have resulted from so many years of itinerant questing and of the rootlessness that was my parents' legacy. This has served to enhance my own inclination to appreciate diversity of vision and of understanding, and made it probable that my interactions with Rolland G. Paulston would, as noted, lead to the emergence of the mapper within me, and that the very notion of reconceptualization would have such tremendous appeal for me.

This anecdotal offering, this self-disclosure, is meant to assist my reader to decipher, complicate, and critique the work presented here. In the pages that follow, I offer further insights into social cartography, interweaving these with a discussion of the interrelations depicted in the maps (there are two) and implications of the mapped (illustrated) autobiography. I ask my reader to 're-think' the interrelations within the intertextual field and to consider carefully both the conceptual organizers used and their application to a curriculum of possibility for the civic-cultural surround in a nation aspiring to democracy, a curriculum we have yet to envision and enact as a general principle in educational practice, despite Henderson and Kesson's (2004) thoughtful call to do so in pursuit of 'curriculum wisdom.'

I introduce multiple frameworks we might consider to theorize a curriculum connected in moral-political terms with this moment of social change. I provide a reading and critical discussion of the map itself, consider the possibilities of the work and its limitations, and expand upon my initial discussion of this mapping project as properly belonging within the field of curriculum inquiry, working to envision how social mapping might serve the latter by illustrating the deterritorialization of selfhood at the level of the nation. I ask my reader to bear in mind (as I do) Grumet's (1988) caveat: namely, that "our work... is but a picture of the seeing," "no matter what its form" (61).

Finally, I ask my reader to note that I am working from a meta-theoretical perspective to pursue 'ideology-critique' (Kemmis, 1986, 73) as I ponder this moment in our American civic-cultural struggle over meaning(s). I employ this approach to make sense of this disputatious discursive terrain, the intricacies of which may be made both visible and arguable: first, through the elaboration of writing, and second, through the imagery of the map. What is produced by this visual imagery goes beyond the binaries, and elicits a 'naming' of some 'unexplored and unnamed territories between them,' their intertextual field, their interterritorial *space*. That 'naming' makes a claim, but it also invites a dialogue. The dialogue permeates the rhizome, whose offshoots give curriculum studies, for example, an expansive and multi-directional textual reach (see, e.g., Pinar et al., 1995). Such a dialogue requires an approach that embraces diversity in its many forms and therefore I highlight particular strands of this national autobiographic project to consider features of the syntactic structures that support them. I turn first, however, to dimensions of social mapping to provide further insight into this research genre and into my own positioning as mapper.

Paulston and Liebman (1996) offer their envisioning of the role of social mapping in these words:

> As is true of any written discourse, a map begins as the property of its creator. It contains some part of that person's knowledge and understanding of the social system. As a mental construction representing …the ideologies of cultures, maps can be characterized as what Baudrillard's translators describe as "art and life." … While we find maps can shape the system of objects, we suggest that rather than carve out a truth, they portray the mapper's perceptions of the social world, locating in it multiple and diverse intellectual communities, leaving to the reader not a truth, but a cognitive art, the artist's scholarship resulting in a cultural portrait. (14)

This mapping is undertaken, therefore, with an eye to *illustrating* the 'art and life' of this national autobiography. When creating a social map, some discernment is required to decide whether the map—as an expression of the mapper's way of seeing a particular phenomenon, 'the artist's scholarship, resulting in a cultural portrait'—offers some arrangement of meaning that will resonate with the reader. This is particularly important where the map makes a claim to illustrate national autobiography. Paulston and Liebman assert above that the map belongs to its creator, and initially it does because in so many ways it reflects the *artfulness* of its creator, while at the same time reflecting the mapper's scholarly analysis of discursive terrain provided by others.

However, a map is like a thought offered during the course of conversation: once that thought is given expression, it is acted upon, first, by another's reception, and then by response, and becomes changed as it enters the process of conversation itself. In other words, there is a hermeneutic at work, both during the creation of the map and then again, upon its reception by the reader, and it is important not to rob the reader of agency, not to present or position the map as a model. The project of critiquing and re-mapping is an integral link with this agency, the point at which mapping becomes a *conversation* between map-makers and map-readers (see, e.g., Nicholson-Goodman and Paulston, 1996). This is the point, also, where the map ceases to be the mere 'property' of its creator and truly goes 'public.'

If we think about the map as a 'cultural portrait' of a contextual moment or space, then it seems reasonable that this portrait may also resonate in some way—if only by way of evoking opposition—with the reader's experiencing of that moment or space. This resonance is less likely to be found, however, where there is greater distance between the phenomenon mapped and the reader's location within the social milieu within which the phenomenon is taking place. I have deliberately chosen here to focus on a phenomenon that has impacted *all* Americans, and to focus on this contextual moment—the moment of response to a horrific and worldview-changing event—in terms of change and diversity in our civic-cultural ways of seeing our nation and our place in the world.

I have spoken of this moment metaphorically in terms of 'silence,' but the map displays a broad range of ways of seeing civic-cultural struggle relative to the nation/world, opening out to 'perceptual codes' (Huff, 1996, 165)—ultimately conceptualized as *cultures of citizenship*—that we as citizens may cognitively employ to make sense of our imagined community, the nation. Some of these cultures of citizenship reflect civic courage, especially in present context. I employ a civic-cultural framing of autobiographical dimensions and possibilities here, and I use the map to portray the differences that exist within our notions of *America* and *American* because of my interest in exploring the space and shape of civic-cultural struggle, and because civic courage has demanded it in our times. This is both the meaning and the intent of this national autobiography.

Some of us lost, for this moment, the ability to speak freely from our own cognitive spaces. We were pressured to think and speak exclusively from a space of *Orthodoxy* in a civic-cultural form of 'gracious submission' (Pinar, 2004), as if this was our best and only defense, as if 'united we stand' meant that any thoughtfulness or deeper questioning on our parts could cause the nation to falter or fail. In this scenario, the agents of *Control* came out in full force, reinforced by our own reactions to attack and unquestioningly sanctioned by those huddling together for safety in the space of orthodoxy. The rest of us became 'outliers.' This effect of having an authoritarian regime in power in a time of national crisis led me to consider what public, academic, and political discourses offered by way of envisioning social and educational change. A brief description of the conceptual interrelations of these discourses—and thus of the autobiography they speak forth—may be helpful in considering parameters for curriculum theorizing.

In writing where *Reason* serves as a foundation for citizenship, it is evident—either tacitly or explicitly—that there are consequences for speaking out, but that conscience must prevail and risks must be taken. Many were taken by surprise as the nation tolerated shutting down civil liberties in the name of security, and spokespersons for official institutions, political organizations, and mainstream media outlets alike targeted dissent as though it was somehow un-American, even anti-American. This was compounded by the effects of having an administration in office that operated on a 'need-to-know basis, where the people were assumed *not* to need to know and those who questioned or sought information were denied access, stonewalled, or fed breadcrumbs of information under the rolling disclosure strategy (see Prologue). Worse yet, those protesting the secrecy were condemned as 'unpatriotic' because they *resisted* orthodoxy.

In writing where *Perspective* serves as a foundation for citizenship, what is lamented is the lack or loss of voice, position, or space for dialogue—a loss not entirely uncharacteristic of the nation *prior* to September 11th (it must be acknowledged that opening spaces for such dialogue has a long and troubled history in America). This loss, however, was flagrantly supported by the orthodoxies swallowing up greater democratic aspirations in this moment, and so it is loss as a social force that is either tacitly or explicitly evidenced. In the limited space still open, alternative constellations of meaning were aired, but then immediately interrogated and subverted as they came under attack. The message was clear: you are either 'with us' or 'against us.'

In writing where the preferred mode of civic engagement is *Representation*, what is lamented is media filtering (and thus silencing) of dissent, along with an official use of diversionary tactics to downplay and, if possible, undermine any protest, no matter what the scale.[4] Representation seemed to have disappeared as politicians shied away from assuming they had the public on their side if they took umbrage with administration enunciations of public opinion and stood for alternative visions. The result was that we lost that representation as we became, ostensibly, a one-party state. There was a good deal of 'structured silence' (see, e.g., Barry and Lobe, 2002; Chang, 2002; Giroux, 2002; Lapham, 2004), but my concern is for the realm of our 'epistemological unconscious,' where there may have been damage done, and no genuine 'damage control' was forthcoming. I believe that we (I speak of us as a general public) narrowed our range of understandings, our range of visions, to 'fall in line' with state-sponsored media portrayals of the 'party line' defining the mood of the nation. In short, *our eyes made adjustments to the darkness.*

In writing where the preferred mode of civic engagement is *Activism—and where orthodoxy was resisted in its enunciated form*—what is lamented is the failure to use the moment for better purposes, such as awakening the public to new understandings of the dilemmas we face in a post-9/11 world and of the need to correct the deficiencies of the past in order to meet the challenges of the future. The triumphal enunciation itself co-opted the language, for instance, of communitarian discourse as communal identity was boxed in by nationalistic rhetoric and the enunciation itself—as an approved *newly remembered* (or reinvented) national identity—was enforced with hypernational zeal. At the same time, any criticism of national failings was kept from the public eye; the mantra of accomplishment and arrival as a democratic nation of exceptional resolve, strength, and unity ruled the moment. What usurped its place was, in fact, a celebration of the 'deed' based on speech acts (Barthes, 1989) that pronounced the democratic project complete and our national character perfected.

Constructs of citizenship have been shifting for a long time, and are now deeply embedded in complications emerging in the twenty-first century milieu. Thirty years of 'cold war culture wars' (Rich, 2001) have been responsible in part, but so have identity politics and globalization. In fact, America's divergent reactions to twentieth-century totalitarianisms (i.e., the Nazi regime in Germany, Italian fascism, and Soviet communism) contributed over time to the development of the 'left-right' culture war, in part, as an ideological conflict over appropriate political-philosophical responses to protect ourselves against such threats (Ciepley, 2006). What has resulted is a scenario where each side sees the rhetoric of its opponent as a form of fascistic subterfuge, and says so in a fashion consistent with Nairn's view of nationalism as having a 'Janus-face,' i.e., "the fact that it is both communal and authoritarian, friendly and bellicose, all at the same time" (Brennan, 1990, 45), which profoundly complicates and inhibits any genuine conversation between the two. The outcome is, therefore, ironic, and the resulting epistemology of resentment operates in a field of endless contestation with no positive potential resolution.

I suspect that the events of September 11th and its aftermath brought the schisms already present in the 'epistemological unconscious' of a diverse and divided culture to the surface *at the same time* that we were 'rediscovering' ourselves as a nation through trauma, perhaps producing an internal culture shock of some importance. Coupled with grief and anxiety, that could, to some extent, explain self-imposed silence(s). As I pondered what that silence meant, and why so many felt its power, I began to suspect that it might be due to a cataclysmic realization of civic-cultural difference even as unity was ubiquitously and aggressively invoked. That realization of difference turned how we think about who we say we are or will become as a nation into high drama, painfully complicated by a genuine connectedness in tragedy and loss, and that is, in part, what I have 'listened for' in these discourses.

Further, because I chose to draw from alternative discourses, i.e., discourses that exhibited civic courage, in the face of this silencing, I feared that I might wind up with a purely 'oppositional' view of the cultural surround, an outcome that would skew the map and suppress some portion of the authentic dialogue, some facet of the autobiographical project. I therefore immersed myself in the discourse and rhetoric of those insisting on adherence to the 'one true America' perspective complicit in the silencing. I spent endless hours studying so-called 'conservative' media dissemination of this perspective—for instance, watching news-talk shows on the Fox cable outlet (e.g., *Hannity and Colmes*), shows that I would normally 'tune out'—in order to understand their message(s). While I fully expected that these 'speech acts' (Barthes, 1989, 128) would reflect a triumphal orientation, I was totally unprepared for how consistently and how forcefully they would reflect hypernational agitation—and *demand conformity* to the triumphal-nationalist agenda.

This immersion served its purpose well as I observed the language strategies through which others are inducted into the society of believers reflected in their audience(s), or, alternatively, castigated as traitors to the nation. To represent their hypernational invective, I selected an advertisement posted in *The New York Times* by William Bennett's group—Americans for Victory Over Terrorism (AVOT)—whose declared aim was to warn 'liberals' that they were subject to the same treatment as the terrorists themselves (including detainment) if they failed to 'rightly understand' the dynamics and dimensions of the new 'war on terrorism' as enunciated by the administration. Ultimately, I decided to include as well the discourse of presidential speech (*State of the Union* Address, 2003) to highlight the 'one true America' positioning reflected in the triumphal narrative of the nation.

Social Cartography: The Conceptual Lens

Just as the media 'mirror' the world for us, so too the adversary and the 'outliers' alike 'mirror' the world the media mirror for us, in an endless circle of reflected images. What we wind up with is a 'through the looking-glass' scenario where we have to try to get inside what is being reflected in the mirror in order to sort out what might actually be real, *if anything*. Such is the postmodern condition. Given such complexity, a postmodern sensibility is helpful for conducting research within such a frame. Nicholson-Goodman and Paulston (1996) explain:

> Postmodern sensibility, from Foucault's view, presents a critical threat both to the illusion of stability and to the illusion of a foundational basis for change. As such, it is subject to villainization as though the sensibility itself, by destroying prior illusion, could destroy either progress or hope of progress. Those who labor within this sensibility encounter themselves as 'other,' and benefit from that encounter, particularly as the encounter itself brings to life new venues for research, and new research processes—the sites and tools of excavation. A kind of watchfulness is necessitated by the process, however—one which demands that we be overseers of ourselves in the moment where we gaze into the looking-glass of otherness. (102)

This presence/absence reflects something about our public sphere and our civic-cultural struggle that should not be overlooked—that we are mired in a 'circle of mirrors' from which escape is hardly an option. Paulston (1996) explains, while sharing his own concerns for his field, and speaking in terms of his "desire to move beyond the sterile polarities of modernist rule-making and poststructuralist nihilism in knowledge work" (354). Acknowledging that there is "certainly space for both rules and irony in comparative studies" (354), he seeks to "privilege the narrative imagination with its power of disclosure which ...marks our basic ethical ability to imagine oneself as another" (354). This notion of narrative imagination is a recurrent theme in many fields of study; Greene (1986, 1988, 1995) speaks of this consistently in her work on naming and confronting mindlessness, numbness, and meaninglessness. For Paulston, empowering imagination is a key to "help us move beyond our present aporia of the deflated sovereign subject" (354).

Elaborating on the changing notion of 'mirror(s),' Paulston contends

> Where the pre-moderns tended to see the image as a *mirror*, and the moderns as a *lamp*, the postmodern model of the image is akin to a circle of *mirrors* where each viewpoint reproduces the surface images of all the others in a play of infinite multiplication. Recent attempts to break out of this so-called postmodern mirror play of simulacra, i.e. reproductions without originals, propose a hermeneutic of imagination that relocates the crisis of creativity in a world refigured or prefigured by our imaginings. ... Today, as we look ahead to the new century ...we require more than ever the power of imagining to recast other ways of being in the world, other possibilities of existence and to wager once again that imagination lives on (Kearny, 1998). [Emphasis in original] (1996, 354)

I approached this curriculum inquiry project through the prismatic lens of social cartography, then, in order to 'zoom in' on the interrelations and interconnectedness of particular imaginaries present in these discourses as I searched for an authentic substance to work with in this autobiography of a nation. The map articulated as a result of this inquiry suggests an initial discursive dispersion of our imagining of the nation in cultural terms and of our positioning on agency within the public sphere as citizens. I believe that the schism in our consciousness about these matters acted somewhat like an earthquake, and that in its breaking up of the bedrock something was exposed that had been working its way through the foundations all along, but perhaps only became fully visible as a result of September 11th. In short, the internal culture shock may have reflected an intensified realization of *difference* in a moment where the call (and the urge) to 'unite' took center stage and where speech acts straying from the enunciation of unity were stifled.

Autobiography based on discursive activity thus provides an intriguing research genre for approaching this difference. Social mapping, secondarily, is used here as a tool for figural-conceptual inquiry, for making sense of, and highlighting, disputed autobiographical claims, and as well for raising questions about our national identity vis-à-vis prospects for the emergence of new social imaginaries and a future for democracy. Mapping as conceived here, as social cartography, however, bears its own unique rhizomatous characteristics, which also require some explanation. Deleuze and Guattari distinguish between the map and a *tracing*:

> It is our view that genetic axis and profound structure are above all infinitely reproducible principles of *tracing*. All of tree logic is a logic of tracing and reproduction. In linguistics as in psychoanalysis, its object is an unconscious that is itself representative, crystallized into codified complexes, laid out along a genetic axis and distributed within a syntagmatic structure. Its goal is to describe a de facto state, to maintain balance in intersubjective relations, or to explore an unconscious that is already there from the start, lurking in the dark recesses of memory and language. [Emphasis in original] (12)

While it might be argued that this 'tree logic' has its place in some of the vistas acknowledged in the autobiography, it is also true that new social imaginaries—and the range of possibilities upon which they operate (Appadurai, 1996)—have deterritorialized older prescriptive reproductions, and for this reason, rhizomatous thinking may be both necessary and useful in these times. Deleuze and Guattari (1987) offer this possibility:

> The rhizome is altogether different, a *map and not a tracing*. ... What distinguishes the map from the tracing is that it is entirely oriented toward an experimentation in contact with the real. The map does not reproduce an unconscious closed in upon itself; it constructs the unconscious. ... The map is open and connectable in all of its dimensions; it is detachable, reversible, susceptible to constant modification. It can be torn, reversed, adapted to any kind of mounting, reworked by an individual, group, or social formation. It can be drawn on a wall, conceived of as a work of art, constructed as a political action or as a meditation. Perhaps one of the most important characteristics of the rhizome is that it always has multiple entryways... [Emphasis in original] (12)

The form the map takes is a mode of representation that demonstrates a dispersion of ways of seeing in smooth space. The map, then, is not a grid, but rather a portrait, an illustration, in this work, of an autobiographic moment. The shape it takes is that of a "diasporic public sphere" (Appadurai, 1996, 21), and it is therefore portrayed as a movement away from the center in any of a number of directions (see Figure 1).

This map reflects as well, I think, broad outlines of what we might want to look at for purposes of inquiring about a curriculum for a democratic future. In this sense, it is essential, once again, to note that the map is merely a vehicle for curriculum theorizing. As such, it may be instructive for considering psychosocial shifts in our thinking about America as we moved into the era of global, postmodern compression of space and time and came to understand that our view of the nation is also a positioning in the world. Most striking is the extent to which our civic-cultural surround has become increasingly porous. We have yet to fully grasp the changing relationship between nation and world in our times, i.e., understanding that we are at once both actors on the national scene and actors in a global world whose civic-cultural dimensions and modes of organizing understandings are changing with shifting imaginaries about culture itself as a result of new global technologies and literacies.

The effects of this cannot be overstated, since the 'changing imaginaries' I am referring to here extend well beyond traditional boundaries that we, as citizens, might affect within the nation, *and yet are intimately connected to our daily lives*. I believe that September 11th brought that home to us in no uncertain terms, although we have yet to really look at what that means for *currere* (Pinar, 1975, 1994, 2004), the question of who we say we are or will become. This is essential to determine what is required in order to achieve 'release from our arrest' (Pinar, 1994, 61).

Reading the Map: Essentials of Conceptualization

I conceptualized the map as a porous and essentially transparent field (the transparency is meant to indicate that we are exploring constructs of *nation* and *citizen* in discursive terms, that they are porous, and nothing more). This porous quality is also indicated by the broken outer lines of the figure. Based on my analysis of the discourse, I selected two conceptual organizers: a horizontal axis denotes epistemological *foundations for citizenship* (seeing the nation from a space of *Orthodoxy*, of *Reason*, or of *Perspective*); and a vertical axis denotes axiological dimensions of *civic engagement* (perceiving our participation as citizens from a positioning that values *Control, Representation*, or *Activism*). The use of these axes enhances my ability to analyze the vistas reflected in the writing in such a way as to distribute these vistas along continua, or trajectories, in what amounts to open, or smooth, space (Deleuze and Guattari, 1987).

I have placed *Orthodoxy* at one end of the horizontal continuum to denote a nationalistic end of the pole where writing is firmly anchored in symbols that coincide with the state as the repository of national identity, legitimacy, and power *as defined and represented by* authority. Authority may be construed as the power of the state, of hegemonic belief, or of providential Authority (God, the Creator, etc.). In this space, the state and nation are conflated in the writing; i.e., they are taken to be 'one,' so that the nation-state is itself *reified*.

I have placed *Reason* in the center of the horizontal continuum to denote an anchoring in respect for the Constitution where writing reflects its espoused ideals, values, and principles, on the one hand; and its democratic processes of governance and a free and communicative public sphere, on the other. For many, it is these ideals, values and principles that are the repository of national identity, legitimacy and power. In this space, the nation represents a diverse public, not the apparatus of the state itself, which is merely a device for governance. This is a national domain not necessarily linked to nationalism, but rather linked to support for reason as the 'foundation' upon which the nation as a construct rests. Further, in this space civic debate and civic conscience play major roles, since there is no specific orthodoxy being handed down from 'above.'

I have placed *Perspective* opposite orthodoxy at the other end of the horizontal axis to denote inclusion of global and/or nodal anchors that complicate and may even contradict how the nation is defined or understood. Writing in this space recognizes the connection between diversity and the nation's symbolic power, but may do so in relation to the world beyond. This writing may thus also reflect the concerns of citizens who situate themselves as 'global citizens,' or alternatively, as 'nodal citizens' who have strong ties with (and allegiances to) places beyond our borders. In that sense, they form a diasporic public sphere requiring our attention and understanding (Appadurai, 1996, 21). This space, as noted, represents the *complication* of the national domain, as well as the *contradiction* of the nationalistic domain.

The vertical axis represents an axiological range of preferred modes of civic engagement, and I use it to problematize the horizontal axis—that is, to look at how we engage as citizens from within any of the narratives elaborated above—and here three modes emerge: *Control*, *Representation* and *Activism*. The *Control* mode, at one end of the continuum, involves writing whose vistas reflect 'government *for* the people,' and its operative feature is *sanction*. Narratives positioned here put their trust in the powers that be to 'do the right thing,' and tacit support is granted to the government to do its best 'for the people,' without undue concern for or consideration of difference or of either particular or supranational needs. The engagement of citizens in this location is anchored in support for authority, leaving the government in charge of, or in control of, the nation.

The *Representation* mode, at the center of this continuum, involves writing whose vistas reflect 'government *of* the people,' and its operative feature is *legitimacy*. Narratives located here reflect trust in the *process* of representation, exhibiting the expectation that the system will work as representatives respond to the needs of all, not just the privileged few, that is, that citizen engagement in the public sphere will result in a negotiation of *legitimacy* that will work to serve all. Where conflict and difference emerge in terms of what is best for the nation, the expectation here is that accommodations may be made that will alleviate the problem(s). There is a trust here not only in the system itself, but also in civic conscience as it is enacted through the citizenry of the nation. A free and meaningful public sphere is a necessary player in this mode.

The *Activism* mode, opposite *Control*, involves writing whose vistas reflect 'government *by* the people,' and its operative feature is *empowerment*. Narratives that speak from this end of the continuum hold the people accountable for change through citizen participation and response (including resistance) to government policy and practice as they work to transform both. In order to have meaningful participation and response, citizens must be informed about issues, needs and problems, and, again, the public sphere becomes a central focus of concern.

The convergences formed by these two axes produce an interesting range of 'perceptual codes' (Huff, 1996, 165), framed here, as noted, as *cultures of citizenship*, each reflecting particular aspects of our national psyche, and folded together, these may be taken to compose a national autobiography (albeit an autobiography that is anecdotal, tentative—in the sense both of being incomplete and of constituting a "provisional representation" (Paulston, 1996, xxi)— and framed in the temporal terms of a specific social moment). They include the following: *triumphal, voyeurist, vigilant, pluralist, globalist, reparationist, communitarian*, and *hypernational*.

Figure 1 reflects what I see as the terrain of competing understandings of national being/becoming—our varying understandings of civic-cultural struggle in a changing world (dis-)order discourse—that directly impacts how, as Americans, we conceive of our nation and therefore how we relate to each other as citizens, and to the world as well. It is our national autobiography *illustrated* (see Figure 1).

Reading the Map: A Cultural Portrait

The figure, as noted, is not a model—i.e., it is not meant to enunciate a reality, but rather to explore the interrelations of a variety of perceived 'realities'—it is the "scholar's artistry resulting in a cultural portrait" (Paulston and Liebman, 1996, 14). It is critical to the process of autobiography not to "subordinate the lived present to an abstract, analytical grid" (Pinar, 1994, 26), and I remind my reader that while the figure may appear to be such a grid, it is just one conceptualization of difference resulting from discourses that describe lived realities in a moment of social trauma and social change. I use social mapping as a means of illustrating that the selfhood of the nation is problematic, i.e, that it is diverse, contradictory, and 'contains' within its contours multiple personalities that relate uniquely to being American in this social moment.

To assist my reader in making sense of the figure, let me explain its conceptual spaces in terms that return us to considering their portrayal of constructs along continua representing epistemological and axiological variances. Here it is my hope that the figure comes into clearer focus as we think about what it might mean to abide and educate in each of these conceptual spaces. To bring this into focus, I utilize some basic assertions about the specific socialization towards civic-cultural struggle (even where either the civic or the cultural aspect is *ignored*) indicated for each space within the autobiography, as well as its 'discursive mode,' its envisioning of the relations between state and nation, and, finally, its primary feature. Features of the terrain might be considered topographic, and their inclusion here is meant to demonstrate coherence, rather than claiming correspondence; they simply describe features of the plateau, taken to constitute a *vista*. Here I draw from Eisner's (2002) notion of "*imaginative extrapolation*":

> Imaginative extrapolation involves using what one sees to generate theoretical interpretations that give the particular situation a fresh significance. Facts never speak for themselves, and when unrelated to a broader theoretical structure they are likely to be little more than bits and pieces that do not add up. Imaginative extrapolation provides the material through which new perspectives are made available, facts are made meaningful, and coherence is made possible. (153)

In Eisner, "artistically crafted research" can be both "powerful and illuminating" as it provides "coherence, imagery, and particularity" as the "fruits of artistic thinking" (153). The figure, then, is presented here as having a storyline articulating particularities of civic-cultural being and becoming that emerged through discursive analysis of texts, or writing, bodies of discourse taken to compose an autobiography of the nation. What follows is a brief synopsis of facets of the autobiography depicted in greater detail above (see Chapters 5 and 6).

Where *Orthodoxy* is a framework for citizenship, citizens defend the character of the nation as defined or construed by authority, in which case the nation and the state are taken to be conflated, perceived as though they were one, thus reifying the nation-state itself. In this narrative, then, the voice of authority is understood to *be* the voice of the nation. The discursive mode here is *consensus*—and this is the fount of silencing for anyone not included, or not willing to be included, in a consensual conflation of state and nation. In this space, there is no vision of the nation different or apart from the vision expressed by those who hold power over the state. The primary feature in this space, then, is a kind of conformity that can only be produced by adherence to *doctrine*, This space has consistently been aggressively advocated, advanced and promoted by the New Right, and the difficulty their dedication to their orthodoxy poses for curriculum inquiry is how to realistically and productively acknowledge the space of their convictions, while staving in the imposition of their doctrines, especially on that portion of our population still in its formative stages, our young.

Where *Reason* is a framework for citizenship, citizens question and seek information so that they might support the good of the nation as defined by foundational principles, civic debate and civic conscience. In this case, the nation represents a diverse public. This public may be viewed as a 'community of belonging' based on fundamental ideals, values and principles held by the general populace, or may be more intimately related to the lived experiences of people in specific places and the ideals, values and principles they share and/or debate. The discursive modes here are *debate and dissent*—and when debate and dissent become muted or thwarted through intimidation or for other reasons, silence prevails. In this space, debate and dissent form the voice of the nation, and contestation within a principle-based or local knowledge terrain serves to legitimate both the project of democratic governance *and* divisions/diversity within the culture of the nation.

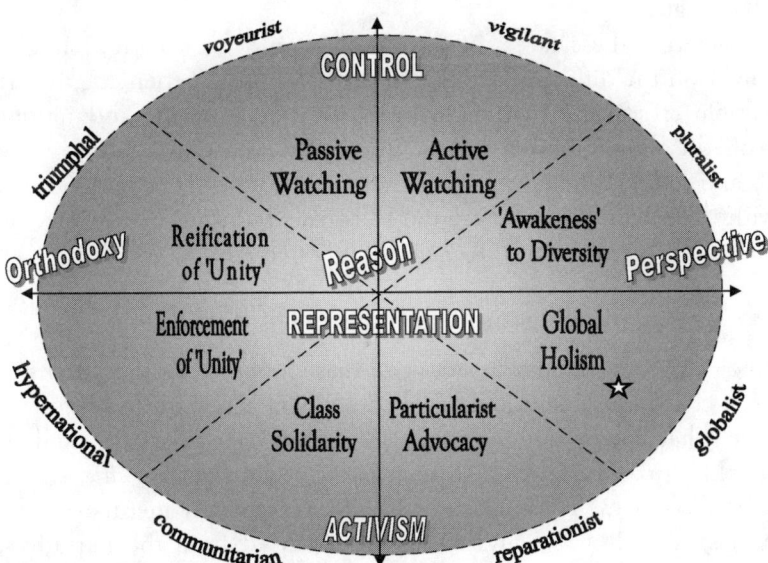

Figure 1 Civic-cultural portrait of post-9/11 American Autobiography.

Where *Perspective* is a framework for citizenship, citizens consider alternative—either broader or more particular—gestalts of community and act in good faith toward a more global sense of community or toward particular 'communities of sentiment' (Appadurai, 1996) whose sensibilities *transcend* national limits. In this case the nation may be seen as a 'global citizen' in its own right, or simply as one node on a trajectory along which home lies elsewhere. This is smooth space (Deleuze and Guattari, 1987), and the discursive mode here is *dialogue*. Silencing is generally weakened by the multiplicity of perspectives and their out-of-country linkages, which render consensus a moot point. However, under rare circumstances such as those that prevailed in this contextual moment, this space of being/becoming may actually be the *most* vulnerable, since the threat of force *can* produce and/or impose silence. In this space, the project of governance is complicated by a multiplicity of perspectives that may be immutable, thus eroding the nation's perceived ability to operate as a discrete entity that can 'contain' all of its parts.

The sense of the nation, then, is transformed, because the 'whole' exceeds the sum of its parts. The narratives most intimately connected with this space tend to be holistic in terms of the world within which the nation is positioned, since they open to the world. This space is one where citizens identifying with "globalization from below" (Kellner, 2005), or aspiring to participation in *CivWorld* (Barber, 2004) and its embodied forms, as well as advocates for particular world causes, global ecological and environmental issues, and so forth, might be located.

Considering these facets of our autobiography as a nation should shed some light on the differences and difficulties we are experiencing in this time of multiple crises, and each facet bears its own emphasis and rationale in terms of educating for a democratic future. We expect, in a diverse nation, to absorb and reflect difference. At the same time, we often experience encounters with those who do not share our sense of what it means to be American, let alone what our civic-cultural responsibilities entail.

Reading the Map: Cultures of Citizenship

If we look closely at the interrelations of these foundations for citizenship and modes of civic engagement and listen carefully to the narratives that lay claim to them, what emerge are convergences within the larger surround. I have identified four convergences that open out to eight *cultures of citizenship* drawn from the discourses. These cultures of citizenship are sometimes explicit in, sometimes 'hinted at' by, and sometimes inferred from the narratives, and they are framed in this work as *vistas* (views of America as a particular kind of civic-cultural landscape). Some of them hold promise for the functioning of democratic society, while others pose serious challenges. They all occupy space in our socio-cultural (and therefore, our moral/political) fabric and play a part in our autobiographical project. I briefly outline these cultures of citizenship here, but I remind my reader that these are not discrete, abstract units, but rather vistas of national autobiography forming plateaus that together constitute the rhizome of our national psyche, which is always in flux. Further, although categorized here as 'cultures of citizenship,' they are the slippery ground from which sliding (and sometimes colliding) identities may emerge.

Triumphal and *Voyeurist* Cultures of Citizenship

At the convergence of *Orthodoxy* (where nation and state are conflated) and *Control* (where the operative feature is *sanction*), there is a civic-cultural orientation that plays out in one of two ways, either in a *triumphal* or in a *voyeurist* culture of citizenship. The difference between the two is subtle. The first of the two, the *triumphal* culture, is the product of an enunciation that proclaims that America has succeeded in reaching its goals and that it is an exceptional society inspired and blessed by God—in short, that democracy as these narratives claim the Founding Fathers envisioned it is a *fait accompli*. This is the culture of citizenship we find in President George W. Bush's speeches and most pronouncements and elaborations by the New Right (and this is what they want taught in the schools). From their vantage point, all citizens should participate in this celebration of the 'deed' (namely, having achieved, accomplished, arrived). This culture of citizenship defines *itself* as the patriotic view.

On the other hand, this celebration for some may be merely a spectacle not involving active participation, but resulting rather from indifference, acquiescence, resignation, submission, etc. Where there is no acknowledgment of debate, dissent or difference, the state may set the tone and the agenda for civic engagement. Since our experience of the nation is often media-controlled and largely media-derived, this culture of citizenship is *voyeurist*—i.e., reflecting passivity based on the uncritical absorption of media images, verbal or otherwise. That is, this sense of nation and citizen involves a passive 'watching' of events as they are portrayed by the media and, through the media, by the state. This culture of citizenship amounts to manifested consensual silence, framed by sanctioned control based on acceptance of an *orthodoxy* in which the nation is defined by authority.

Hypernational and *Communitarian* Cultures of Citizenship

At the convergence of *Orthodoxy*, with its anchoring in doctrine, and *Activism*, which reflects *empowerment* as its operative feature, another pairing of cultures of citizenship appears to emerge: *hypernational* and *communitarian*. The *hypernational* advances an orthodoxy intimately connected with the triumphal narrative, but because it embraces (anti-dissident) *activism*, it is a space where *coercive* consensus emerges and manifests in terms of the state-as-nation conflation, with the state defining civic-cultural propriety. This culture of citizenship supports the *triumphal* narrative and assumes *control* as a mode of governance, not only advancing the verity of the triumphal view of America, but also seeking to *enforce* it. The coercive feature of this domain is imposed upon all 'outliers' as it declares that there *is* only 'one true America,' and that all other views are 'treason' (AVOT, 2002; Coulter, 2003). Since *orthodoxy* is its anchor, its position appears 'reasonable' to its adherents, in spite of its migration away from the space of *Reason*.

On the other hand, there are those within this convergence whose faith in the egalitarian ideals America was created to advance is sufficiently strong to sustain hope in their eventual achievement, those who embrace the narrative of the *communitarian* culture of citizenship, which is also connected to *orthodoxy* and *activism*, but in its own unique way. Adherents to the communitarian ethic are also inclined towards *activism*, but their devotion to the nation includes recognition of *reason* and *representation*. That is, narratives in this space may exhibit the solidarity of the triumphal and the hypernational cultures, but their interests are aligned with an activism that attends to the unmet needs of disenfranchised persons and communities rather than with claiming superior, exceptional status for the nation. This culture of citizenship is attuned to, and seeks to engage with, the whole community—i.e., the *collective*—rather than with the individual as a locus of concern. Its attitudes and approaches to solidarity are also in contradistinction to the attitudes and approaches of the hypernational. Nevertheless, it shares with the latter the connection with *orthodoxy*, and this poses a dilemma because, like the triumphal and hypernational, it seeks to foment consensus around its own espoused principles and ideals.

Vigilant and *Pluralist* Cultures of Citizenship

At the convergence of *Control* and *Perspective*, a third pairing of cultures of citizenship emerges: *vigilant* and *pluralist*. While *sanction* is the operative feature of control, its basis in *Reason* and its attention to *Perspective* impact the culture of citizenship profoundly. A *vigilant* culture operates in a somewhat muted fashion relative to dissent and difference, but attachment to *reason* leads to a different kind of 'watchfulness' than what is found in the *voyeurist* culture of citizenship. Looking to authority to set the standard and pace for change, the effects of *reason* lead to an awareness of civic responsibility, and the accountability of government becomes a concern due to attachment to *Representation* as well. Here there is a tacit expectation that the citizen is 'sovereign,' that responsibilities accompany the privileges of citizenship, and that the government is not mythic, as in the triumphal or hypernational cultures, but is, in fact, 'answerable' to the people.

However, attachment to *perspective* may also produce a profoundly different effect, and texts reflecting a *pluralist* culture of citizenship reflect the perception that one may be a nodal citizen who lives as a member of both the nation and some 'other' imagined community. This 'other' imagined community may be based on race, gender, ethnicity, religion, sexuality, geographic origin, or other form of embodied identity. Narratives here therefore show a clear recognition of difference and highlight hegemony as a malefactor. The influence of *perspective* plays a major role, then, in the perceptual code that results. Those who speak from this space may also reflect acknowledgment of an accelerated proliferation of the hybridization effects of globalization so clearly highlighted in Appadurai (1996), but they do so from *within* the domain of American national identity.

Globalist and *Reparationist* Cultures of Citizenship

At the convergence of *perspective* and *activism*, a fourth pairing of cultures of citizenship emerges: *globalist* and *reparationist*. Since perspective is a space where citizens consider alternative gestalts of community, whether broader or particular to a specific cultural node, and since activism embraces *empowerment* as its operative feature, the resulting cultures in this convergence are highly dynamic, in part due to the effects of globalization. The *globalist* culture of citizenship may be manifested in a global or nodal sense of belonging that relates to engagement with an enlarged global perspective or to nodal causes and communities connected or related to out-of-country linkages or transnational activity. This culture of citizenship evokes anxiety in America's conservative sectors because it necessarily includes those who look *beyond* the nation for both authority and legitimacy in terms of 'belonging' and 'community' (Bhabha, 1994). This is a convergence where particularist groups seek to live according to their own cultural values and traditions, holding allegiances beyond the nation. In this space also are those who have supranational concerns such as environmental degradation, human rights, women's or children's rights, global health, etc. This culture of citizenship includes those as well who have been empowered by technology to establish global connections, professional or otherwise, to engage with any of a multitude of issues, interests, or concerns.

Another culture of citizenship within this convergence is the *reparationist* culture. Like the pluralist culture of citizenship, the reparationist culture is connected to *perspective*. However, due to its concern for *representation* and *reason* and its clear valuing of the civic mode of *activism*, this culture works to 'repair' and undo the historical legacies of civic-cultural injustice that are so much a part of our nation's history. The distinction between a reparationist culture of citizenship and a communitarian culture of citizenship is, again, a subtle one. The distinction can probably be most clearly expressed in terms of influence and intent. The influence of *perspective* may render the reparationist culture more attentive to the needs of particular groups or nodes, while the influence of *orthodoxy* on a communitarian culture of citizenship may render this culture more coherently attentive to the needs of the community taken as a whole.

Reading the Map: A Final Word

This map shows interrelations of a dispersion of ways of seeing national being and becoming within a broad intertextual field. The point of the mapping is to reflect the complexity and the diversity of our various narratives as they speak to the question of who we say we are or will become as a nation. In the contextual moment under study, civic courage was required to stand up to the triumphal culture as the dominant discourse. The power of orthodoxy as it was coupled with control in the face of terror, shock, loss, and grief enabled those in power to redefine the nation and reformulate its ideals, values and principles—in full public view, with the hypernational lending both laudatory support of the reformulation *and* coercive manipulation of 'dissenters.' Those situated in the voyeurist culture of citizenship, for whatever reasons, submitted to this revision of the nation, leaving all others to stand or fall as 'outliers.' In this scenario, the enunciations that were 'getting daily press' were those emanating from the space of orthodoxy, and its convergence with either (assumed) control or (anti-dissident) activism, leaving the public sphere all but empty of alternative possibilities or imaginaries about the will, character and desires of a nation under attack.

If we think about this map as a cultural portrait drawn from discursive activity following the attacks of September 11th, and we contrast the portrait as a representation of civic-cultural being/becoming with the behavior of our media and the state during this moment, we can see attempted censures or erasures of certain elements of our national psyche. The first to come under attack were those who spoke out against orthodoxy, whether reparationist or globalist, who were almost immediately branded as unpatriotic, anti-American, pro-terrorist, and ultimately by some, as traitors, as noted. Many of the texts informing the autobiography portrayed here testify to this effect (see Chapters 5 and 6), as noted. In this first wave, those who espoused sensitivity to issues potentially underlying the attacks were *defined as* 'the problem.' Those at American colleges and universities who had dissented from a policy of retribution and revenge, for example, were labeled 'Blame America First-ers.' Those who had expressed anti-war sentiments were castigated as 'divisive,' even pro-terrorist. Those who had entreated the rest of us to understand the tensions and problems of the Middle East before engaging in aggression were characterized as 'soft-on-terrorism.'

There was a progression from this first attack towards a second censure/erasure. The second area of our national psyche that came under attack in this whitewashing of American foreign policy and overstatement of national interest camouflaged by the declaration of America's 'exceptional' purity and goodness were those who responded with alarm or with reservations about the censure/erasure of reason itself (see, e.g., Carter, 2005; Gore, 2007). As long-standing democratic principles were washed away in a flood of insecurity, fear, and anxiety, those who spoke out about protecting our rights and our freedoms, our 'civil libertarians,' were also equated with being anti-American and weak, and were rebuked for not caring about the safety of their fellow Americans. Note that this included both liberals *and* conservatives (see, e.g., Safire, 2001). The finger of blame was pointed at this culture of citizenship with substantial success in discursive terms, and the result was that even those who had reservations about the dismembering of our Constitution ultimately appeared to cave in to that pressure, holding their tongues.

In this contextual moment, then, civic courage was required and portrayed by those who worked discursively to hold on to the empowerment and the legitimacy of their ways of seeing and enacting their citizenship in their relationship with others, with the nation and the world. Ultimately, what was left to us of the America we had 'known' was what power would allow. Our tripartite system of government, with its precious checks and balances, lost its checks and its balances. The Judiciary was initially bypassed as surveillance and detainment out-of-country 'occupied' our civil codes and derailed them. Congress was left out of the loop on crucial information, and ultimately caved in to the presumed 'wisdom' of those who had the greatest Intel as well, leaving us with a one-party system in control of the whole works, from top to bottom.

Belief in God (and in the Almighty's sanctioning of America's course) began to take the place of rational thought, civic debate about principles, and the good nature of our citizens. What was enunciated by power during this period was a new thing. We were told that this is a 'Christian' nation that is *good* because it is willing to tolerate those of us who are *not* Christian. The depravity of our culture disproves this, and the pronouncement that all good comes from those who operate from a space of the 'fear' of God took some of us by surprise. We were told to go to church, to worship and mourn together, to lift up our fellow countrymen in the name of God, and to look to God for solace and for wisdom. (What I am indicating here is *not* that we should avoid such comforts, but rather that it is not the *place* of the state to tell us to do so.) We were told that the God of the *triumphalists* was on our side, but that wasn't necessarily comforting for all of us. We were also warned by some (e.g., Falwell, 2001; Robertson, 2001) that God had abandoned us because of our sinful ways. In the blink of an eye, religion became the primary indicator of governmental policy and intent in America. Not only had the state *become* the nation, but it was now reified as holy (God's State), and belief in the nation appeared to *require* belief in God as a new form of theocratic nationalism took hold (see, e.g., Hedges, 2006; Phillips, 2007; Taylor, 2005).

Under this kind of pressure, and under the pressure of a massive display of symbolic imagery in the form of flags, anthems and other patriotic paraphernalia, those who continued to speak out against prevailing, or conventional, 'wisdom' were demoted as citizens unworthy of the name, their dissent deterritorialized. As John Ashcroft's Justice Department accessed newly acquired powers of surveillance and worked outside the parameters of what was previously considered acceptable either in legal *or* ethical terms, the rule of law took a back seat to power. The abuses attached to this transition became even more startling as his replacement, Attorney General Alberto Gonzales, took hold of the reins of 'justice' in what we can now clearly see amounted to a total perversion of Constitutional intent (let alone, international law). Under his authority, but presumably according to superior direction, the rule of law moved from a back seat to power to the wastebasket of oblivion. This is a red-flag issue that also must be addressed by those seeking to educate for democratic aspirations and a democratic future, and cannot be ignored. The space of 'through education' must address this event, given its implications for the future.

We may never know how many detainees there were, who they were, or what ultimately happened to them. We will always know, however, that what happened violated the wisdom of those who stood proud to call themselves American because theirs was a land of reason and representation, a nation built on principles and ideals, suffering the (as yet still unjust) rule of law in order to reach towards its democratic aspirations. In this newly revised landscape, this post-9/11 America, some of us found ourselves abruptly immersed in a new American wilderness. No longer was the nation that we loved recognizable, and the result was an amazing confrontation with a new kind of terror—the terror of a state that felt itself threatened and that responded to all perceived threats, both real and imagined—with 'full force.' The effects of this re-visioning were heightened by the publication and proclamation of such doctrines *without critique* throughout the mainstream media of the land. Journalism, some said, had died.

The map used to illustrate the autobiography shows a range of vistas of how we envision our nation as citizens, and how we enact our citizenship, but alterations to the figure might demonstrate how this map was affected by the contextual moment. The narratives composing the autobiography, as well as a growing body of writing over time, confirm the worst of our apprehensions, our anticipation that these alterations would be forthcoming, our fear that they would remain in full force. Figure 2 shows the angst resulting from these censures/erasures, revealing the ultimate view of post-9/11 America given the continued, and uncontested, domination of the 'one true America' narrative, i.e., of its continued enforcement as *the* national ideology. Note what is gone. Note what is left. This map reflects the fears of many of our citizens today; it is a *post-democratic* view of America (see Figure 2).

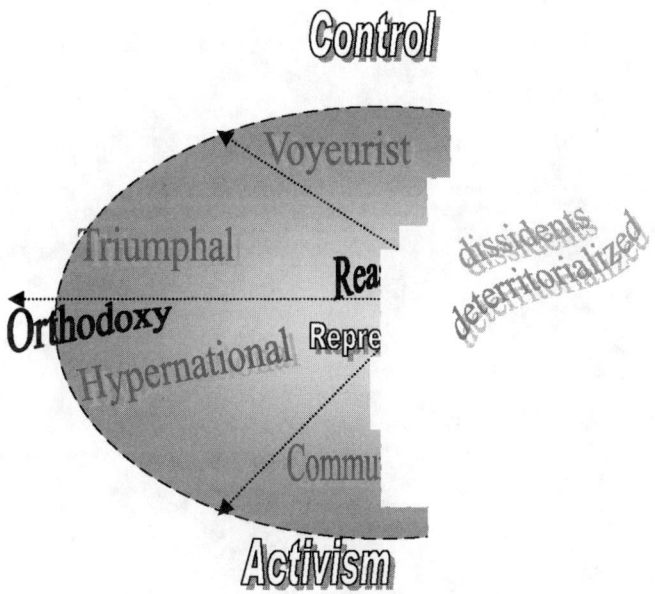

Figure 2. Mapping Feared Effects of
Censures/Erasures on the Post-9/11 American Psyche

Part Three
Ongoing Fragmented Dialogues

8

The Public Sphere: Risk, Uncertainty, and Techno-Culture

In this chapter, I sketch problematiques of the (now global) public sphere in our times. This is the space of the *beyond*, but it is worth mentioning that what happens in the beyond does not stay in the beyond, but rather, reaches into daily life in numerous ways and impacts our ability to *see* who we are and who we are becoming as a nation. I confine myself here to just a brief outline of some social changes promising to impact curricular change, since the body of work about these changes has grown to unmanageable proportions. First, I address Porter's (1999) thoughts on educational change in an 'era of uncertainty,' an era in which, as a result of neoliberalism, the school's role as a change agent is 'diminished.' Second, I argue that America has become a prototype of the ultimate risk society following September 11th because the risk paradigm that enveloped the world as a result of environmental degradation and the global dissemination of health hazards and environmental risks in the 1980s and 1990s signaled that major societal and political changes were afoot. The events of September 11th masked their effects, even as they pointed to a new and urgent need to understand them.

These changes, some of them more recently exacerbated as a result of our response to attack, have transformed both the political and the quotidian aspects of life. Finally, both of these somewhat alarming paradigm events converged at a time when the public sphere itself was undergoing revolutionary changes as a result of the emergence and establishment of the 'techno-culture thesis,' a thesis declaring that new technologies held promise for revitalizing the public sphere and thus democracy in the Information Age. I examine, in this respect, the early dialogue about what was then thought of as e-democracy and its promise of renewal, considering disputes over this claim in some detail. I begin, however, with a short discussion of Porter's analysis of epochal change vis-à-vis educational policy and practice.

An 'Era of Uncertainty'

In his work, *Reschooling and the Global Future* (1999), James Porter describes a transformation of thinking about educational policy and practice that occurred as a result of the emergence of neo-liberalism. He characterizes this transformation in terms of a shift from an 'era of confidence' to an 'era of uncertainty.' The broad outlines of this dynamic change in public thinking and social and political re-ordering—which Giroux (2004) characterizes as 'proto-fascism' (9)—raise a multitude of questions to explore. However, a very brief introduction to neo-liberalism as 'public pedagogy' (Giroux, 2004, 105) should suffice to set the stage for discussion. Giroux paints a rather stark picture of the emptiness of civic-cultural space in this 'new' social order:

> The breathless rhetoric of the global victory of free-market rationality spewed forth by the mass media, right-wing intellectuals, and governments alike has found its material expression both in an all-out attack on democratic values and in the growth of a range of social problems including virulent and persistent poverty, joblessness, inadequate health care, racial apartheid in the inner cities, and increasing inequalities between the rich and the poor. Such problems appear to have been either removed from the inventory of public discourse and social policy or factored into talk-show spectacles in which the public becomes merely a staging area for venting private interests and emotions. Within the discourse of neoliberalism that has taken hold of the public imagination, there is no way of talking about what is fundamental to civic life, crtitical citizenship, and a substantive democracy. (xix)

Porter (1999), speaking from 'the English experience,' speaks of the same concerns as Giroux, warning that beliefs we held in the past about "the importance of independent and democratic education and the free flow of ideas" (27) have undergone substantial change:

> In their place is a policy increasingly driven by the widespread acceptance of a particular economic orthodoxy—that of 'the market.' ...While detailed attention to issues of nationalism, and more recently, globalism, have been considered relevant concerns for educators, there has been a tendency for those concerned with school education to accept the economic system as a 'given.' The assumption is that teachers and pupils must make the best of the economic circumstances prevailing at the time. However, it is becoming clear that continued acceptance of the neo-liberal theories espoused by politicians and dominant elites, constitutes a major obstacle to educational progress. (27)

Porter highlights features of the neo-liberal terrain, beginning with an historical sketch of its origins that takes us back to "the right-wing administrations" in the U.K. and America in the 1980s, to the administrations of Margaret Thatcher and Ronald Reagan:

> They were influenced by the idealized capitalism of free enterprise promoted by ideologically motivated economists such as Friedrich von Hayek, Ludwig von Mises and Milton Friedman. The link to education was powerfully expressed in the USA by

the National Commission on Excellence that reported in 1983. Set up by President Reagan, the report was dramatically titled *A Nation at Risk: the imperative for education reform*... and asserted that "a rising tide of mediocrity threatens our very future as a Nation and as a people". Social-democratic governments in Australia, France, New Zealand and Spain were strongly influenced by the crude but powerful message of the free marketers. They also adopted most of the policy agenda of Margaret Thatcher and Ronald Reagan. In Britain, the implications for education were profound... (29)[1]

Porter breaks down "the essence" of free-market economics as offering "a clear and robust model of what governs human behaviour," a model wherein "the human being is a trader, persistently engaged in making judgments about the advantages and disadvantages of various courses of action" (29). There are, however, hidden assumptions in this theory that are troubling, as follows: first, that human behavior in general "can be related to a ranking of economic choices" based on cost-benefit analyses; second, "that the choices are made by the idealized rational economic man of economic theory"; third, "that the various transactions are optimal for everybody and balance out," known as "the theory of competitive equilibrium" (29). Porter indicates that this 'market theory' "has been the driving force behind the politics of the last two decades in the most affluent countries of the world," that "the influence of the model has been astonishing," and that this is a principle that "has been extended into every walk of life" (29).

Having outlined what neo-liberalism *is*, Porter makes several complaints against this theory as a model of human behavior. First, he offers, it fails to consider sociological and cultural frameworks, citing "Mrs. Thatcher's claim 'that there is no such thing as society'" (30). Second, it fails to take into account the "introduction of uncertainty" as a result of "the development of non-linear techniques now central to modern scientific analysis" so significant in environmental work, techniques that also point to "the inherent difficulty of prediction" (30). Its value system, moreover, is based on "a powerful legitimising framework for the continued existence of privileges that in themselves demonstrate the inequality and imperfection of the market" (30). Further, its "political policies," which Porter sees as deriving from "the New Right," "have led to an increase in the gap between the richest and the poorest," so that "the effects of the pursuit of a pure market economy has [sic] led to a value system based on exclusion and inequality" (30). Most importantly, for my purposes here, is that "the operation of a market economy is incompatible with collective responsibilities" (31).[2]

Turning his attention to education as a public sector, Porter maintains that "the simplistic market economics" we've endured in recent years "have had a strongly limiting effect" on the space of 'through education,' which Porter treats as its "scope" (32). He sees governments that apply this economic ideology as trying "to limit education to its economic function" (32) in such a way that

> Education and training are seen as the key to the achievement of a sound national economy. Further, governments also argue that the formal education service itself can not be maintained unless it sustains a highly productive work force. Anxious about the social and economic effects of growing unemployment and the political dangers of a reduction in the standards of life of their electorate, major political parties in all democracies are making education the focus of their attention. ... Getting education "right" is now seen as the most important policy objective of many Western countries. (32)

Porter warned that "continuing to base political decisions and associated welfare and educational policies on such assumptions can only worsen a situation that is approaching anarchy" (33). But what does all this mean for the curriculum of schooling? To answer this question, he compares our present 'era of uncertainty' with a prior 'era of confidence' (prior to the 1970s) in which the following characteristics were prominent:

- an ongoing expansion of education coupled with belief in the power of schools to transform society;
- education as the highest priority;
- emphasis on teacher training and education put teachers at the center;
- education was child-centered and there was an improved understanding of child learning and development; and
- a growing awareness of structural features of society relative to race, class, and gender was present. (15-17)

Pointing to a change in the educational policy-making climate from the 1970s on, he characterizes this shift as an 'era of uncertainty' that includes:

- an emergence of concerns about both progress and social cohesion;
- the disappearance of consensus;
- the emergence of an adversarial relationship between policy-makers and practitioners, leading to less influence for schooling;
- schooling redefined in economic terms;
- the notion of standards as problematic and accountability as key;
- more centralized control over schools, more detailed control over the work of teachers;
- schooling as a market and thus the commodification of education;
- government assessment of 'product quality' and public use of the results. (22-24)

What Porter concludes from the features of this transformation is that a 'diminished' role for schooling is the result in this 'era of uncertainty,' where government policy in most countries in Europe, North America and Australasia has been increasingly based upon the view that comprehensive state funded welfare provision could not be afforded, that support for public services should be reduced and that individuals should assume greater responsibility for their welfare. In school education there has been an increase in bureaucratisation and politicization. Officials, whether operating in centrally [sic] systems as in Sweden or comparatively decentralized systems such as the Federal Republic of Germany, have increasingly intervened directly in the schools. (24)

According to Porter, this "new political ideology" has been centered in the idea that "the State should encourage the fullest expression of a free market" (24), and that it was this view that

> led to the belief that all schools should narrow their concerns to the mere production of citizens for a highly competitive market economy. The change has resulted in a system of control which transforms the transaction between teacher and learner and marginalises the role of the educator. (24)

The nature of these reforms are not news to us as educators, since we live with the imposition of their strategies and with the repercussions of their aims, but what is truly and deeply disturbing about this shift in public and official views of education is that its reach is *global*—i.e., that it is hegemonic at the global level, since it has been transferred from developed to developing nations via international aid agencies:

> Most developing countries have been forced to enter into agreements with the International Monetary Fund (IMF) and the World Bank for assistance. These agreements have come with austerity packages of 'structural adjustment' that have usually diminished financial support for the school, reinforced authoritarian regimes and failed to create democratic structures conducive to educational freedom. (24)

Porter notes the precise outcomes of both the neo-liberal transformation among developed nations and the transference of its agenda to developing nations in terms of the world's "educational agendas," which are "deeply influenced by the growing awareness of a global economic system" that is "even more heavily biased" in favor of the rich (and, in his thinking, of their countries) "than it was before" (24-25):

> Internationally, the outcome has been the isolation of the school, the deprofessionalisation of teachers and a dramatic diminution in the function and potential of the school. ...any new policy for a national system of schooling must confront the realities of economic policy and the influence of globalization on the nation state. (24-25)

Porter sees schooling as "the most widespread and critical of all the networks in contemporary civil society," and argues that "a truly democratic society requires a vigorous, critical and independent school system with the priority to educate for the fullest participation in democratic institutions and in the political decisions that influence all aspects of social life" (63). Perhaps this possibility is yet on the horizon, around the corner, offering its long-promised hope; perhaps not. Beck's (1992) work on the 'risk society' muddies this hopeful prospect even further.

Risk Society Dynamics and the Public Sphere

> Along the path from a public critically reflecting on its culture to one that merely consumes it, the public sphere in the world of letters, which at one point could still be distinguished from that in the political realm, has lost its specific character. For the "culture" propagated by the mass media is a culture of integration. It not only integrates information with critical debate and the journalistic format with the literary forms of the psychological novel into a combination of entertainment and "advice" governed by the principle of "human interest"; at the same time it is flexible enough to assimilate elements of advertising, indeed, to serve itself as a kind of super slogan that, if it did not already exist, could have been invented for the purpose of public relations serving the cause of the status quo. The public sphere assumes advertising functions. The more it can be deployed as a vehicle for political and economic propaganda, the more it becomes unpolitical as a whole and pseudo-privatized. (Habermas, 1991, 175)

Apart from Habermas' classic work, *The Structural Transformation of the Public Sphere*, from which the quotation above—under a section subtitled "The blurred blueprint: Developmental pathways in the disintegration of the bourgeois public sphere"—is taken, Beck's (1992) work on the *risk society*, I believe, is one of the most important works on the transformation of the public sphere for our times. Beck addresses social and political change occurring as a result of the real-world intrusion of a risk paradigm on modern societies, and, although his analysis is based on *environmental* risks and hazards, the outcomes he foresees look strikingly similar to the outcomes we are observing as we watch our current transformation into a security state. Because his analysis is complex and covers a great deal of ground, I focus here on the hollowing out of the political, or, per Habermas (1985, cited in Beck), the 'new obscurity' (190). In other work, I have attended to some of Beck's other viable notions for our times: the emergence of the catastrophic society as a result of the 'exceptional condition' becoming the norm, the vacillation of the public between hysteria and indifference, the loss of social thinking and lack of responsibility, and the 'Not-Yet-Event' as a stimulus to action (see Nicholson-Goodman,

2007). I focus here, therefore, specifically on the transformation of the political.

Beck offers four theses, each of them leading exquisitely to the next. They lay out before us a vista of what social change might look like in such a society. I find this vista helpful in my quest to understand, via new conceptual tools, more of what is happening in and to post-9/11 America. This is new terrain, and it is wilderness to us. A growing portion of our population is quietly, silently moving in a slow, but steady downward spiral, into a state of being where human dignity is debased and human lives deemed worthless. We have a new solidified and powerless underclass growing inside the U.S. that draws together the poor, the working poor, and those exiting the middle class in a downward spiral of loss and displacement, and we as a nation have so far been relatively silent about this, in spite of a healthy body of discourse examining issues of social justice relative to education. Rather than formally reviewing Beck's theses, I use his words to paint a picture of risk society transformation, beginning with his sense of the originating principles of democracy, but quickly moving to the status of technological innovation vis-à-vis the political:

> The axial principle of the political sphere is the participation of citizens in the institutions of representative democracy... Decision-making, and with it, the exercise of political power, follow the maxims of legality and the principle that power and domination can only be carried out with the consent of the governed. The actions of the *bourgeois* and the spheres of techno-economic pursuit of interests, by contrast, are considered *non*-politics. This design is based first on the equation of technical and social progress; then on the assumption that the direction of development and the results of technological transformation follow... inescapable *techno-economic objective constraints*. Technological innovations increase the individual and collective well-being. The negative effects (deskilling, risks of unemployment or transfer, threats to health and natural destruction) have always found justification in these rises of the standard of living. *Even dissent over the 'social consequences' does not hinder the accomplishment of techno-economic innovation.* That process remains in essence removed from political legitimation. [Emphasis mine] (184)

"That process," according to Beck, "possesses a power of enforcement virtually immune to criticism," so that "*progress replaces voting*" and "becomes a substitute for questions, a type of consent in advance for goals and consequences that go unnamed and unknown" [emphasis in original] (184). This establishes, for Beck, the prospect that "the innovation process that is enforced by modernity against the predominance of tradition is *split in two democratically* through the project of industrial society," with each of two parts "of the decision-making competencies that structure society" taking its own direction (184). One part is subject to the political; the other "is removed from the rules of public inspection and justification and delegated to the freedom of investment of enterprises and the freedom of research of science" (184). Both have their drawbacks, but only one is *visible*. Beck elaborates a "political stand-off" between the two (185), and describes the landscape of unfettered technological innovation in these words:

> Waves of current, announced or emerging changes pass through and convulse society. In their scope and depth, they will probably overshadow all the reform attempts of the last few decades. Thus, the political stand-off is being undermined by *hectic changes* in the techno-economic system that put human imagination to a test of courage. Science fiction is increasingly becoming a memory of past times. ...society is caught in a whirlpool of change that richly deserves the title 'revolutionary'... This social transformation, however, occurs in the form of the *non*-political. [Emphasis in original] (185)

Beck asserts that "techno-economic development," however, "loses its character as non-politics" as the "scope of its potentials for change and endangerment" increase (185-186):

> Where the outlines of an alternative society are no longer seen in the debates of parliament or the decisions of the executive, but rather in the application of microelectronics, reactor technology and human genetics, the constructs which had heretofore politically neutralized the innovation process begin to break up. (186)

What results from this 'break-up,' which occurs even as "techno-economic action continues to be shielded by its own constitution against parliamentary demands for legitimation" (186), is that it "becomes a third entity, acquiring the precarious hybrid status of a *sub*-politics, in which the scope of the social changes precipitated varies inversely with their legitimation" so that "*the political becomes non-political and the non-political political*" [emphasis in original] (186). Beck posits "a new political and moral dimension," one that he responds to with this image:

> The game with the roles of politics and non-politics reversed, while the façade remains unchanged, is becoming ghostlike. Politicians have to be told where the path devoid of plan and consciousness is leading—and told by those who *do not* know either and whose interests are directed at something quite different and therefore *also* attainable. Then, with the practiced gesture of fading trust in progress, they must present this journey into unknown alternative country to the voters as their own invention... because from the beginning there was and remains no alternative. The necessity the non-decidability of technological 'progress' becomes the bolt securing the process to its democratic (non)legitimation. The 'anarchy' (Arendt 1981) of the (no longer) unseen side effect takes over power in the developed stage of Western democracy. (187)

The problem with this entire scenario, according to Beck, is that "the fixation on the political system as the exclusive center of politics continues to exist" (187), in spite of our location on a trajectory where "the path devoid of plan and consciousness" (187) is the path we are compelled to follow, for lack of any other serious option. Beck's vista is one of a world, then, in Barber's words, that is "spinning out of control" (Barber, 2001, 5). The word Beck uses for this is anarchy, and this is yet another feature of our civic-cultural struggle that profoundly complicates the prospects for a curriculum of possibility, let alone a future for democracy. I turn now to a discussion that focuses on electronic media as its own unique form of public sphere.

Cultural Citizenship and the Electronic Public Sphere

Curran's essay, 'Rethinking the Media as Public Sphere' (Dahlgren and Sparks, 1993), considers the public sphere from a radical democratic perspective, pulling together what he sees as some "eclectic elements" to offer a 'theory.' He elaborates a schema that "cuts across the best-known modern representation of the media and the public sphere—the historical analysis advanced by Jurgen Habermas" (27). His reasoning is that Habermas' work (1974) "has rightly triggered widespread debate," and Curran "follows a detour by evaluating his arguments in the light of subsequent historical research" (27). Curran's goal is to show "the way in which historical research—the neglected grandparent of media studies—can contribute to the debate about the role of the media in liberal democracies" (27).

For Curran, a "democratic media system" should fulfill a basic obligatory purpose:

> ...that it represents all significant interests in society. It should facilitate their participation in the public domain, enable them to contribute to public debate and have an input in the framing of public policy. The media should also facilitate the functioning of representative organizations, and expose their internal processes to public scrutiny and the play of public opinion. In short, a central role of the media should be defined as *assisting the equitable negotiation or arbitration of competing interests through democratic processes.* [Emphasis in original] (30)

Curran provides a schema of "alternative perspectives of the media" in the British context showing differences in political perspective relative to six elements: (1) a characterization of the public sphere; (2) the political role of the media; (3) a characterization of the media system; (4) the journalistic norm employed; (5) its view of entertainment; and (6) its view of reform. From the radical democratic perspective he is espousing, the public sphere is seen as a "public arena of contest," the political role of the media is seen as "representation/counterpoise," the media system is characterized as "controlled market," the journalistic norm employed is "adversarial," its view of entertainment is "society communing with itself," and its view of reform is "public intervention" (see Curran, Table 1.1). This schema presents us with an interesting way to think about the media and its public(s) in relation to dialogue within the nation.

Dahlgren, in his 'Introduction' (Dahlgren and Sparks, 1993), addresses "some troublesome ambiguity at the core" of Habermas' work on the public sphere, reflecting on "the renewal of the concept" (1). Noting that one or another "version of... the public sphere has always existed as an appendage to democratic theory," he presents a view of the public sphere that reflects its foregrounded and normative position:

> It becomes a focal point of our desire for the good society, the institutional sites where popular political will should take form and citizens should be able to constitute themselves as active agents in the political process. How well the public sphere functions becomes a concrete manifestation of society's democratic character and thus in a sense the most immediately visible indicator of our admittedly imperfect democracies. (1-2)

The public sphere is read, in Dahlgren, as the space where 'the people' receive pertinent information and prepare to have their say in the affairs of life and government within democratic systems. The commodification of news, the complications of its market positioning, and the plurality of sites for its portrayal and interpretation exacerbate the tensions within this space.

Explaining Habermas' public sphere as an "analytic category," Dahlgren then incorporates and modifies it "within new intellectual and political horizons" (3). Habermas' analysis of the public sphere, for instance, was based on the activity of the bourgeois classes—the propertied, literate, liberal and therefore universalist elite of the late-teen centuries, and addressed transformations of that sphere based on *laissez-faire* capitalism and related social developments—e.g., "industrialization, urbanization, the growth of literacy and the popular press, ...the rise of the administrative and interventionist state" (4). Here is the link, in Dahlgren, with the present:

> The consequences of these developments included a blurring of the distinctions between public and private in political and economic affairs, a rationalization and shrinking of the private intimate sphere (family life) and the gradual shift from an (albeit limited) public of political and cultural debaters to a mass public of consumers. (4)

Radical democratic desire for an engaged and informed active public notwithstanding, Dahlgren has to agree with Habermas' analysis of the impact of the rise of the welfare state in the twentieth century:

> Journalism's critical role in the wake of advertising, entertainment and public relations becomes muted. Public opinion is no longer a process of rational discourse, but the result of publicity and social engineering in the media. (4)

This characterization—of a public sphere both eroded and manipulated by commercialism—is not where Dahlgren ends up, however. He goes on to point to considerations that now have to be scrutinized when analyzing the role of the media in society. Ultimately, he articulates four strands in modern society that complicate the notion of the public sphere. These are: "the crisis of the nation-state, the segmentation of audiences, the rise of new political and social movements, and the relative availability of advanced computer and communication technology to consumers" (12). Each of these plays a role in the condition of and 'pull' on the public sphere. While all of these are important concerns, I address here, briefly, the nation-state problematic first, and then consider the implications of technological availability within a more specific discourse on electronic democracy.

Dahlgren argues that today's nation-state is "in deep crisis," not only due to "fiscal dilemmas," but also in terms of "problems of legitimation" (12):

> This crisis of course goes in tandem with the transnationalization of capital and the dispersion of production within the international economy. Economic control of the economy within the nation-state's borders increasingly resides outside those borders. Internally the state is facing a stagnation of national parliamentary politics, where the margin of administrative and political manoeuvrability are [sic] contracting and the consequent political programmes of the established parties are tending towards dedifferentiation. (12)

His analysis of the crisis of the nation-state is deeply troubling, but hardly surprising. Few, if any, of our citizens are completely unaware of the inroads and erosion of national boundaries that came with the globalization of the economy, since it impacted us locally (and continues to do so). Many of us are also deeply aware of an aggravated state of social dislocation—people out of work, losing homes, losing the means to live and to work, even the means *to* survive—that further complicates the role of the nation-state in terms of the political, or legitimacy. Given that he was writing in the early 1990s, when things were *perceived* to be arguably 'better' for many citizens in the U.S., we need to consider carefully the nexus between the economic-political agenda of our leadership—past *and* present—and the relative civic action/non-action tendencies among the greater part of the population. Dahlgren argues that

> in Reagan's USA... the resultant social dislocations have generated still more political stresses at the popular level. Here particularly we see the emerging contours of the 'two-thirds society'—a form of social triage where the system can seemingly provide for the well-being of approximately two-thirds of the populace while sacrificing the remaining third and allowing it to solidify into an underclass. Party loyalty and participation in the arena of official politics understandably recedes. Reagan... came to power with just over one-fourth of the popular vote: about half the electorate did not feel that participation was meaningful. In such a situation, the ideological success of the powerful in the public sphere is at least being passively contested to a degree not manifested three decades ago. (12)

Is silence—from this perspective, as acquiescence to public authority based on a resignation to powerlessness—simply a signal that the public understands that it has no role in making change(s)? Dahlgren appears to think so. Further, warning that we cannot take the interplay of these multiple and complex factors too lightly when considering the role of the media, Dahlgren leaves us with this thought:

> ...our understanding of the public sphere must... be of a practical nature, attuned to the flow of the relevant discourses in the media. Close familiarity with what is said and not said, and how it is said—the topics, the coverages, the debates, the rhetoric, the modes of address, etc.—are a prerequisite not only for an enhanced theoretical understanding but also for concrete political involvement within—and with—the public sphere. Nobody promised that citizenship would be easy. (19)

If Dahlgren's analysis leaves us with the idea that we must become students of media discourse capable of analyzing even the silences, or vacant spaces, within that discourse in order to exercise the rights and responsibilities of citizenship, Gitlin (1993) takes us in a different direction.

In his essay, 'Bites and Blips: Chunk News, Savvy Talk and the Bifurcation of American Politics' (Dahlgren and Sparks, 1993), Gitlin asks whether the fact that "American television has been for some time compressing politics into chunks, ten-second 'bites' and images that seem to freeze into icons as they repeat across millions of screens and newspapers" (119) has "caused democratic politics to explode" (120). Arguing that our culture is one in which the spectacle is favored over substance, and that the media are complicit in this effect, Gitlin articulates the scenario this way:

> The premium attitude is a sort of knowing appraisal. Speaking up is less important—certainly less fun—than sizing up. Politics, real politics, is for 'players'—fascinating term, for it implies that everyone else is a spectator. To be 'interested in

politics' is to know how to rate the players—do they have good hands? How do they do in the clutch? How are they positioning themselves for the next play? ... Savviness flatters spectators that they really do understand; that people like them are in charge; that even if they stand outside the policy elites, they remain sovereign. Keeping up with the maneuvers of Washington insiders, defining the issues as Washington defines them, savviness appeals to a spirit both managerial and voyeuristic. It transmutes the desire to participate into spectacle—one is already participating, in effect, by watching. (125)

Taking us through a stunning tour of American campaign history (and Gitlin *is* focusing on 'campaigns' and 'races'—both military and sports metaphors), he raises another interesting question: is the bifurcation of television and newspaper coverage (*The New York Times* vs. *The New York Post*, or the MacNeil/Lehrer *NewsHour* vs. Geraldo Rivera—his choices) also complicit in the decline of democratic participation? His answer is chilling:

...metacoverage for the *cognoscenti*, concocted pageantry for the *hoi poloi*. But pageantry only mobilizes the population under two conditions—they must believe there is something at stake, and they must be drawn into some form of participation. As the spectacle becomes more scripted and routine... more people turn off. Thus television inspired political withdrawal along with pseudo-sophistication. As campaign coverage proliferates, and the pundits and correspondents pontificate in their savvy way, they take part in what is increasingly a circular conversation—while an attuned audience, wishing to be taken behind the scenes, is invited to inspect the strategies of the insiders. Savviness is the tribute a spectacular culture pays to the pleasures of democracy—middle-class outsiders want to be in the know, while the poor withdraw and fail to vote... Politics, by these lights, remains a business for insiders and professionals. (132-133)

Gitlin's message is clear: we are inculcating passivity and an impotent withdrawal into voyeurism *vis-à-vis* our own political, social and cultural world. Does this apply in the face of national tragedy and loss? Perhaps, but it seems appropriate to me that each of us should answer that on our own. We certainly were provided with metacoverage if we would watch, and Americans definitely engaged with television news and newspapers more than ever, but I wonder: to what extent did that *simulate* participation, when it might really have been more accurately depicted as spectatorship?

What about our young? Looking to the future, Gitlin worries that there may be a "music video generation" of

younger viewers [who] are more likely, when they watch television, to pay attention to disconnected images; to switch channels, 'watching' more than one program at once; and to spin off into fantasies about images. Of all age-groups, the young are also the least likely to read newspapers and to vote. (133)

For Gitlin, the crux of the problem lies here:

> ...the promotion of ignorance coincides with the emptying out of the public sphere—the paucity of forms through which political energies could be mobilized. In the end, what is most disturbing is not ignorance in its own right, but, rather, the coupling of ignorance and power. When the nation-state has the power to reach out and blow up cities on the other side of the world, the spirit of diversion seems, to say the least, inadequate to the approaching millenium. Neither know-it-alls nor know-nothings are likely to rise to the occasion. (135)

For Gitlin, the 'coupling of ignorance and power' is the essential moment of anxiety. I share that anxiety, especially in our present circumstances, and construe the silence to be more than oppression (or repression), but rather to be frighteningly and intimately connected to ignorance and uncertainty, caused both by a lack of essential information and an unhealthy distance from power (i.e., disempowerment). The 'spirit of diversion' is a dangerous one, *especially in the parent culture*, and our voyeuristic tendencies have taken their toll over time.

I turn now to the promises and problems of the *electronic* public sphere relative to the notion of "cultural citizenship" (Stevenson, 2001, 1). Here we have a relatively new prospect that is coming into clearer focus as citizens of the nation realize their vulnerability and the potential impacts of the choices our government makes. Gitlin's 'conditions' have a role to play here (there *is* something at stake *and* citizens *are* being drawn into participation).

Stevenson (2001) explains that "to talk of cultural citizenship... invites a dialogue across disciplinary boundaries and maps out some of the key developments currently taking place within the modern world" (1). He offers us some 'food for thought' as he begins to elaborate the dimensions of cultural citizenship:

> ...demands for cultural citizenship both focus on the spheres of media and education and have been influenced by the dual processes of postmodernization and globalization. The partial break up of previously assumed homogeneous national cultures has opened questions of cultural inclusion and exclusion. To be excluded from cultural citizenship is to be excluded from full membership of society... 'cultural' citizenship needs to include dimensions other than the recognition of difference. ...while the recognition... of our right to be different remains key, cultural citizenship also requires a set of public institutions that are both democratic and protected from the excesses of the free market. (3-4)

Stevenson points us to "a new breed of claims for unhindered representation, recognition without marginalization, acceptance and integration without 'normalizing' distortion" and he works to "trace out... key questions at stake in this arena" (4). Arguing that these questions "focus our attention on questions of rights, democratic participation and notions of duty," he sees that in the past decade, "questions of citizenship have come increasingly to the fore" (4):

> This has been widely recognized as being connected to the growing crisis of the welfare state in Western democratic nations, the demise of actually existed socialism, the critical questioning of liberalism and social democracy and the development of informational capitalism. All of these social developments and others have helped put citizenship studies on the map. (4)

Stevenson indicates, however, that thinking about citizenship in these terms is "both at once important and overly narrow" (4). A more viable conceptualization of citizenship would truly center on a critique of the cultural power inherent in current practices and institutions:

> Social movements in respect of race and ethnicity, gender and sexuality, disability and others have all sought to interrupt the construction of dominant cultures. These movements have sought to challenge widely held stereotypes that once permeated the symbolic cultures of civil society. The deconstruction of ideas that have been associated with the 'normal' citizen has sought to widen the 'inclusive' fabric of the community while creating space for difference and otherness. Questions of 'cultural' citizenship therefore seek to rework images, assumptions and representations that are seen to be exclusive as well as marginalizing. (4)

This 'reworking' of the 'master code' propels the approach I have taken here, namely, to look for "other stories of what could be" (Fine, 2002, 138). For Stevenson, this question of 'cultural citizenship' has obvious results with regard to the public sphere, since "the discursive construction" of this ongoing dialogue "has a further 'cultural' dimension" (5), namely, that

> the arena in which they are mostly [sic] likely to be fought out is within the media of mass communication. The progressive enframing of key political debates within print and radio, and the dominant medium television has been one of the major 'cultural' transformations of the twentieth century. The development of a sophisticated array of visual codes and repertoires that interrupt the agendas of more hegemonic institutions and cultures is an essential armament within the semiotic society. To have access to cultural citizenship therefore is to be able to make an intervention into the public sphere at the local, national or global level. (5)

The public sphere, as a space of 'intervention,' then, serves as a mediator of civic-cultural struggle through its 'array of visual codes and repertoires' and plays an important role in the negotiation of citizenship. In Stevenson, we are faced not only with "the increasingly political nature of cultural questions," but also "the diversity of arenas that debate and represent these questions" (5).

The fount of consciousness derives from multiple dimensions and directions, all highly politicized and conveyed through 'images, assumptions and representations' that complicate both understanding and portrayal. Access is required at some level, whether local, national or global.

Stevenson attends to globalization with specific concerns for its impacts on cultural citizenship as they play out in the public sphere. He argues that "the 'cultural' aspects of globalization," with which we are now very familiar, include "a number of processes" related to the mobility "of people and symbols" across the borders of nation-states, and that the result has been to foster several "complex and often contradictory developments," among which "the growing penetration of the cultural sphere by economics and instrumental reason" (5) is first and foremost:

> Huge conglomerates specializing in the production of a range of cultural goods now dominate world markets. However, new levels of cultural intermixing partially breaking down older more homogeneous cultures have also coupled this development. This has helped foster claims for cultural rights from a variety of sites... An increasingly commercial as well as a more multi-cultural public sphere has produced claims for special protection from the domains of high culture and minority cultures alike. Processes of globalization then can be read ambivalently in that they have provided new zones of cultural intermixing while progressively commodifying the cultural realm. These claims for rights will primarily be addressed towards the nation-state, despite recent reports of its demise, as well as more trans-national and local levels of governance. (5)

What Stevenson addresses here is the erosion of national boundaries and, more importantly, the erosion of the logic behind their ultimate determination of cultural belonging, or citizenship. The 'growing penetration of the cultural sphere' has enormous impact on the nation as an imagined community particularly, while 'new levels' of cultural intermixing' impact not only 'the cultural realm' itself, but our sense of the nation and the degree to which it is granted "emotional legitimacy" (Anderson, 1991, 4). Where, then, is the dialogue that is required to sustain a democratic nation to be found? His answer is that we should expect to find this dialogue in "a pluralistic and electrically charged public sphere" (5), and that public space in terms of

> places where ideas, perspectives and feelings can be shared in modern societies is crucial for the development of the self, the creation of social movements and the fostering of a critically informed public more generally. Again the spaces and places where this sort of interaction can take place may combine different kinds of communication from face to face interaction to that of a more mediated variety. Open-ended and reflexive forms of dialogue can be as much a part of the Internet as it can the local town hall. However there are many other pressures within modern society that would seek

ideological closure and ensure topics for debate ...do not receive the chronic forms of scrutiny they evidently deserve. (5-6)

For Stevenson, providing such spaces, "in terms of a genuinely 'cultural' citizenship," means that we need to augment and preserve the relative autonomy of such spaces or places "against more colonizing influences" (6). The emergence of an 'electronic public sphere,' while it may serve the purposes Stevenson is advancing, is a double-edged sword, as we shall see. Nevertheless, it does constitute a public 'space' which potentially offers hope for achieving the dialogue so essential to democracy. Here, however, the potential threat of electronic surveillance, along with other issues, makes the promise of this segment of the public sphere also highly problematic.

Turner's (2001) 'Outline of a General Theory of Cultural Citizenship' considers this problematic, and others, in terms of the considerations involved in conceptualizing a social theory of cultural citizenship. He offers that

> The notion of cultural citizenship raises two interesting problems. The first is a sociological issue about the unified character of the cultural foundations of the nation-state, namely the problems of multi-culturalism and postmodernism. The second problem is a philosophical one. If one can in fact articulate a notion of cultural rights, is there a cultural obligation which corresponds to or matches this assertion of rights to cultural resources? (13-14)

Citing O'Neill's (1990) work, Turner raises *her* question: "how are we entitled to express ourselves?" (14). This is an essential point that is pivotal to our discussion, since Turner's sense of what O'Neill demonstrates is that while "cultural rights are typically couched within a rights discourse," they might be "more effectively" (14) derived from

> an ethical theory that takes obligations rather than rights as its foundation. Indeed much of the debate about cultural rights has been dominated by a tradition of individual liberalism which excludes the notion of obligation in favour of an individualistic theory, thereby concentrating on freedoms. In this approach, O'Neill argues that legal institutions which only address these individualistic freedoms without a corresponding notion of obligation produce a collection of rights which are merely shams. (14)

He takes O'Neill's work to point out "the possibility of cultural risk and the growth of a communications environment which is hazardous and culturally contaminating" (14). This position leads him to consider Beck's (1992) work, which articulated a social theory of risk for environmental hazards, but failed to consider cultural dimensions in the way that Turner means to do. What is at stake here, Turner insists, are the kinds of risk that Beck ignores:

"the contamination of cultural heritage, the simulation of authentic traditions and the erosion of cultural authority" (14). For Turner, O'Neill's work is important because

> Communicative obligations in a democracy are associated with maintaining the conditions for public communication as such. She notes that 'languages can be debased and killed: cultural traditions, dispersed and vulgarized; technologies can be introduced and others displaced in ways that destroy possibilities of communications without coercing or deceiving individuals' (O'Neill, 1990: 167). Communicative obligations directly raise questions about the ownership of the media, the shaping of the public sphere, the silencing of minority opinion, and the manipulation of information by powerful sectors of the communications industry. (14-15)

Wrestling with the philosophical question of an ethical foundation for determining the cultural rights and obligations of citizens leads Turner to conclude that an analysis of this kind "would help to develop the notion of corporate citizenship, namely the idea of a corporate responsibility for genuine and critical public debate rather than a cynical policy of communication management" (15). This is a hopeful note on an otherwise dim horizon, and it is this 'genuine and critical public debate' that I have in mind as I proceed.

Turner, who speaks to a "traditional debate over cultural imperialism and cultural rights" (22), therefore looks both to Bell's (1974) "sophisticated theory of the information revolution" and to McLuhan's (1964) "imaginative analysis of the media revolution" (22). Where Bell saw "the centrality of the university and tertiary education systems" (22) to the production and control of knowledge in terms of "the axial principle of the centrality and codification of theoretical knowledge" as the "basis of economic growth and social stratification" (22), McLuhan argued "that the medium is the message," that "the form of the media actually is constitutive of the content of the message itself" (23). Turner questions whether "a revolution in the means of communication" (23) has occurred

> such that all previous modes of thinking about communication and information are rendered obsolete and irrelevant. If McLuhan's argument is correct, then we need to re-think not only the specific idea of cultural citizenship but the basic premises of democratic theory as such. McLuhan's theory of communication indicates that we need to reconceptualize democratic theory in order to understand the impact of globalized electronic media on identity, participation and culture. In general, much conceptualization of democratic citizenship... still assumes the dominance of print-based culture. This recognition underlines the importance of the discussion of electronic democracy. (23)

Pointing us to the work of Barber (1984), Lanham (1993), Poster (1994) and Becker (1993), Turner heralds "the enormous scope of the digital-satellite-electronic media of communication and their interaction for a revitalization of democratic participation" (23). For these scholars, the advent of 'virtual community' or 'virtual democracy' is welcome news:

> Social theorists of the global media believe not only that we have arrived at a new cultural threshold, but that we have arrived at a unique opportunity to sidestep the legacy of the administrative state and to revive participatory democracy through an extension of the impact of electronic communication systems to the wider community. (23)

"Each of these writers," Turner offers, "welcomes rather than laments the arrival or intervention of technology in modern civil society" because

> an electronic commonwealth can be realized through the use of numerous cable and satellite services, and television- and consumer-based formats of interaction. Such a commonwealth would bring together individuals otherwise largely disenfranchised from political life by powerful institution elites and media systems, that way reinstating the political subject into modern life. (23)

Turner's analysis addresses the spatial concern—the loss of public space—and he suggests that

> the new media of the communication revolution can overcome a fundamental problem of modern democracy, namely space. The classical democracies of Greece and Rome could be participatory because, in principle, face-to-face dialogue was possible. In the ancient polis, space did not prohibit dialogue, which was the medium of character development for the citizen (Dahl, 1989: 14). (Turner, 2001, 23-24)

Does that mean, given its transcendence of physical limits and its virtual reach, that the electronic commonwealth is the key to renewing democracy? Unfortunately, he indicates a number of concerns about "the spatial or geographical impact which electronic democracy might have on existing definitions of democracy" (24). First, there is the matter of whether "the electronic commonwealth will indeed constitute a de-territorialized and de-nationalized entity," a problem that "is neither posed adequately nor successfully analysed" (24). That is part of what I have taken up here as I seek the source(s) of national autobiography, i.e., the source(s) via which we imagine the nation *together*.

Second, Turner highlights two problems raised by Poster (1994): namely, the concern that such technologies have not yet been "fully constituted as cultural practices" and the possibility that "the information super-highway will be restricted in the way the broadcast system is restricted" (24). According to Turner, for Poster, the indication is that such "restriction will most likely be culturally consonant with wealthy, white male values and ideas" since "new technologies, even after two decades of the new social movements, are likely to have been conceived, designed and produced by white males" (24). Turner also echoes Varn's (1993) concern "that citizens may drown in a sea of irrelevant data and information churned out by inordinate distribution points in large bureaucracies and government agencies," and that "opinions will override political action if electronic roads to democracy are taken" (24).

Turner also considers Becker's (1993) work, pointing out that he "was one of the earliest advocates of electronic democracy and localistic experiments in electronic dialogues and teledemocracy,"

> namely 'democratically aided, rapid, two-way political communication' and he envisages that 'advances in interactive electronic communication technologies would empower the American citizenry and lead to a much stronger democracy at the national, regional, state and local levels' (Becker, 1993: 14). ...His advocacy of electronic democracy preceded the contemporary fascination with the Internet and sparked off numerous debates and analyses of the possibilities for democracy of these developments. (Turner, 2001, 24)

Reviewing Barber's (1984) work on electronic democracy, a work that "shows more reserve than Becker," Turner offers that

> he recognized its important contribution to the debate on ...the argument that contemporary politics is in significant need of redevelopment and resuscitation by such new media of dialogue, communication and interaction. Indeed the very foundation of the American republic was always about the problems of communication in a nation of strangers. Barber's work is a useful contribution to how citizenship can be empowered by these technological modes of dialogue, exchange and policy construction. (25)

Turner sorts through the implications and problems of such promising technology in Barber's work:

> Within his 'strong argument' for democratic citizenship lies an appropriation of the techno-culture thesis which advocates, such as Becker, have developed in the United States for the last decade. The creation of the medium to facilitate civic participation in an active democratic programme would require significant linkage among neighbourhood assemblies that permitted equal discussion of shared concerns as well as national and indeed international discussions among individuals on national and local initiatives. (25)

Turner is concerned with the implications of a medium that appears to foster 'thin association' rather than 'thick' community, an issue which he takes up in his conclusion. What do these 'advances' offer/threaten as we move into their realm of 'reality'? Turner highlights three "broad areas of criticism" (29), citing Rheingold (1993):

> First, there is the commodification of information, resulting in the erosion of a public sphere. Secondly, there is the argument that high-bandwidth interactive networks increase the level and sophistication of political surveillance, resulting in a loss or decline of personal liberties. Finally, there is the view that we have already moved into a hyper-reality, where the politics of spectacle and entertainment construct the citizen as a passive, hypnotized subject, resulting in a simulation of political reality. ... The nature of 'community' in the modern electronic world becomes a crucial issue in political theory and public debate. (29)

This question of "the nature of community'" is the core of our concerns here, since the removal of community from place in electronic space, or cyberspace, raises the question of who "the strangers" are in this "communion in the electronic commonwealth" (29):

> The electronic (thin) community and cool communication can be an association of strangers, who never physically connect with each other, share only a computer language, and 'visit' each other's sites merely out of idle curiosity. The modern web site, in this respect, could be regarded as the modern equivalent of the 'market' which dominated nineteenth-century discussions of association versus community. The contemporary Internet could be regarded as a global market of strangers exchanging information and as a consequence creating a thin community. As local cultural identities thicken in response to decolonization, political networks extend through thin channels of exchange. (29)

As a scholar-practitioner, I am concerned, of course, with the erosion of the public sphere and also with highly sophisticated political surveillance that foreshadows the arrival of (at the same time that it betrays the presence of) Big Brother, but in my thinking, the primary problematic of this 'social space' is its hyper-reality. When I think about 'communities of sentiment' (Appadurai, 1996) and the nation as an 'imagined community' (Anderson, 1991), it worries me deeply that we connect and converse (in the virtual world) with strangers as though they were friends or neighbors, and, thus, that we are losing the thickness and the richness of community life. This is a particularly salient issue where cultural citizenship emerges as a thread of continuity throughout our increasingly media-controlled sense of the nation, and where globally linked, external 'sodalities'—sodalities that may or may not be 'friendlies'—can use this thin association to strengthen their commonality in a virtual world.

Tompaine.com, for instance, is a 'virtual' magazine. It is probably best described as a 'little' magazine in electronic format. The people who contribute are 'real' flesh and blood folks, and because of this, the virtual aspect of the venue does not appear to transform it in any visible way. Nevertheless, it *is* a virtual magazine—one to which I subscribed electronically for the purpose of conducting this research. The aspect of the venue that troubles me is that it reflects a 'thin' community, mostly utilizing 'cool' talk, and it offers, by virtue of its location within e-culture, a virtual conversation. No matter how intense its critiques, they are only experienced to the extent that one is 'subscribed.' There are entire communities of people left out of this e-universe of discourse, as is true for any other of our e-avenues for gathering and sharing information, insights and opinions. It troubles me that the critique and dialogue presented by commentaries in this venue are meant to find resonance among members of the general public, thereby strengthening the public sphere, but the public included here is exclusively an electronically connected one—only those who are 'wired' (or have 'wireless' access) are invited. This, of course, reflects a small part of the critique of the techno-culture thesis raised above. There is, however, a second dimension to this venue that worries me more, and that is the issue of *surveillance*.

Vinson and Ross (2003) draw attention to the emergence of a *spectacle-surveillance* paradigm manipulated and exploited to drive public opinion and policy towards a business-knows-best agenda vis-à-vis public schooling, thus constraining the potential for change in the future. For Vinson and Ross, the use and abuse(s) of image and watching form the core of the problem(s). They argue that

> The contemporary convergence or coexistence of surveillance and spectacle forms in part the context within which image attains its power. Yet this state of affairs poses specific and critical threats to the enactment of meaningful schooling and to the evolution of global society. These threats include those related to democracy, authenticity, anti-oppression, and the collective good, current and historical goals of public education, and those commitments that might effectively challenge the problematics of disciplinarity. (70)

Vinson and Ross, moreover, argue that there are "specific architectural consequences" of this disciplinary regime, and that they are harmful to schooling and to its participants and benefactors (society).

While the role of schooling may in fact be diminished relative to social change and its effects (Porter, 1999), knowledge workers cannot ignore our need to rethink and to respond to educational needs in present context, whatever such changes may portend for the future. Power over the production and commodification of culture and cultural change (and the extraordinary artifice that is presently involved in their propagation) leads us to question the surround within which we are being re-packaged and re-presented (marketed) to ourselves (Twitchell, 2004), and what is happening to our humanity as a result (Berman, 2000). Knowledge workers in various fields, theorizing space, spatial relations, and the visual, have been providing new, postmodern tools for analyzing this cultural surround vis-à-vis power for some time now; I have space to offer just a few examples here, as outlined in Vinson and Ross.

Foucault's (2000) disciplinary power of 'Panopticism,' Vinson and Ross contend, consists of "continuous individual supervision, in the form of control, punishment, and compensation, and in the form of correction... the molding and transformation of individuals in terms of certain norms" (45), or normalization. Vinson and Ross offer that "in its purest and most perfect form Panoptic discipline operates invisibly, unverifiably, and automatically, and as such is unrivaled in its efficiency, insidiousness, and effectiveness" (46). "What was new" in this scenario, Vinson and Ross indicate, and "what was most dangerous and potent, was its ability to produce at the same time both "silent" (or "docile") and "obedient" (or "useful") bodies" as "the individual's time, space, and movement" were manipulated and controlled to serve the purposes of the surveilling institution, whether prisons, asylums, factories, hospitals, or schools.

Vinson and Ross also underscore DeBord's (1967/1995) notion of 'the spectacle' as "a social relationship between people ...mediated by images" (48) as a space where "reality unfolds in a new generality as a pseudo-world apart" so that "the former unity of life is lost forever" (48). In this "immense accumulation of *spectacles*," "all that once was directly lived has become mere representation" [emphasis in original] (48). Thus, for Vinson and Ross, "spectacle defines a society in which everywhere reality (and 'real' human experience) is replaced by *images*—images that obtain and pursue a 'life of their own' dinstinct [from] (not merged with) reality," so that we are presented with "a form of capitalist-induced alienation in which 'being' means 'appearing' and where the image, as commodity, as distorted and disconnected, mediates all social relationships" [emphasis in original] (48-49). Vinson and Ross note as well that "spectacle... maintains its own regime of control and discipline, ...one rooted in the fact that it exists purely for its own reproduction and thus subordinates all of human life to its needs" (49).

Finally, Vinson and Ross offer for our consideration Baudrillard's (1995) notion that we endure "a system of deterrence, in which the distinction between the passive and the active is abolished," where a setting of "hyperreality" exists and simulacra replace the real, such that we are always on the other side of the gaze, "far from the strategy of transparency," and there is only "'information,' secret virulence, chain reaction, slow implosion" (50). This creates a setting in which "the differences between the image and the real collapse," where "hyperreality" sets in, and "frequently the existence of the image is more real than the real itself," so that "at some point images live in the absence of any 'authentic' original (or reality)—as *simulacra*" [emphasis in original] (52).

Movement that truly represents 'release from our arrest' (Pinar, 1994, 61), then, is made all the more difficult and requires a good deal more civic courage than we might expect in a 'spectacle-surveillance' paradigm that seeks to normalize, to deter, to mystify, and thereby to confuse the public and to alter the very meaning of 'experience.' These are dark images, but they are highly relevant considerations in our times. However, before postmodern perspectives, concerns, or sensibilities may be effectively exercised to address these issues, they will need to face and respond to the "intense academic and mainstream criticism" leveled against them (Kincheloe, 2006, 224). 'Lines of flight' research, in this respect, must find its 'anchors' in order to contribute to change. Reynolds (2004) puts the matter this way as he posits that "we live in the time of the looking-glass" (19):

> We want to be as warm on [the] side of postmodernity as we were before we stepped through whatever looking glass it was and away from the modernist notions of self, truth, and meaning. Perhaps we are afraid that we will find on the other side of the mirror what Neo in *The Matrix* found when the mirror covered him and there was, indeed, the matrix. So, we deal with the uncertainty of our time and theorize about the possibilities of more meaningful times ahead. That is one of the many dilemmas of postmodern existence. (20)

The work I have undertaken here is an initial iteration of what we might consider vis-à-vis reuniting the *within* and the *beyond*, of restoring DeBord's (1967/1995) 'unity of life' (Vinson and Ross, 2003, 48), in our search for a (democratic) nation imagined together in new ways and with new understanding, as will hopefully become evident as I imagine contours of a curriculum for post-9/11 America, our new American wilderness (see Chapter 9).

9

Contours of a Curriculum for the New American Wilderness

> Curriculum expresses the desire to establish a world for children that is richer, larger, more colorful, and more accessible than the one we have known. Perhaps it originates in what Sartre has called "negation," the creative refusal of human consciousness that says, "not this, but that." Perhaps it begins with a gesture to the future, with pulling back the curtain, opening the window, letting in more light. And then, too soon, we look at the window rather than through it, and negation collapses into prescription. I am not suggesting that this contraction of hope into resignation is inevitable, for it is an expression of historic and particular oppositions, the individual and the community, the family and the economy, the transcendental and the embodied, desire and renunciation. (Grumet, 1988, xiii)

> ...if the world we give our children is different from the one we envisioned for them, then we need to discover the moments when we, weary, distracted, and conflicted, gave in, let the curtain fall back across the window, and settled for a little less light. (Grumet, 1988, xv)

I have worked here with Grumet's caution in mind: that is, not to let negation, or refusal, collapse into prescription. I have worked, as well, to 'discover the moment' when we 'gave in' and 'settled for a little less light.' This I sought to achieve by elaborating on the public dialogue that emerged in the early period following September 11th, before repression set in, questioning who we say we are or will become as a nation. The main consideration here, for me, is not the way those in power cynically and in their own self-interest exploited the moment, although they clearly did, and this, too, has repercussions that cannot be ignored. My concern, rather, is with the failure of the American public in this moment, a failure that I read as paralysis in the face of disorientation and disinformation, a psycho-social slippage of gigantic proportions. I have sought here to pull back the curtain to let the light in, as Grumet suggests. I therefore explore in this chapter the work of some who have struggled with the quest for a curriculum for democracy, past and present.

Curriculum Inquiry as Metatheory

Stephen Kemmis (1986), in *Curriculum Theorising: Beyond Cultural Reproduction*, offers an analysis of curriculum as a field of study, reviewing Schwab's (1969) call for a 'practical turn,' which declared that curriculum as a field of inquiry had become 'moribund' because it had taken flight from a consideration of practical action to what he termed the 'theoretic,' or, in Kemmis' terms, the 'technical' (Kemmis, 1986, 13). Schwab was influential in pointing to the need for a reconceptualization of the field (Pinar, 1975) and in drawing curriculum discourse back from technical considerations to practical argumentation (or contestation), but much of the field of curriculum today remains deeply submerged in concerns for technique and procedure. As a result, a chasm has emerged between those who engage in curriculum development and those who engage in curriculum theory, or curriculum inquiry. The result has been to leave those who concern themselves with the 'technical' in charge of curriculum development.

Kemmis indicates that in order to understand the migration, expansion, and transformation of curricular concerns we need first to understand the difference between 'the practical' and 'the theoretic':

> ...practical action, and the mode of thought associated with it, is *doing* action. It is essentially risky; it is guided by general and sometimes tragically conflicting moral ideas of the good for humankind; it involves weighing circumstances and making judgments so that one can act rightly in particular human and social situations. It refers to the kinds of moral judgments people make when they want to act wisely. Practical action is exemplified whenever people make value-laden judgments about how to live through social situations... (14)

By contrast, the technical (or 'theoretic') is understood to be based on a view of education as a form of 'applied science' informed by 'foundational' fields and modeled on natural scientific theory. Kemmis explains:

> Especially after the 1920s, educational theory began more systematically to seek guidance from these 'foundations' disciplines, and to lose its distinctive character as educational thought—educational theory about educational problems. And as that version of theory modelled on the natural scientific view of science developed in psychology, sociology, economics, linguistics and other fields, so educationists turned more and more to these fields for guidance, coming, eventually, to regard those other fields as foundations for education itself. In the process, education as a field began to lose its distinctive character: its problems became the 'applied' problems of psychology, sociology and the rest—and finding solutions to educational problems came to be regarded as the work of applied psychologists, applied sociologists, applied economists and applied linguists who happened to have a specialist interest in education. (15-16)

The practical turn that Schwab advocated is interpreted by Kemmis as a return to an "older and still living tradition of educational thought and action," since

Schwab speaks against the theoretic from an older tradition of the practical, reviving the arguments and distinctions of philosophers and theorists from a venerable tradition, and reminding his contemporary audience of values and concerns still current—the living values and concerns of a society whose history is founded in its own particular traditions, including its particular views on such matters as truth and truthfulness, justice, democracy. (17)

Kemmis explains that the conflict between the two "put the whole debate on a new level—the level of metatheory" (20), which he characterizes in these terms:

> Unsurprisingly, this arrogance of the 'scientific' view was challenged by advocates of 'the practical' because the practical recalled and revitalised older conceptions of curriculum thought... and conceptions of what it meant to be human, to be a member of a society, and to be an educator (involving judgments about educational and social values enacted daily in classrooms and schools as teachers aimed to make wise decisions about the good for humankind, and the best interests of students and society). (19)

Kemmis identifies essential distinctions between ideas about the purposes of schooling to make sense of curriculum work. I employ Kemmis' analysis because he approaches curricular disputes in terms of their broader philosophical and historical underpinnings, and because he uses a metatheoretical lens, ultimately turning the conversation in the direction of 'ideology-critique' (73), which suits my purposes here.[1] His discussion centers on disagreement and confusion over the foundational basis for educating our young:

> Contemporary views of what should be 'in' the school curriculum reflect ideas from three different periods in recent history: ideas from the period of relatively high social consensus (the late 1950s), from the period when this consensus broke down (the 1960s and 70s), and the current period in which strenuous attempts are being made to re-establish consensus about the nature, needs and problems of society. Coming over such a brief historical time span (only 30 years), ideas from these different periods all present themselves as 'contemporary' to curriculum developers in government agencies and in schools, yet they embody very different views of education and society, and also embody different views about the nature, needs and problems of contemporary curriculum theory. (Kemmis, 1986, ix)

Understanding social change is essential, then, for considering curriculum from this vantage point. The social order retains no fixed relationship with curricular intent or direction, but does involve a constant struggle between various interest groups over the purposes of schooling.[2] Curriculum, then, is 'historically embedded' (23). Because of this relationship between education and competing interest-groups within social contexts, 'the representation problem' (Lundgren, 1983, cited in Kemmis) emerges. Kemmis notes that

> ...the central problem of curriculum theory is to be understood as a double problem of the relationship between theory and practice, on the one hand, and of the relationship... between education and society, on the other. These relationships have been interpreted and enacted in different ways through history and, at any time, competing views of the whole set of relationships can be found contending against one another. [Emphasis in original] (22)

Because the terrain is contested and these relations between education and society are in continual flux, understanding the dynamics of civic-cultural struggle in a given contextual moment is crucial to understanding curricular change(s) and curricular dispute(s). Articulating changes in views of educational purposes, Kemmis details the intricacies of education-society relations and maps vistas of educational purpose from each of three perspectives.

Arguing that "the choice of what aspects of the life and work of a society should be represented in the curricula of its schools and other educational institutions remains crucial, not only to educationists but to society as a whole," Kemmis warns against the misconception that there is any fixed referent for curriculum study. He posits instead that meanings are temporally fixed, often unconsciously, "within the framework of particular metatheories." Therefore, "it is this metatheoretical perspective that must be illuminated before we can begin to ask any questions about what curriculum is or what curricula should 'contain'" (23). Kemmis makes it clear that both curriculum theorizing and curricular practice have evolved, that "curriculum is a product of human and social history, and a means by which powerful groups have exerted a very significant influence on the reproduction processes of society by influencing and perhaps even controlling the processes by which the young were and are educated" (32). Therefore, he maintains that

> Curriculum theorists need a wide historical perspective on curriculum as the object of their studies, because the object of their studies is not constant across history, but, like society itself, has changed in response to the historical circumstances, economic and political structures, and the human interests and self-interests of the makers of curricula. The object of their studies is a human and social construction which has been made and remade through history. (32)

I highlight this point because it illustrates the importance of attending to our current civic-cultural upheaval, the contested reconstruction of our national autobiographical project, and the power of discourses and of state-centric media, in particular, to reframe or reconstruct our identities as individual citizens, the identity of our nation in terms of its aspirations, character, and ideals, and the *enactment* of education through schooling (what I would call the 'face' of education) as a result. This is a matter of no small concern. By its very nature, according to Kemmis, the study of curriculum is contextual, tentative, and temporal.

I map our discursive autobiography in a specific social moment for purposes of highlighting 'how ideas and ideals are reformulated', bearing in mind Kemmis' imperative that "to understand curriculum, we must also become historians, social theorists, philosophers" (34). I use a *reconceptualist* (Pinar, 1975) notion of curriculum theorizing that enhances our ability to apprehend social changes we are facing and what they mean for the public educative experience and the ideas and ideals of curriculum they foster as we face past and present, and peer as well into an uncertain future, a future that promises continuing civic-cultural struggle. As a result, I seek here to address social change as it impacts curriculum—using national-discursive autobiography as both (slippery) ground and catalyst—and heed Kemmis' notion that

> curriculum theories are social theories not only in the sense that they reflect the history of the societies in which they arose, but also in the sense that they entail ideas about social change and, in particular, about the role of education in the reproduction and transformation of society. [Emphasis in original] (35)

Kemmis reviews Lundgren's (1983) "outline history of curriculum codes" which demonstrated that such codes are "products of their times" (31). Lundgren's analysis posits five discrete codes, each based in a specific period of social change or growth. The first of these is the *classical curriculum code* of the Greeks and Romans, which sought to balance the intellectual, physical, and aesthetic development of the individual. The second is the *realistic curriculum code* produced by the Renaissance, which redirected emphasis toward knowledge acquired through the senses and scientific knowledge. During the eighteenth and nineteenth centuries, the *moral curriculum code* emerged, which was related to the rise of mass education and also arose as a "response to the needs of new nation-states for a committed citizenry and a concern for training citizens in their duties within the framework of the state" (31).

This was followed, in the twentieth century, by the *rational curriculum code*, which reflected pragmatism, a concern for the individual, and the idea that scientific notions could provide a rational basis for societal organization. Further, the latter sought to supplement the 'moral code' by "instilling the values of liberalism—values also well suited to the demands of burgeoning national economies in the Western world" (31). Finally, in the present period, we have what Lundgren terms the *'invisible'* curriculum code, one in which the explicit ideals and aspirations of earlier curriculum codes have become implicit, in which state control of education and curriculum development is sufficiently well advanced that the key value questions of education are now the responsibility of technologists of curriculum (curriculum developers in state education bureaucracies), leaving teachers and students with a curriculum whose values have been predigested, ...and where curricula appear, by contrast with curricula of former times, relatively value-neutral. (Kemmis, 1986, 31-32)

Pointing out that "it is not until the late nineteenth century that educational theorising began to take the form of modern curriculum theory," Kemmis highlights a crucial distinction of this new form:

> Whereas in the past, educational theorising concerned the *general relationships between education and society*, expressing views about the good for humankind, about the nature of the good society, and about the role of education in fostering both the good for persons and the good for society, in the late nineteenth century educational theorising became more specific and more detailed in its prescriptions for teachers and schools as it was harnessed to the needs of the modern industrial state. (36)

It is here that we recognize the intrusion of invisible state control, with its political, social and economic priorities, into the arena of education such that

> one group of emerging curriculum theories began to take for granted that the role of schooling was to produce a qualified labour force and to achieve the reproduction of society—reproduction in later generations of the values and forms of life and work which together characterized the economic, political and cultural patterns of the modern state (Lundgren, 35, quoted in Kemmis, 36)

What was lost in this reproductive process, according to Kemmis, was any understanding of "how open and philosophically unresolved these larger questions are" (36). For him, the result is that

> ...there are substantial conflicts over educational values, and in our century schooling has been harnessed in the service of totalitarian values as well as liberal ones. Not only in its totalitarian phases, but also, in more subtle ways, schooling has been both a means for the enlightenment and development of the individual and a means for achieving the purposes of the state. (37)

What Kemmis highlights is the *illusion* that we already have the answers to these 'larger questions,' or alternatively, the *assumption* that the questions themselves have been answered. Within that scenario, the intrusion of nationalist-triumphal state purposes as a controlling factor relative to the curriculum within educational institutions poses a danger to the space needed to develop civic-cultural dialogue and civic courage, for the nurturing of alternative imaginings of 'what could be.' This is especially troubling because the code itself is 'invisible,' and therefore masks the questions that might be raised by consideration of the practical, questions vital to the life of our society. Further, the stultifying effects of such a scenario within educational settings work to 'muzzle' attempts on the part of educators themselves to work through the 'larger questions' inherent in the 'practical turn.'

Given such a muzzling, what are practitioners to do? Kemmis finds his answer in "*ideology-critique*," a process deriving from "what Habermas calls critical social science" (73). Kemmis explains:

> Ideology-critique consists in undertaking enquiries whose aim is to 'map' our contemporary historical and social circumstances (either as a general analysis of society and culture or as a specific analysis of one's own local situation), ...and to use the process of mapping not only to identify the key landmarks and symbols in the social territory 'out there' (in the world around us) but also to identify the key landmarks and symbols in the way we understand the world (for example, in the language we use, our values, the significances we place on things, and the forms of social relationship and production through which we interact with the world). It looks both outward to illuminate the social world and 'inward' to illuminate the formation of our ways of seeing and being in the world—our consciousness. Because its subject matter is the relationship between these two orders of knowledge, the subject matter of critical social and educational science is *ideology*. [Emphasis in original] (73)

What Kemmis has described here is what I intend when I speak of the *within-beyond*, and a point of contact, I believe, between Kemmis' metatheoretical view of curriculum and Pinar's use of *autobiography*. I undertake ideology-critique here by mapping autobiographical discourse at the level of the nation in this contextual moment, using 'key landmarks and symbols' found within the intertextual field. The resulting map provides some highlights for our consideration that may not necessarily be self-evident, pointing to the potential of mapping to make the 'invisible' visible.

To approach ideology-critique, Kemmis employs Habermas' organization of social research forms based on 'knowledge-constitutive interests,' an organization that led Habermas to theorize three distinctive 'thought positions': the technical, the practical, and the emancipatory. The *technical* is based on "an interest in controlling and regulating objects (things); it is characteristically sought through empirical-analytic science" and "its products are scientific explanations of the causal type" (Kemmis, 71). The *practical* "is an interest in educating human understanding to inform human action; it is characteristically sought through the hermeneutic sciences" and "its products are interpretive accounts... of social life, and it frequently adopts the method of *verstehen* (the 'understanding method'...) which aims to illuminate the historical and social processes which frame the thought and action of actors..." (71). The *emancipatory*, in contrast, "is an interest in rational autonomy and freedom, emancipating people from false ideas, distorted forms of communication and coercive forms of social relationships which constrain human and social action" (72).

While the technical thought position has as its aim "the regulation and control of social action" and the practical thought position "aims to interpret the world for people," the emancipatory "aims to reveal the way social processes are distorted by power in social relationships of domination and coercion, and through the more 'invisible' operation of ideology" (72). Further, the emancipatory 'thought position'

> does not rest content with illuminating social relationships ...but aims to create conditions under which distorted existing relationships can be transformed by organised, collaborative action—a shared political struggle towards emancipation from irrationality and injustice... (72)

Based on these understandings, Kemmis outlines three distinct orientations to curriculum: '*vocational/neo-classical*,' '*liberal-progressive*,' and '*socially-critical*' orientations. These orientations, he claims, contend with one another in schooling.

He views the vocational/neo-classical orientation as dominant, arguing that

> It reflects and recreates a view of education as a preparation for work. It uses ability-grouping on the basis that the division of labour in society distinguishes meritocratically between workers, and the school plays an active part in meritocratic selection and allocation of opportunities. ...it recognizes endowment early, selects appropriately, and prepares students efficiently to participate in the society awaiting them beyond school. It is 'vocational' in the sense that it prepares students for work and that it aims to identify and develop a sense of vocation in students; it is 'neo-classical' in the sense that its view of education is based on the classical humanist tradition that the culture 'contains' certain worthwhile knowledge and skills which schools must transmit. (104)

The liberal-progressive orientation challenges the vocational/neo-classical conceptualization:

> It sees schooling as a preparation for life rather than for work. Its guiding image is of the student as a developing person. It sees education as the development of the 'whole person,' and rejects the instrumental view of school knowledge and work. It sees society as open to reconstruction, and aims to support the process of reconstruction through the development of morally-informed citizens. It aims to recognise and develop each child's sense of the true, good and beautiful. It takes an individualistic

view in its social philosophy and sees the development of autonomous persons and authentic action as the aim of education. It takes the view that society is in need of improvement, and believes that society will be improved by the right action of men and women of good will. (104)

Finally, Kemmis presents the socially-critical orientation, which "is less sanguine about the improvement of society *through education*" [emphasis mine] (105). For proponents of this view, the unequal (and I would argue, fragmented and diasporic) playing field makes it unlikely that education alone can improve society. Instead, Kemmis puts forth a vision of education in which change can only be achieved through emancipatory means:

> To educate students in such a society must be to *unmask* these social processes and to offer forms of social and political action which offer ways of understanding and struggling to overcome the social structuring of inequity. The first task of education is to assist students to develop the forms of critical enquiry which will enable them to understand how our society has come to have the structures it has... and on this foundation, to assist students to develop forms of action and reflection which enable them to participate in the struggle against irrationality, injustice and deprivation in society. To achieve this, the socially-critical school offers students projects which require the collaborative development of knowledge and discourse, democratic organisation and socially-useful tasks. It engages the wider community in the work of the school, and rejects the bureaucratic barriers which separate the life and work of the school from the life and work of the wider society. They involve students in reflection on society and in self-critical reflection on their own knowledge, ways of organising and action. [Emphasis mine] (105)

From this 'socially-critical' perspective, the 'invisible' ideology of the present is brought into the open for critique and for action. This is crucial if the state's control and manipulation of social imaginaries is to be broken, and ownership *and* imagination returned to those most intimately involved in the community of interest surrounding the schools, namely the *public*.[3] For Kemmis, it is equally important that educators "attempt to restore a sense of curriculum as *problematic*," and that this problematization occurs "in the context of a particular contemporary debate among teachers, school communities, and in society generally" (106).

One crucial part of the picture for us to consider, Kemmis asserts, is the extent to which the educational system is 'reified' (81). This 'imaginary' is a feature that complicates the process of theorizing the terrain itself, and cannot be ignored. Kemmis argues that our current state systems of schooling, with their extended bureaucracies, serve to rob teachers (and others connected with the work of schools) of 'local control.' The system itself looms larger than life, its requirements "are so extensive and so pervasive" (81), that we come to take the system itself for granted, replacing (again, in an imaginary sense) real actors and real problems that might emerge, given space and voice:

> It is reified as 'the system'; it is no longer understood in terms of human relationships affecting those who participate in the educational process but as an entity—a large, impersonal organization, composed of rules, procedures, authority structures and characteristic patterns of operation; it is regarded by participants as real... This reification of 'the system' permits and encourages its participants to believe that it exists as a real, controlling entity, with its own agency and power, and to forget... that the system is in fact constituted by their own work within the system and by their own socially-negotiated agreement to adopt its characteristic patterns of relationship and interaction. (81)

Once the system is "reified," Kemmis tells us, "its participants accept the assumptions and values" it presents as "natural," so that working within the system means taking "these values and assumptions for granted—as part of the 'contract' of agreeing to work in it" (81). Kemmis therefore offers that

> While practical curriculum theorising has traditionally been concerned with formulating answers to the central curriculum question 'What is the role of education in society?', and providing answers to this question in the form of practicable curriculum proposals, technical curriculum theorising has taken its answer to this question as *given by the state*... [Emphasis mine] (85)

This is problematic because the prevalence of the technical approach, in my view, may represent the death of ideas—of *imagination*—as these give way to the will of technicians reflecting the will of the state. The crisis confronting us, the real danger, may be the loss of imaginative capacity—a capacity informed only with the acquisition of knowledge, awareness, understanding, and openness to critical questioning and creative activity, all of which depend upon a healthy public sphere, which includes our schools. It is a loss that the nation should not countenance, given our need for new possibilities, and therefore, for renewed 'hope to fight' (Freire, 1970, 80) for a better future. The problem with silencing critique and 'muting' dissent (other than the obvious moral-political dilemma this poses for a democracy) is the loss of voice that costs us much-needed vision for new solutions to our many problems. This has special implications for institutes of 'higher learning,' as Kemmis notes:

> Once schools became instruments for the reproduction of social, political and economic life in the state, harnessed and regulated by the state, certain educational values were put at risk. In universities the value of academic freedom is sometimes invoked to sustain the independent right of universities and university researchers to pursue truth, no matter how unpopular or politically subversive the enquiries may

seem. (Note, however, that Sharp, 1985, argues that the onward march of technical rationality is rapidly placing the independent status of universities at risk) (84-85)

Kemmis makes a clear distinction, however, between universities as sites of knowledge production where academic freedom is still protected, and K-12 schooling, which faces dilemmas based on a history of state control:

> Schools have not traditionally enjoyed this freedom. Research into whether schools actually deny certain educational values (like rationality and truth) under the influence of the state, especially if such research is conducted by schools and teachers (rather than university academics) is therefore likely to be controversial. Examining the political theories which underlie contemporary schooling is likely to be disquieting to some. Yet, contemporary schools clearly embody and explicitly teach social and political values, they function to reproduce certain aspects of social, political and economic life in society, and, in adopting roles assigned to them by the state, they adopt theories of politics and social change legitimated by the state. (85)

Kemmis' view of this socialization—reflecting the adoption by our young of "theories of politics and social change legitimated by the state" (85)—is made even more problematic where the state has gone awry, has become ideological, self-interested, has abandoned its obligations to the people it is meant to serve, or is a fraudulent cover for anarchy. This poses the problem I began with in this work, the failure of the state itself and, as importantly, of the public to respond to such events (see Prologue). The fact that the state has become unreliable (and now, increasingly, unpredictable) is therefore highly salient, but so is the condition of the public. In a democratic society (if we are to become one), it is absolutely necessary that 'theories of politics and social change' are neither legitimated nor dictated solely by the state, and in America perhaps more than anywhere else, diversity *is* our wealth and our heritage, however troubled the waters of difference may have been, or may continue to be. The struggle for emancipation must have some recourse against a false consensus, or a false consciousness, to use Kemmis' terms, instituted and enforced by the state. Therefore I turn first to Greene's (1978) 'landscapes of learning' and her (1986) advocacy of critical pedagogy to engender a quest for new meanings as alternatives to the 'given,' and then to Pinar's (2004) case for autobiography as revolutionary act, that is, as a means for this process to occur.

Maxine Greene: Landscapes of Learning and Critical Pedagogy

> The image of self we have inherited was defined in the 18th century, at a moment of high optimism and faith in human rationality. The American ("that New Man," as de Crevecoeur called him) was described as indeed "noble in reason," much like the Renaissance man. Moreover, he was thought to be distinctively self-

> determining and almost infinitely perfectible. Even today that delineation possesses a concreteness, as if it referred to something objectively real, an actual personality. There is a sense in which Americans are loath to question its validity, in spite of all their present experiences of personal diminution and their doubts about their effectuality. (Greene, 1978, 7)

In *Landscapes of Learning* (1978), Greene situates her discussion of critical pedagogy within the realm of an American sense of self, a sense that she believes 'possesses a concreteness' that derives from 18th century thought. She contrasts this sense of the American as "that New Man," one who is exceptional and 'perfectible,' with a modern sense of the American as a disempowered being:

> ...people are experiencing themselves being worked on by forces as invisible as they are impersonal—red dyes in food, asbestos in the workplace, listening devices on the telephone, behavior modification in the school; phenomena of this sort are constantly being (*ex post facto*) disclosed. People struggle to cope with official agencies, with the telephone company, or with the justice system. They confront bureaucracy wherever they turn, "a form of dominion," Hannah Arendt said, characterized by "rule by Nobody." No one takes responsibility; yet individuals feel that their rights and liberties are being eroded by people more adept, efficient, and powerful than they can ever be. And, in a mysterious way, all this seems linked to science as much as to ubiquitous technique. (Greene, 1978, 10)

Greene (1978, 1988, 1995) consistently focuses on mindlessness, numbness, and meaninglessness, offering that transcendent meaning(s) constructed both by individuals and groups of persons in their intersubjective interactions, can give new meaning to the quest when it is conducted at the level of the *collective*. What I read as the 'paralysis' of the public in the post-9/11 social moment has, in fact, a history that precedes this moment by decades. The impacts of social forces related to the late stages of modernity have been contributing to public dismay for some time now, and some of these impacts have become so familiar to us in our daily lives, have become so much a part of the 'taken for granted,' that one might think that they require no further elaboration. Greene (1978) offers that "even for the relatively uninformed, there is a lived experience of what Jacques Ellul calls 'encirclement' by impersonal technique" (9).

Greene, of course, argues that elaboration is precisely what is needed, since naming 'the wall' (Hughes, 1968, cited in Greene, 1988, 88) that stands between us and our dreams of a better way of being-in-the-world, of better possibilities yet to be imagined, is a necessary step on the road to 'wide-awakeness' (1978, 153). Nevertheless, Ellul's (1967) notion of 'encirclement' rings true not only for our struggles in daily life, but more particularly for those laboring in the fields of education, as the technical *consumes* the space of the practical and the emancipatory:

> No technician anywhere would say that he is submitting men, collectively or individually, to technique. ... The individual is broken into a number of independent fragments, and no two techniques have the same dimensions or depth, not does any combination of techniques (for example, propaganda plus vocational guidance) correspond to any part of the human being. The result is that every technique can assert its innocence. Where, then, or by whom, is the human individual being attacked? Nowhere and by no one. Such is the reply of technique and technicians. (Ellul, 1967, cited in Greene, 1978, 9-10)

This notion of being attacked "no where and by no one" speaks to the invisibility of the code, but also of fragmentation and, ultimately, of disintegration of order. Greene's concern for praxis, for action that can make a difference is evident, and she cites Dewey for support:

> More then half a century ago, Dewey talked about the tendency to build castles in the air when energies are "checked by uncongenial surroundings." When people construct imaginary worlds, they often allow them to "substitute for an actual achievement which involved the pains of thought." He went on to discuss the split between mind and conduct and the ways in which this can characterize an entire social situation. There are times, he said, when the social situation throws those normally given to reflection back "into their own thoughts and desires without providing the means by which these ideas and aspirations can be used to reorganize the environment." (Greene, 1978, 13)

This concern for imagination as abnegation, as withdrawal from thought leading to withdrawal from action, leads her to a concern for heightened interiority manifesting in cynicism:

> Under such condition, men take revenge... upon the alien and hostile environment by cultivating contempt for it, by giving it a bad name. They seek refuge and consolation within their own states of mind, their own imaginings and wishes, which they compliment by calling both more real and more ideal than the despised outer world. (Dewey, cited in Greene, 1978, 13)

This notion of 'the despised outer world' presents an avenue that needs further exploration, posing an interesting entryway for thinking about the clash between *Jihad* and *McWorld*, and about *American Jihad* as well, a term Barber (2001) uses to characterize the fundamentalist-conservative movement here at home. For Greene, this problem must be addressed if we are to experience freedom in a positive, constructive sense. There is an in-between in play here, the meeting place between the *within* and the *beyond*, which becomes a site of struggle:

> In the United States today, we know what it is to feel dominated and constrained. We have to struggle for our emancipation; some of us are familiar with the feeling of a chain in the mouth. But the problems will not be solved by the invention of new either/ors, by forced choosing between the outer and the inner. No one's self is ready-made; each of us has to create a self by choice of action, action in the world. Such action, if it is to be meaningful, must be informed by critical reflection, because the one who is submerged, who cannot see, is likely to be caught in *stasis*, unable to move. But the kinds of choices that are necessary can only be made when there are openings, when appropriate social conditions exist. So the matter of the diminution of self is two-pronged: it demands reflective thinking on the part of individuals, and it demands social change. Even as we think about dignity and transcendence, therefore, we need to think of human *praxis*, or the kind of knowing that surpasses and transforms, that makes a difference in reality. (Greene, 1978, 18)

For Greene, this delicate balance between development and enrichment of the individual, on the one hand, and intersubjective interaction to achieve the 'possibility of freedom' collectively, on the other, reflects the importance of the public sphere:

> It seems eminently clear that the freedom of wide-awakeness has to be expressed in intentional action of some kind. ... The possibility of freedom has always to be acted upon; it is grounded in our being what we are and not mere imitators of each other, and so it has continually to be achieved. This cannot happen in a vacuum. Situations must exist or be created that will permit the release of individual capacities, that will permit persons to identify themselves. To identify the self is, in a sense, to understand one's preferences; to understand them is to be able to reflect upon them in the light of some standard, some set of values, some norm. ... One has to be with others actively, reflectively, at least some of the time, in a space one knows is a shared space, and one has to care. (Greene, 1978, 153)

Greene's (1986) search for a critical pedagogy reflects frustration with "blankness" and "a nameless inertial mass" (427). She seeks "the sources of questioning, of restlessness' as she expresses an increasing desire for "traces of utopian visions, of critical or dialectical engagements with social and economic realities" (427). She describes what she sees as "an administered and media-mystified world," where

> we try to reconceive what a critical pedagogy relevant to this time and place ought to mean. This is a moment when great numbers of Americans find their expectations and hopes for their children being fed by talk of "educational reform." Yet the reform reports speak of those very children as "human resources" for the expansion of productivity, as means to the end of maintaining our nation's economic competitiveness

and military primacy in the world. ...the world we inhabit is palpably deficient: there are unwarranted inequities, shattered communities, unfulfilled lives. (427)

The weight we live under, as Greene sees it, poses a problem for those seeking to create space for emancipatory struggle in American education as they 'face off' against this 'administered and media-mystified world,' signalling an erosion of the public sphere. And yet, as we have seen, this sphere is not eroded for *all*—the autobiography mapped in this text lends credence to our understanding that there *is* yet something to be said. Those contributing their voices to this autobiographical text 'bear witness' to the silence, but demonstrate the civic courage needed to move through it, to *refuse* its forcefulness.

The conceptual mapping I have articulated here signals that ranges of attitudes and perspectives within this 'inertial mass' do exist, that there are different ways of being American and different modes of envisioning and expressing our civic-cultural struggle. This is not, to be sure, an extraordinary finding, but it does reveal aspects of our national will, character and desire—features of our nation as an imagined community—that may serve to further both humanist illumination *and* critical pedagogy. My concern is for the curricular contours within this autobiographical project and how they might serve to illuminate a curriculum of possibility that takes into account our civic-cultural struggles in past and present context to shed light on future possibilities. Here illumination might pave the pathway for emancipatory praxis, for the work of resuscitating democratic aspiration. This is, after all, one trajectory of civic courage in the face of adversity.

Greene (1986) considers the origins of the American public sphere, framing it in terms of a *disruption* of what William Blake referred to as "mind-forg'd manacles":

> The American tradition originated ...in the critical atmosphere specific to the European Enlightenment. It was an atmosphere created in large measure by rational, autonomous voices engaging in dialogue for the sake of bringing into being a public sphere. These were, most often, the voices of an emerging middle class concerned for their own independence from anachronistic and unjust restraints. Their "rights" were being trampled, they asserted, rights sanctioned by natural and moral laws. ...Liberty, at the time of the founding of our nation, meant liberation from interference by the state, church, or army in the lives of individuals. For some ...liberty also meant each person's right to think for himself or herself, "to follow his intellect to whatever conclusions it may lead" in an atmosphere that forbade "mental slavery." (430)

Greene speaks here of an important heritage; indeed, it is the heritage of my home and hearth. But although this heritage may hold for those who take their sense of the nation from the space of *Reason* and *Representation*, a space that Greene sees as the rationale underlying the republic, other frameworks exist as well, as we have seen.

There are, for instance, those who hold onto *Orthodoxy* as the central rationale for the nation, and this is increasingly problematic as the so-called right-wing (and those in power, who have found right-wing rhetoric useful for their own purposes) promulgates a 'new' theocratic nationalism as a distinctly American identity and agenda for our times (see, e.g., Hedges, 2006; Phillips, 2007; Taylor, 2005). As we have seen, this goes hand in hand with the triumphal narrative that some are so fond of hailing as our remembered/forgotten heritage. There are those who simultaneously hold on to other kinds of attachments from whatever *Perspective* they may adhere to. For instance, for the globalist, the nation itself plays the role of *citizen* in a global world, while others cling to, or maneuver around and through a diasporic public sphere where their sense of America is conjoined with their own fond (and sometimes romanticized) remembering/forgetting of a prior homeland. We see citizen behaviors moving in any of a number of directions: *sanctioning* government policy and practice based on their desire for *control*; debating *legitimacy* on an ad hoc basis to affect *representation*; or working for *empowerment* through collective *activism* to advance or oppose particular policies or practices. Such is the life, the struggle, the *imagining* of America as nation.

Greene's (1986) account of the search for a critical pedagogy also entails looking at issues of power, and for this she moves to a consideration of Arendt's work:

> The founders were calling, through a distinctive critical challenge, for opportunities to give their energies free play. That meant the unhindered exercise of their particular talents... To be able to do so, they had to secure power, which they confirmed through the establishment of a constitutional republic. For Hannah Arendt, this sort of power is kept in existence through an ongoing process of "binding and promising, combining and covenanting." As she saw it, power springs up between human beings when they act to constitute "a worldly structure to house... their combined power of action." When we consider the numbers of people excluded from this process over the generations, we have to regard this view of power as normative as well. It is usual to affirm that power belongs to "the people" at large; but, knowing that this has not been the case, we are obligated to expand the "worldly structure" until it contains the "combined power" of increasing numbers of articulate persons. A critical pedagogy for Americans, it would seem, must take this into account. (430-431)

Acting to compose or create 'a worldly structure' through which citizens might put their 'combined power of action' to good use lies at the root of many of these cultures of citizenship, and yet for some, neither power nor action are desired; neither, in fact, is sought. I might argue that this civic-cultural lethargy is artificially induced—i.e., that "in an administered and media-mystified world" human agency appears to dissolve (Greene, 1986, 427). Alternatively, I might argue that this is simply a fact of human nature—that is, that we are *not* all interested in, or engaged with, the betterment of self, nation, or world. Our *voyeurist* culture of citizenship, for instance, is a space of weakness that exhibits indifference, ignorance, resignation, acquiescence, etc., confirming concerns about the emergence of a Huxleyan world, or, as Postman (1985) put it, a scenario where we are 'amusing ourselves to death.' Regardless, we who teach in the public eye don't have the luxury of ignoring the ramifications of what we do and how we do it. Further, we have an aggressive faction of (self-?) interested 'officials' operating as public education critics and policing teacher work in public educational institutions as though we were the enemy, as though we were the 'problem' with American society.

I have chosen a framing that borrows from social epistemology—and its focus on studying speech as the 'effects of power' (Popkewitz and Brennan, 1998, 9)—coupled with a mapping of social imaginaries to approach and attend to the 'epistemological unconscious' (Bourdieu, 1992, 47) of our society in these times in terms of civic-cultural struggle. What has resulted is a discursively derived cultural portrait of the contextual moment, an autobiography of post-9/11 America, the new American wilderness. Recalling Blacker (1998), I have worked from a 'worm's-eye view' to theorize aspects of the surround that might help to inform curriculum theorizing in such a way as to avoid positioning myself 'above the fray.'

Nevertheless, the issue of power is not negligible. I have simply worked to avoid positioning myself within a theoretical avant-garde, per Bourdieu (1992). In short, I have attempted to work here within the constraints of a self-imposed 'theoretical modesty' (Blacker, 1998, 357). That does not mean, however, that I am either ignorant of or indifferent to the moral-political aspects of what I do and how I see. Illumination is no more welcome in a culture constrained by orthodoxy and control than is emancipation, and I work here to integrate the two—as I 'slither horizontally' between them—in order to synthesize a space of disruption for this very reason: namely, because the art of mapping, while a non-innocent political strategy, is also an illuminative tool which may be used for emancipatory purposes when, for instance, it is linked to the autobiographical project as a 'revolutionary act' (Pinar, 2004).

Greene speaks of an emancipatory discourse that can open space for critical pedagogy, a pedagogy that doesn't ignore power, but finds a way to resist it, stretching towards *humanization* (Freire, 1970, 1998):

> We cannot negate the fact of power. But we can undertake a resistance, a reaching out towards becoming *persons* among other persons, for all the talk of human resources, for all the orienting of education to the economy. To engage with our students as persons is to affirm our own incompleteness, our consciousness of spaces still to be explored, desires still to be tapped, possibilities still to be opened and pursued. ...We have to find out how to open such spheres, such spaces, where a better state of things can be imagined; because it is only through the projection of a better social order that we can perceive the gaps in what exists and try to transform and repair. (Greene, 1986, 440-441)

Greene's sentiments are echoed in Pinar (2004), who restores the within-beyond to a space that is simultaneously private and public, collapsing the split to heal the wound inflicted on the psyche:

> Curriculum theory asks you... to consider your position as engaged with yourself and your students and colleagues in the construction of a public sphere, a public sphere not yet born, a future that cannot be discerned in, or even thought from, the present. So conceived, the classroom becomes simultaneously a civic square and a room of one's own. (37-38)

Bringing her focus to formal education, Greene (1986) expresses similar hopes for humanization in her search for a critical pedagogy—desires that are close to my heart as well:

> I would like to think of teachers moving the young into their own interpretations of their lives and their lived worlds, opening wider and wider perspectives as they do so. I would like to see teachers ardent in their efforts to make the range of symbol systems available to the young for the ordering of experience, even as they maintain regard for their vernaculars. I would like to see teachers tapping the spectrum of intelligences, encouraging multiple readings of written texts and readings of the world. (431)

What Greene is advocating here is a 'hermeneutic of imagination' that can 'make the range of symbol systems available,' and I bore this in mind in this curriculum inquiry project. Her call to open space for exploring 'wider and wider perspectives' in quest of a greater range of understandings resonates with my own desires as a scholar-practitioner and as a mapper. She advocates an engagement with new social imaginaries deriving from learners' lived experiences and common life-worlds, and a pedagogy based on imagination as socio-cultural practice that could re-structure, re-invent and rebuild new, more expansive "world structures" than those we tolerate and suffer at present.

Her spirit *is* the spirit of civic courage, as she shows us what it might mean to take such a forward step:

In "the shadow of silent majorities," then, as teachers learning along with those we try to provoke to learn, we may be able to inspire hitherto unheard voices. We may be able to empower people to rediscover their own memories and articulate them in the presence of others, whose space they can share. Such a project demands the capacity to unveil and disclose. It demands the exercise of imagination, enlivened by works of art, by situations of speaking and making. Perhaps we can at last devise reflective communities in the interstices of colleges and schools. Perhaps we can invent ways of freeing people to feel and express indignation, to break through the opaqueness, *to refuse the silences*. We need to teach in such a way as to arouse passion now and then; we need a new camaraderie, a new en masse. These are dark and shadowed times, and we need to live them, standing before one another, open to the world. [Emphasis mine] (1986, 441)

Although this piece was written in 1986, it speaks to us as well today, perhaps with a more urgent voice than ever before. Once again, we face the silence. Once again, we must find voice to speak, 'standing before one another, open to the world,' no matter how horrific the view. In doing so, we will open space for a currere for tomorrow's world that our young can appropriate and transform on their own terms. That space must be a portal for democracy, because 'tomorrow's world' is no utopia. It will yet be, regrettably, a world laden with fear, with anxiety, with deprivation and loss, with confusion, and with the terror of our difference from those who appear or pretend to speak with the 'one true voice,' and we must speak against it, regardless of what power they might wield or what terror they might inflict. This will require a kind of civic courage we have not yet begun to imagine, let alone to muster. I have begun, then, by showing how this autobiographical text is situated in a surround that fosters, sustains, and/or enforces this silence, while at the same time making space to include other articulations of what might be, and I turn my attention therefore to Pinar's (2004) sense of autobiography as a revolutionary act.

William F. Pinar: Autobiography as a Revolutionary Act

In Pinar's (2004), *What Is Curriculum Theory?*, we encounter the following:

> Indirect autobiography—an autobiography of alterity (Gilmore 1994)—subjectifies intellectually the process of social psychoanalysis. The official story a nation or culture tells itself—often evident in school curriculum—hides other truths. The national story also creates the illusion of truth being on the social surface, when it is nearly axiomatic that the stories we tell ourselves mask other, unacceptable truths. What we as a nation try not to remember—genocide, slavery, lynching, prison rape—structures the politics of our collective identification and imagined affiliation. The pretensions of the Founding Fathers and their colleagues were not only pretensions; they were, as well, aspirations. (38)

It is these 'unacceptable truths,' those things we try *not* to remember (and therefore do not teach), those that lie beneath 'the social surface' that need to be faced in order to restructure 'our collective identification and imagined affiliation.' Without acknowledgment of past failings, how could we possibly move towards greater democratic aspirations? Pinar constructs a pathway between currere and social reconstruction:

> The method of currere... provides a strategy for students of curriculum to study the relations between academic knowledge and life history in the interest of self-understanding and social reconstruction. (35)

Pinar asserts that in this process that weds self-understanding to social reconstruction, "*currere* becomes a version of cultural criticism" (36) and that cultural criticism is always a product of the perceptual space from which it is spoken:

> "Cultural criticism," Christopher Lasch (1978, 16) notes, "... at its best showed that the attempt to understand culture has to include the way it shapes the critic's own consciousness." (36)

Pinar, far from advocating currere as an approach to curriculum theory that is narcisstic or solipsistic, sees autobiography as a project always in the making relative to a 'collective,' since our perceptual space is formed through our interrelations with others:

> In contrast to psychologistic conceptions of self-knowledge, what Boler (1999, 178) terms "collective witnessing is always understood in relation to others, and in relation to personal and cultural histories and material conditions." ...self-knowledge and collective witnessing are complementary projects of self-mobilization for social reconstruction. (37)

Pinar speaks in soothing tones of the healing this reunion can bring, of the *possibility* of being 'open to the world,' even in these "dark and shadowed times" (Greene, 1986, 441):

> When autobiography is understood phenomenologically, "distancing" and "reconstituting" need not be, strictly speaking, compensatory. These gerunds can also refer to the process of excavation, and to the architectural rebuilding of a self, with materials previously excluded (now excavated), a self more spacious, more inviting, especially to "others," like women, children, African Americans, who become, now, no longer "others" and no longer invisible. (Pinar, 2004, 51)

Finally, he speaks of the unmasking—an unmasking that can set us free from the past once we have confronted and rebuked the masking, and returned to ourselves as transformed beings, our aspirations remembered and revived, the 'wall' (Hughes, 1968, cited in Greene, 1988, 88) 'torn down.' Here is a portal worth entering:

> The progressive phrase [sic] of *currere* may be understood as a kind of free-associative "futuring" during which one seeks the revelation of one's fantasies of what one might be. These imaginings are expressions of who one is not now, of material felt to be missing, sought after, aspired to. The possibility in this phase... is to discern how who one is hides what one might become. These fictive representations of who I might be, what world I might inhabit in the future, these fictional versions of who I might be someday but am not now allow us to feel our way through the obscurity of the present. They are the means by which we midwife what is not yet born, in ourselves, generated by others. They change where we are, how we feel, what we think; they become... discursive passages, what Rorty calls a "vocabulary" by means of which we move into new lived space. We become different selves, and in so doing, we become different in the world that itself becomes transformed by our presence there. (55-56)

What Pinar articulates here is a quest to consciously and articulately enter the space of this 'new obscurity' (Habermas, 1985, cited in Beck, 1992, 190) and to effectuate self in the meeting-place between the within and the beyond, in a place where 'the civic square' and a 'room of one's own' meet and intertwine.

A Word about Educating for Democracy

A growing advocacy movement supporting 'educating for democracy' (Campaign for the Civic Mission of Schools, 2004)—has called attention to a growing sense of the need to prepare our young to take their places in the civil polity (Boston, 2005). Concern for the preservation of democracy 'through education' is strong, and it is a hopeful sign that such movements are coalescing into a full-throated cry for the needs of a democratic polity in our times, but a multitude of questions remain, as noted (see Prologue) about the meaning(s) of such a call.

Westheimer and Kahne (2004), for instance, studied ten educational programs in the U.S. "that aimed to advance the democratic purposes of education" (237) and derived a typology to answer the question: "What kind of citizen?" they might be generating. The authors reported three types of citizen promoted by these programs: the 'personally responsible,' the 'participatory,' and the 'justice oriented' (238). They found that the 'personally responsible' approach could as easily serve the needs of a totalitarian state as those of a democracy (244). Students experiencing a 'participatory' orientation "tended to downplay or ignore explicitly political or historically contentious issues" and were unable "to talk about how varied interests and power relationships or issues of race and social class might be related to the lack of consensus on priorities and the inability of varied groups to work effectively together" (261). The authors state that

> the narrow and often ideologically conservative conception of citizenship embedded in many current efforts at teaching for democracy reflects neither arbitrary choices nor pedagogical limitations but, rather, political choices that have political consequences. (237)

Because 'democracy' has become a 'master term' with multiple meanings and interpretations (Appadurai, 1996, 37), considering the politics of the call to 'educate for democracy' is warranted. Rather than focusing on these particular types of citizen, I offer that it might be useful to begin with the 'collective witnessing' (Boler, 1999, cited in Pinar, 2004, 37) offered by American voices in this moment, the autobiography of a nation in distress. This may be useful as a means for bypassing the ideologies of citizenship depicted in Westheimer and Kahne's study.

Increasingly, other realms of discourse raise equally pertinent issues vis-à-vis the category of the civic, each of them worthy of study, each bearing significantly on the complexity of the category of the civic and on the need for cultural exchange and understanding, as well as broadened gestalts of belonging. There are, for example, the following to consider: Banks' (2004) concern that "students develop thoughtful and reflective cultural, national, and global identifications and attachments" (1), expanding the category of the civic appreciably; Castles' (2004) concern that they "be educated in ways that will enable them to function effectively in multiple communities" (1); and Ong's (2004) concern with the tension between "the production of a democratic citizenry and the production of neoliberal subjects" in U.S. higher education (2). Carson (2006), on the other hand, is concerned with "the fragmented curriculum" of citizenship and questions whether it produces a citizen who is "a lonely and self-interested individual, one who is... likely resentful of the demands of community" (26). Pinar (2006b) argues that "the very category of the civic is saturated with the sexual and the racialized" (103) as he seeks to unmask 'unacceptable truths' (2004, 38). Smith (2006) urges that "global citizenship must come to terms with... one nation-state being determined to control the terms of citizenship itself" (131) in his concern for 'a time of great untruths.'

Scholarly discourse attending to the category of the civic as a cultural issue is growing exponentially. I have confined my focus here to ways of seeing the civic-cultural surround in terms of the autobiographical propensities we must face and acknowledge if we are to move towards a democratic future, but the need for careful consideration of effects of the dispersion of meanings within the realm of civic-cultural struggle at the global level—effects on the category of the 'civic'—remains. This is work I will continue to pursue in the future.

10

Epilogue

As I ponder what has happened under the rule of the current powers-that-be (both as prior problematic policies have been continued and as new policies stand in stark contrast to any known in recent history), I am, like many others, left floundering for hope. Nevertheless, I place my hope in public imagination as it is moved by a revival of 'democracy talk,' offering that democracy itself rests on some basic civil and civic assumptions, the highest of which, to me, is aspiring to a condition such that *all citizens* are assisted in enlisting freedom as their ally—regardless of race, ethnicity, class, gender or gender identity, religious or non-religious proclivities, or any of the many other facets of our existence as human, cultural beings—in their quest for positive human self-realization so perfectly captured in the guarantee of "life, liberty, and the pursuit of happiness." This must now be *envisioned* and *enacted* to become, once again, a way of being-in-the-world for us as we learn to *live* democracy in our own interactions with others (Henderson and Kesson, 2004). Yet we struggle within an authoritarian social order where power has unfettered social, cultural, political and economic control, and we do so within the complications of a risk society paradigm in an era of uncertainty.

My primary intent here has been to elicit from an autobiographic framing of public discourses what our vistas of the nation, our autobiography of being and becoming, might teach us about a curriculum of possibility for democratic aspirations. I lean towards believing that our proper understanding of ourselves—and of our differences—would be better celebrated and would lead to less strife if we could see ourselves as species beings who have in common, above all else, planetary belonging and the need to acknowledge interdependence to survive. Learning to work across differences in the face of staggering challenges is, to me, just good old-fashioned common sense, but it is obstructed by the politics of resentment (Bourdieu, 1992).

This stance places me in the *globalist* culture of citizenship. It is also congruent with an adaptive neo-postmodern orientation that seeks to celebrate difference while embracing the notion that each of us individually and all of us together need to work creatively and responsibly to work to settle conflicts that readily attach themselves to (and are attracted by) ideologies. Ideology-critique (Kemmis, 1986), as noted (see Chapter 9), is one way to expose the dynamics of the civic-cultural surround within which such a dialogue may play out. What we need are spaces to speak, and these are spaces we must create for ourselves and with others (Miller, 1990, cited in Pinar et al., 1995) wherever we may find opportunity.

My secondary intent here has been to focus on the events in our times that put an authoritarian stamp on the triumphal narrative of the nation (and its hypernational forward guard), and that reveal the inner workings of a theory that may well take us down the road that leads to fascism, while exploring features of the contextual moment that reveal how such a thing might occur. I therefore briefly share some thoughts from work that I am currently exploring.

A Theory of Authoritarian Government and Christian Nationalism

Sovereign is he who decides on the exception. (Schmitt, 2005, 5)

I remember laughing out loud when I first watched Jon Stewart's (Comedy Central, *The Daily Show*) parody of President George W. Bush's claim: "I'm the decider." It wasn't just because Jon was working out a pretty good (and funny) imitation of the president himself, but because Stewart humorously held that claim up for public scrutiny without the melodrama that might have preceded such action in the mainstream media, had they been astute enough to grasp its importance. It became obvious, over time, however, that the full meaning of this claim had not made itself apparent to me either, and that mistaking it for simple hubris was naive. I now believe, in fact, that it may have been a statement of political faith. As I studied the many troubling facets of this administration's maneuvering, manipulation, and aggrandizement of power, I realized that while George W. Bush's public discourse was carefully crafted to present him as a homey American folk hero (Bumiller, 2002), his position statements represented very real clues to political convictions (doctrines, actually) that contained much deeper and more sinister undertones. This is an issue that cannot be ignored, especially since the doctrines underlying our presumed leadership's selling of their triumphal narrative align with the work of theorists, philosophers, and professors in the field of jurisprudence whose political theology is implicated in the ascension to power of the Nazi regime in Germany in the 1930s. What I am suggesting is that the powers that be charted a course without regard for the shape of its actual destination and without any apparent ethical concern about the means being used, ignoring (or perhaps exploiting?) history. Perhaps this alignment is the reason for the political culture shock the nation's concerned citizens have been enduring over these past eight years. However, even as I observe and consider what can be understood about our present state of affairs, even as I consider whether a totalitarian ideology has been applied in post-9/11 America and share the apprehension that has resulted, I am haunted by Deleuze's remarks in "Intellectuals and Power," a conversation between Michel Foucault and Gilles Deleuze (Foucault, 1977):

> I would venture the following hypothesis: the thrust of Marxism was to define the problem essentially in terms of interests (power is held by a ruling class defined by its interests). The question immediately arises: how is it that people whose interests are not being served can strictly support the existing power structure by demanding a piece of the action? Perhaps, this is because in terms of *investments*, whether economic or unconscious, interest is not the final answer; there are investments of desire that function in a more profound and diffuse manner than our interests dictate. But of course, we never desire against our interests, because interest always follows and finds itself where desire has placed it. We cannot shut out the scream of Reich: the masses were not deceived; at a particular time, they actually wanted a fascist regime! (214-215)

I am disturbed as I am reminded that the locus of real fascism (not the kind we like to imagine and use as epithets to hurl at our adversaries) is not just the elites who grab power and discard ethics to attain their satisfactions, but a totalitarian movement that draws its strength from 'the people' (Arendt, 1968). Moreover, I am deeply distressed by the re-emergence of the threat of this tendency of the public in our times. The issue of a fascistic trend underlies the intent of this autobiography, which is to open space to diverse visions and understandings of America as a means to decenter one particular enunciation of 'Truth' for the nation, and thereby to resist its enforcement. Livingston (2004) refers to 'the fascism of modernity's truth fetishes,' and has this to say about the importance of cultural practices:

> Gilles Deleuze and Felix Guattari made the claim that what most people really want is fascism (Deleuze and Guattari, 1989). Their definition of fascism is not confined only to the workings of government. Rather, fascism, explicated in a broader sense, means a positivistic imposition of truths into discourse through hegemonic cultural formations. These truths are manifested in everyday discourse as binary relations such as god/man, nature/culture, mind/soul, conscious/unconscious, and so on. According to Foucault, these truths become reified in the social structure through continuous repetition of cultural practices. These historically reified cultural practices appear to be real to those invested in that particular social discourse. In this way, fascism comes to mean structuralism (Deleuze and Guattari, 1989). (37)

The use of repetition, which pundits call 'staying on message,' is a political-rhetorical feature of our times. The use of repetition to lie, to make the untrue true by virtue of repeating the same deceptions over and over, without conscience, until all that rings in the ear is the lie, is another matter. In a very real sense, what this accomplishes is to give structure and strength, reality and veracity, to useful fictions, and, as Schmitt said, "Sovereign is he who decides the exception" (2005, 5). This, too, is a sign of our times, and this is a sign that must be confronted.

I want to briefly visit as well a less blatantly sinister (albeit equally troubling) scenario. The power grab of this cultural clique may well have another side to it, one less odious perhaps, but equally effectual and offensive in that it also circumvents democratic principles and processes. What if all that triumphal discourse was not a matter of political theology, but rather a market approach to re-conceptualizing a nation in such a way that it stands apart as a new kind of America, a new *brand* for the nation? James B. Twitchell (2004), in *Branded Nation: The Marketing of Megachurch, College Inc., and Museumworld*, addresses the idea that our identities, especially cultural identities, are actually the products of branding:

> Much of our shared knowledge about ourselves and our culture comes to us through a commercial process of storytelling called *branding*. The process starts early. A marketing professor estimates that 10 percent of a two-year-old's nouns are brand names. ...There is no need to recite the dreary litany about how the Marlboro Man is better known than George Washington; how more people recognize the golden arches than recognize the Red Cross; how Mickey Mouse, Coke, or Tom Cruise are part of the With-It! Nation, while the United Nations, elective democracy, or the Peace Corps are part of the Huh? Nation. And no need to mention how American foreign policy and politics have been hijacked by brand meisters. We all know that. (2)

Twitchell moves quickly to the site of institutions themselves to show just how pervasive this phenomenon has become:

> As well, we now appreciate that institutions that were always thought "above" market pressures, such as the law, have been deeply affected. As Richard Sherwin has shown... the goal of modern mega-tele-trials... is to make the case fit a compelling story, branding it as melodrama, mystery, heroic suspense. Gerry Spence, renowned defense attorney, has said as much: winning is just a matter of "finding the right story." (2)

In a world where almost everything is pre-packaged and marketed in some way, is nothing authentic? Is nothing sacred? What about our cultural values, beliefs, identities? What about our sense(s) of ourselves as a nation? His response is enlightening, to say the least, as it frames the reach of the impacts of popular culture—which may be framed as a manufactured product—into our lives as citizens:

> But what we may not appreciate is that the most successful recent branding exercise has had to do with how *high* culture is currently being created and shared. Branding in the nineteenth century became the meaning-making motor of consumerism, the key to concentrating the consuming desires of almost every human in the West toward manufactured items. What might not be so obvious is that in the middle of the twentieth century the branding process started to enter the marketplace of cultural values and beliefs. Schools, churches, museums, hospitals, politics..., living space, even the judicial system went pop! They—the successful institutions—started *self-*

> *consciously* using techniques of branding not just to make their ideological points and generate cultural capital but to distribute their services at the highest possible return. The admen entered the sacred groves, and, rather like the police in your bedroom, once inside, they are difficult to get to leave. (3)

This has immense significance, I believe, for the space of 'through education,' representing its *colonization*. The process of autobiography, therefore, as a process of re-humanization and re-socialization of the self, both by the self and with others, is perhaps uniquely suited to explorations of currere in our new experiencing of the postmodern condition.

Ultimately, I am forced to wrestle with the question of my own (and others') tolerance for diversity of vision when it comes to the so-called Right: How tolerant can we afford to be of a culture of citizenship that uses intolerance coupled with power writ large to silence, censure, and debase difference? I argue that such contests for being heard are an American tradition, one that we must not let die, but rather must revive with a new energy and more expansive vision, but also towards new ends, and with greater inclusion than ever before. We, the people, must step up to the plate, as they say. We need to reweave a moral fabric for our society (Greene, 2008), and we need to do so together, *somehow*. At the same time, we need to keep the spirit of freedom and purpose alive, and that includes encouraging social critique as we work to understand social change(s). Then, and only then, will we have something authentic and honest to *tell* our young about democracy.

I believe that the answer to addressing the complexities and the ambiguities of our times—the only answer I can both conceive and support as a teacher educator—is to work towards a praxis that should be at the very core of any schooling performed in the name of democracy, and that should always and everywhere begin with a quest for knowledge and understanding as the form that learning experiences should take, and an authentic openness to difference, as expressed in classroom, school, and community culture. Time and life must teach us the rest, which I fervently hope will be wisdom. As I pursued this work, a number of possible avenues for further exploration occurred to me. I have discovered between these pages what it means to recognize the depth of my ignorance and in doing so I have discovered my limits. I have, however, considered streams of inquiry I might seek to navigate.

One of these streams is political philosophy. As I worked to better understand the dynamics of the scenario I was narrating here, images of authoritarianism, fascism, and totalitarianism began to plague me. In fact, I had to do a walkabout of sorts (intellectually) to see if I could withstand my own dark intuitive sense of where we were headed and continue to write for hope. I began to wander down one of those intellectual streams by taking a look at the writing of and about Carl Schmitt and his student, Leo Strauss. This led me to more fully explore not only a greater shard of work in political philosophy, but also to find myself exploring Schmitt's (1996, 2004, 2005) political theology and its related philosophy of jurisprudence. This is a slow cruise that may take a while. But as I began the exploration, and as streams of thinking began to coalesce in my understanding, I realized that what we are most lacking in our culture and in our schools well may be that sense of being on a quest, that somehow thirsting is the answer, that we should gather knowledge to us as our wealth, and pursue understanding as we might some other virtue. I am speaking with the langue of another time, another world, I know. But I am here, very much alive, contending with all the forms of adversity that all human beings bear in this new era, and contending with its changes, its displacements, its forced sacrifices, its willingness to mindlessly cause pain rather than to consider alternatives, and, above all, its forgetfulness.

Remembrance... where has it gone?

My task, then, has been to 'locate' a curriculum drawn from autobiography—to teach against silence and silencing—in a manner consistent with excavating this terrain, the terrain of a *national* 'we, the people,' considered a myth by some in these times. The silence of which I speak suppressed discussion of issues—and access to trustworthy information that might have informed such discussion—in the name of national security, and was too often, too blatantly cloaked under the mantle of unity while covering a political agenda that may truly be considered *anti*-democratic. This tendency—and the failure of the public, this "utter failure of democracy" demonstrated by the public's silent sanction of this administration's radical revolution (Shenkman, 2008)[1]—requires exploration of questions related to totalitarian movements and totalitarian regimes, an area which I am studying (Arendt, 1968).

Only when we understand what we have allowed, only when we pull back the curtain to let the light in (Grumet, 1988, xiii), to acknowledge, accept, and face our 'unacceptable truths' (Pinar, 2004, 38), only then can we see more clearly where we are in this predatory age, and where and how we might make inroads for a democratic future. Only then will we find space to confront the worst of our fears as we create space to see them with fresh vision, to imagine 'other stories of what could be' (Fine, 2002, 138). This is the work of a nation, an imagined community fashioned from various vistas of belonging, one that needs to open to new understandings of coherence and community. When we have done *this* work, then we will have something to *show* our young about democracy

Notes

Chapter 1

1. I use the term 'America' here to indicate Americans in the U.S., with apologies to other Americas and other Americans, whether they be North, Central, or South Americans. I do so because this is the name by which we call ourselves, and by which we are called by others around the world.
2. *Es muss sein* translated literally means 'It must be.'
3. According to the Lincoln Library (1968), "The polonaise of modern times has the character of a stately march." (1529).
4. Among those science fiction narratives that immediately come to mind are George Orwell's *1984*, Aldous Huxley's *Brave New World*, and Margaret Atwood's *The Handmaid's Tale*.
5. There is a large and growing body of work, largely trade books, documenting the trends and event I speak of here, much of it written by those who were, at some point, on the 'inside' as these events were transpiring; my references in this section are therefore carefully limited to just a few works warranting my claims about the new American wilderness.
6. Greene (2008) indicated that what Dewey meant by 'culture' was actually *experience*.
7. The fugue is a "contrapuntal composition which consists of an elaborate interweaving of one or more themes by the different parts at various intervals of pitch" (Lincoln Library, 1545).
8. Beck, however, writing in the 1990s, characterized the changes then being recognized as a *shift* from the former to the latter.
9. This notion of 'the exception' lies at the root of much of the political philosophy and even the philosophy of jurisprudence that was evidenced in discussions about the Weimar Republic in pre-Nazi Germany in the 1920s and 1930s (see, e.g., Agamben, 2005; Meier, 1995; Scheuerman, 1997; Schmitt, 1985, 2004).
10. The rondo is "a direct offshoot of the *song form*. It contains a *principal theme*, one *subordinate theme*, and the *recurrence* of the *principal*" [Emphasis in original] (Lincoln Library, 1529).
11. See Nicholson-Goodman (2007) for further discussion of the use of propaganda.

Chapter 2

1. For a fuller discussion of Lundgren's (1983) work on curriculum codes and Kemmis' (1986) incorporation of this work in his own approach to ideology-critique, see Chapter 9.
2. Bachelard taught at the Sorbonne while Foucault was a student there. Bachelard's work is focused on ruptures, or breaks, in the history of science and changes in conceptions of reason as a result of these breaks. He constructed a model of scientific change by dividing epistemological phenomena into three categories: *breaks* between scientific cognition and everyday experience; *obstacles*—concepts or methods preventing such breaks; and *acts*, the genius leaps that interject the unexpected into the realm of inquiry. He concluded that there was no single, unified conception of rationality, but rather that regions of rationality prevailed historically in scientific thinking.
3. Beck's concern was with the re-ordering of society and the political as a result of the production and distribution of *environmental* risks and hazards, which he saw as a shift away from the production and distribution of wealth as a primary focus, since environmental risks and hazards are disseminated without regard for class or any other discriminating factor (ergo, the wealthy stand to suffer just as much as the poor, Beck reasoned, in a risk society. The same may be said to be true of the risks associated with terrorism). The risk

Chapter 3

1. My thanks to Noreen B. Garman for this personal communication.
2. My understanding of Berger and Luckmann is such that I see their categories as mutable, as open to revisioning, and in this sense their work has served to enhance my

Chapter 7

1. Rolland G. Paulston, sadly, died in 2005.
2. I had already been studying and working to undetstand the dispersion of environmental discourse across a broad range of ways of seeing for many years.
3. Noreen Garman, also at APS, is Professor of Education and Coordinator of the Social & Comparative Analysis of Education (SCAE) program.
4. As millions protested around the world against our pre-emptive strike against Iraq, President Bush indicated publicly that taking such protests into account would be like forming policy based on a "focus group" (Brecher and Smith, 2005).

Chapter 8

1. For further understanding, see D. Harvey (2005), *A Brief History of Neoliberalism*, who adds Deng Xiaoping's efforts to transform China's economy and Paul Volcker's initiatives at the U.S. Federal Reserve to curb inflation to the Thatcher-Reagan agendas (1).
2. Habermas (2001), additionally, sees neoliberals as "prepared to accept a higher level of social inequities," and who therefore "differ in their appraisal of this situation from those who recognize that equal social rights are the mainstays of democratic citizenship" (51).

Chapter 9

1. Alternative curricular frames that have been considered here include: the approach of Pinar, Reynolds, Slattery, and Taubman (1995), who map curriculum discourses as texts dispersing into what has become an expansive field; Marshall, Sears, and Schubert (2000), who link curricular changes to cultural changes and trace curriculum connections and concerns, framed as 'turning points'; and Kliebard (2004), who traces the history of advocacy about the purposes of schooling, which he calls 'the struggle for the American curriculum,' in terms of interest groups: humanists, social efficiency advocates, developmentalists, and social meliorists, or social reconstructionists.
2. For further insight into such struggles in America, see Kliebard (2004), *The Struggle for the American Curriculum*.
3. This idea is complicated, however, as Gutmann and Thompson (1996) point out, by the reality that moral disagreement is a constant in a democracy, and that resolution is only possible through compromise that is consensual.

Epilogue

1. Shenkman indicates that we need to attend to the following: the myth of 'the people, the 'failure of the public,' and the exploitation of myths. But Shenkman complains that we are silent about this failure and argues that it should be on the national agenda.

References

Academy for Educational Development for the Campaign for the Civic Mission of Schools (2004, November). *Advancing the civic mission of schools: What schools, districts, and federal and state leaders can do.* Authors: Washington, D.C.

Agamben, G. (Trans. K. Attell) (2005). *State of exception.* Chicago: The University of Chicago Press.

Ahmed, Z. N. (2000). Mapping rural women's perspectives on nonformal education experiences. APS Conceptual Mapping Project Research Report. Occasional Paper Series. Department of Administrative & Policy Studies, School of Education, University of Pittsburgh.

Americans for Victory Over Terrorism (AVOT). *The New York Times* (Advertisement), 2002, March 10, WK, 7.

Anderson, B. (1991). *Imagined communities: Reflections on the origin and spread of nationalism.* London: Verso.

Anderson, W. T. (1990). *Reality isn't what it used to be: Theatrical politics, ready-to-wear religion, global myths, primitive chic, and other wonders of the postmodern world.* San Francisco: Harper & Row.

Appadurai, A. (1996). *Modernity at large: Cultural dimensions of globalization.* (D. Gaonkar and B. Lee, Eds., Public World series, *1*). Minneapolis: University of Minnesota Press.

Apple, M. (1975). Autobiographical statement. In W. F. Pinar (Ed.), *Curriculum theorizing: The reconceptualists* (pp. 89-93). Berkeley, CA: McCutchan.

Arendt, H. (1968). *The origins of totalitarianism.* San Diego, CA: "A Harvest Book"; Harcourt, Inc.

Arendt, H. (2006/1977). *Between past and future.* New York: Penguin Books.

Banks, J. A. (Ed.) (2004). *Diversity and citizenship education: Global perspectives.* San Francisco: Jossey-Bass.

Barber, B. R. (2001, Rev. ed.). *Jihad vs. McWorld.* New York: Ballantine Books.

Barber, B. R. (2004). *Fear's empire: War, terrorism, and democracy.* New York: W. W. Norton & Company.

Barber, B. R. (2007). *Consumed: How markets corrupt children, infantilize adults, and swallow citizens whole.* New York: W. W. Norton & Company.

Barry, T., and Lobe, J. (2002, April). U.S. foreign policy—Attention, right face, forward march. *Foreign Policy in Focus*, 1-8. Retrieved May 5, 2002 from http//www.fpif.org.

Barthes, R. (1989). *The rustle of language*. Berkeley: University of California Press.

Beck, U. (1992). *Risk society*. London: Sage.

Berger, P. L., and Luckmann, T. (1975). *The social construction of reality*. Harmondsworth, UK: Penguin.

Berman, M. (2000). *The twilight of American culture*. New York: W. W. Norton & Company.

Berman, M. (2007). *Dark ages America: The final phase of empire*. New York: W. W. Norton & Company.

Bhabha, H. (1994). *The location of culture*. London: Routledge Classics.

Blacker, D. (1998). Intellectuals at work and in power: Toward a Foucaultian research ethic. In T. S. Popkewitz and M. Brennan (Eds.), *Foucault's Challenge* (pp. 348-367). New York: Teachers College Press.

Block, A. A. (2007, February). States of siege: The assault on public education. *Journal of the American Association for the Advancement of Curriculum Studies*, 3 [Online]. Retrieved from http://www.ustout.edu/soe/jaaacs/vol3/block.htm.

Bochner, A. P. (2002, April). Love survives. *The Journal of Qualitative Inquiry*, 8:2, pp. 161-169.

Bollinger, L. C. (2000). The open-minded soldier and the university. In P. J. Hollingsworth (Ed.), *Unfettered Expression* (pp. 31 - 49). Ann Arbor: The University of Michigan Press.

Books, S. (Ed.) (2003, 2nd ed.). *Invisible children in the society and its schools* (J. Spring, Ed., Sociocultural, Political, and Historical Studies in Education series). Mahwah, NJ: Lawrence Erlbaum Associates, Publishers.

Books, S. (Ed.) (2007, 3rd ed.). *Invisible children in the society and its schools*. (J. Spring, Ed., Sociocultural, Political, and Historical Studies in Education series). Mahwah, NJ: Lawrence Erlbaum Associates, Publishers.

Boston, B. O. (2005). Restoring the balance between academics and civic engagement in public schools (S. S. Pearson and S. Halperin, Eds.). Washington, D.C.: American Youth Policy Forum.

Bourdieu, P. (Trans. R. Boyne) (1992). Thinking about limits. In M. Featherstone (Ed.), *Cultural Theory and Cultural Change* (pp. 37-49). London: Sage.

Boydston, Jo Ann (Ed.) (1988). *John Dewey: The later works, 1925-1953* (Volume 13: 1938–1939). Carbondale: Southern Illinois University Press.

Brady, I. (2002, April). Show me a sign. *The Journal of Qualitative Inquiry*, 8:2, pp. 176-180.

References

Brecher, J., and Smith, B. (2005). How the world can help Americans halt Bush administration war crimes. Policy Discussion Paper, *Foreign Policy in Focus*. Retrieved August 10, 2008 from http://www.fpif.org/papers/0506haltbush_body.html.

Bumiller, E. (2002, January 6). America as reflected in its leader. *The New York Times*, WK, p. 1.

Burleigh, N. (2001, September 12). Op-Ed pages trot out the white hawks. Retrieved March 19, 2003 from tompaine.com, TP.commentary.

Carson, T. R. (2004). The lonely citizen: Democracy, curriculum, and the crisis of belonging. In G. H. Richardson and D. W. Blade (Eds.), *Troubling the Canon of Citizenship Education* (pp. 25-30). New York: Peter Lang Publishing, Inc.

Castles, S. (2004), Migration, citizenship, and education. In Banks, J. A. (Ed.), *Diversity and Citizenship Education: Global perspectives* (pp. 17-48). San Francisco: Jossey-Bass.

Chang, N. (2002). *Silencing political dissent: How post-September 11 anti-terrorism measures threaten our civil liberties*. The Center for Constitutional Rights. New York: Seven Stories Press.

Charmaz, K. (2002, April). Tenets of terror. *Journal of Qualitative Inquiry*, 8:2, pp.189-190.

Christina, R., and Nicholson-Goodman, J. (2002, March). Academic responsibility after September 11th, 2001. Paper presented at the Council of Graduate Studies in Education Research Conference, Department of Administrative & Policy Studies, School of Education, University of Pittsburgh.

Ciepley, D. (2006). *Liberalism in the shadow of totalitarianism*. Cambridge, MA: Harvard University Press.

Corn, D. (2001, October 5). The loyal opposition: Far from normal. Retrieved March 19, 2003 from tompaine.com, TP.commentary.

Coulter, A. (2003). *Slander: Liberal lies about the American Right*. New York: Three Rivers Press.

Coulter, A. (2004). *Treason: Liberal treachery from the Cold War to the War on Terrorism*. New York: Three Rivers Press.

Curran, J. (1993). Rethinking the media as public sphere. In P. Dahlgren & C. Sparks (Eds.), *Communication and Citizenship* (pp. 27-57). London: Routledge.

Dahl, G. (1999). *Radical conservatism and the future of politics*. London: Sage Publications.

Dahlgren, P., and Sparks, C. (Eds.) (1993). *Communication and citizenship: Journalism and the public sphere*. London: Routledge.

Danner, M. (2001, October 16). The battlefield in the American mind. *The New York Times*, Op-Ed, p. A23.

Dean, J. (2005). *Worse than Watergate: The secret presidency of George W. Bush*. New York: Warner Books.

Deleuze, G., and Guattari, F. (Trans. B. Massumi) (1987). *A thousand plateaus: Capitalism and schizophrenia*. Minneapolis: University of Minnesota Press.

Denzin, N. K. (2002, April). Week four. *The Journal of Qualitative Inquiry*, 8:2, pp. 199-202.

Denzin, N. K., and Lincoln, Y. S. (Eds.) (2002, April). Editors' introduction: Special partial issue—Qualitative inquiry and the events following September 11, 2001. *Qualitative Inquiry*, 8:2, pp. 133-134.

Dewey, J. (1988/1939). Freedom and culture. In Boydston, J. (Ed.), *John Dewey: The later works, 1925-1953* (Volume 13: 1938-1939) (pp. 65-188). Carbondale: Southern Illinois University Press.

Dewey, J. (1991/1927). *The public and its problems*. Athens: Swallow Press/Ohio University Press.

Dowd, M. (2001, October 24). Going really postal. *The New York Times*, Op-Ed, p. A23.

Eisner, E. W. (2002, Fall). What can education learn from the arts about the practice of education? *Journal of Curriculum and Supervision*, 18:1, pp. 4-16.

Ellis, C. (2002, April). Take no chances. *The Journal of Qualitative Inquiry*, 8:2, pp. 170-175.

Epstein, E. H., and Carroll, K. T. (2005, February). Abusing ancestors: Historical functionalism and the postmodern deviation in comparative education. *Comparative Education Review*, 49:1, pp. 62-88.

Faux, J. (2001, September 20). Three things we learned: On workers, the public sector, and American exceptionalism. Retrieved March 19, 2003 from tompaine.com, TP.commentary.

Featherstone, M. (Ed.) (1992). *Cultural theory and cultural change*. London: Sage.

Fine, M. (2002, April). The mourning after. *Journal of Qualitative Inquiry*, 8:2, pp. 137-145.

Fischman, G. E. (2004). [Review of the book *Social Cartography: Mapping ways of seeing social and educational change*]. *Visual Communication*, 3:1, pp. 111-114.

Fischman, G. E., McLaren, P., Sunker, H., and Lankshear, C. (Eds.) (2005). *Critical theories, radical pedagogies, and global conflicts*. Lanham, MD: Rowman & Littlefield Publishers, Inc.

Flinders, D. J., and Thornton, S. J. (Eds.) (2004, 2nd ed.). *The curriculum studies reader*. New York: RoutledgeFalmer.

Ford, R. (2001, November 1). The worry trap. *The New York Times*, Op-Ed, p. A27.

References

Foucault, M. (Trans. A.M. Sheridan Smith) (1972). *The archaeology of knowledge and the discourse on language*. New York: Pantheon Books.

Foucault, M. (D. F. Bouchard, Ed.) (Trans. D. F. Bouchard and S. Simon) (1977). *Language, counter-memory, practice: Selected essays and interviews*. Ithaca, NY: Cornell University Press.

Foucault, M. (C. Gordon, Ed.) (Trans. C. Gordon, L. Marshall, J. Mepham, and K. Soper) (1980). *Power/knowledge: Selected interviews and other writings 1972-1977*. New York: Pantheon Books.

Freire, P. (Trans. M. B. Ramos) (1970). *Pedagogy of the oppressed*. New York: The Seabury Press.

Freire, P. (Trans. P. Clarke) (1998). *Pedagogy of freedom: Ethics, democracy, and civic courage*. Lanham, MD: Rowman & Littlefield Publishers, Inc.

Garman, N. B. (2007). The impoverished landscape of education. A think piece. XXXXXXXXX

Garman, N. B., and Piantanida, M. (1999). *The qualitative dissertation: A guide for students and faculty*. Thousand Oaks, CA: Corwin Press.

Garman, N. B., and Piantanida, M. (2006). *Authority to imagine: The struggle toward representation in dissertation writing* (W. F. Pinar, Ed., Curriculum as Complicated Conversation series, *11*). New York: Peter Lang Publishing, Inc.

Gergen, K. J. (2002, April). September 11 and the global implications of interpretive inquiry. *Journal of Qualitative Inquiry*, 8:2, pp. 186-188.

Gergen, M. (2002, April). September 11, 2001: Changing the ways of the world. *Journal of Qualitative Inquiry*, 8:2, pp. 150-152.

Giroux, H. A. (2004). *The terror of neoliberalism: Authoritarianism and the eclipse of democracy*. Boulder, CO: Paradigm Publishers.

Giroux, H. A. (2005). War talk and the shredding of the social contract: Youth and the politics of domestic militarization. In G. E. Fischman et al. (Eds.), *Critical theories, radical pedagogies, and global conflicts* (pp. 52-68). Lanham, MD: Rowman & Littlefield Publishers, Inc.

Gitlin, T. (1993). Bites and blips: Chunk news, savvy talk and the bifurcation of American politics. In P. Dahlgren and Sparks, C. (Eds.), *Communication and citizenship: Journalism and the public sphere* (pp. 119-136). London: Routledge.

Goodall Jr., H. L. (2002, April). Fieldnotes from our war zone: Living in America during the aftermath of September eleventh. *The Journal of Qualitative Inquiry*, 8:2, pp. 203-218.

Gough, N. (1993, December). Neuromancing the stones: Experience, intertextuality, and cyber punk science fiction. *Journal of Experiential Education*, 16:3, pp. 9-17.

Greene, M. (2004/1971). Curriculum and consciousness. In D. J. Flinders and S. J. Thornton (Eds.) (2nd ed.), *The curriculum studies reader* (pp. 135-147). New York: RoutledgeFalmer.

Greene, M. (1978). *Landscapes of learning.* New York: Teachers College Press.

Greene, M. (1986). In search of a critical pedagogy. *Harvard Educational Review,* 56:4, pp. 427-441.

Greene, M. (1988). *The dialectic of freedom.* New York: Teachers College Press.

Greene, M. (1995). *Releasing the imagination: Essays on education, the arts, and social change.* San Francisco: Jossey-Bass.

Greene, M. (2008, March). The poet, the city, and curriculum. Invited symposium. Seventh Annual Meeting of the American Association for the Advancement of Curriculum Studies. New York: Teachers College, Columbia University.

Greenwood, D. J. (2002, April). Alone and together: A reflection for *Qualitative Inquiry* on the terror attack. *The Journal of Qualitative Inquiry,* 8:2, pp. 191-193.

Grumet, M. R. (1988). *Bitter milk: Women and teaching.* Amherst: The University of Massachusetts Press.

Gutmann, A. (1999). *Democratic education.* Princeton, NJ: Princeton University Press.

Gutmann, A., and Thompson, D. (1996). *Democracy and disagreement: Why moral conflict cannot be avoided in politics and what should be done about it.* Cambridge, MA: The Belknap Press of Harvard University Press.

Habermas, J. (Trans. T. Burger) (1989/1962). *The structural transformation of the public sphere: An inquiry into a category of bourgeois society.* Cambridge, MA: The MIT Press.

Habermas, J. (Trans. M. Pensky) (2001). *The postnational constellation: Political essays.* Cambridge, MA: The MIT Press.

Habermas, J. (Trans. C. Cronin) (2006). *The divided west.* Cambridge, UK: Polity Press.

Hagler, G. S. (2001, October 25). A worldview on peace and restraint. Retrieved March 19, 2003 from tompaine.com, TP.commentary.

Halstead, T. (Ed.) (2004). *The real State of the Union: From the best minds in America, bold solutions to the problems politicians dare not address.* New York: Basic Books.

Halstead, T., and Lind, M. (2002). *The radical center: The future of American politics.* New York: Anchor Books.

Harvey, D. (1996). *Justice, nature and the geography of difference.* Cambridge, MA: Blackwell Publishers.

References

Harvey, D. (2005). *A brief history of neoliberalism.* New York: Oxford University Press Inc.

Garman, N. (2006). Curriculum leaders as public intellectuals in an impoverished landscape. *Journal of Curriculum and Pedagogy, 3:1*, pp. 73-78.

Hedges, C. (2006). *American fascists: The Christian right and the war on America.* New York: Free Press.

Helvarg, D. (2001, October 29). Consume for victory: Support the war – buy! buy! buy! Retrieved March 19, 2003 from tompaine.com, TP.commentary.

Henderson, J. G., and Kesson, K. R. (2004). *Curriculum wisdom: Educational decisions in democratic societies.* Upper Saddle River, NJ: Pearson Education Inc.

Hersh, S. M. (2005). *Chain of command: The road from 9/11 to Abu Ghraib.* New York: Harper-Collins.

Hollingsworth, P. J (Ed.) (2000). *Unfettered expression.* Ann Arbor: The University of Michigan Press.

Huff, A. S. (2000). Ways of mapping strategic thought. In R. G. Paulston (Ed.), *Social cartography: Mapping ways of seeing social and educational change* (pp. 161-190). New York: Garland.

Johnson, C. (2006). *Nemesis: The last days of the American republic.* New York: Metropolitan Books; Henry Holt and Company.

Kellner, D. (2005). Globalization, September 11, and the restructuring of education. In G. W. Fischman et al. (Eds.), *Critical theories, radical pedagogies, and global conflicts* (pp. 87-112). Lanham, MD: Rowman & Littlefield Publishers, Inc.

Kemmis, S. (1986). *Curriculum theorising: Beyond reproduction theory.* Victoria, Australia: Deakin University.

Kerik discusses post-Katrina leadership (2005, September 8). Retrieved October 27, 2007 from www.msnbc.msn.com/id/9247753/print/1/displaymode/1098.

Kincheloe, J. (1983). *Understanding the new right and its impact on education.* Bloomington, IN: Phi Delta Kappa Educational Foundation.

Kincheloe, J. (1998). Pinar's *currere* and identity in hyperreality: Grounding the post-formal notion of intrapersonal intelligence. In W. F. Pinar (Ed.), *Curriculum: Toward new identities* (pp. 129-142). New York: Garland.

Kincheloe, J. (1983) *Understanding the new right and its impact on education.* Bloomington, IN: Phi Delta Kappa Educational Foundation.

Kincheloe, J. L., and Steinberg, S. R. (Eds.) (1993). *Thirteen questions: Reframing education's conversation.* New York: Peter Lang Publishing, Inc.

Klein, N. (2001, December 19). Legends in our own minds: Ideology makes Christmas shopping so much fun! Retrieved March 19, 2003 from tompaine.com, TP.commentary.

Klein, N. (2007). *The shock doctrine: The rise of disaster capitalism.* New York: Henry Holt and Company.

Kliebard, H. M. (2004) (3rd ed.). *The struggle for the American curriculum 1893-1958.* New York: RoutledgeFalmer.

Krugman, P. (2001, November 25). An alternate reality. *The New York Times,* Op-Ed.

Lakoff, G. (2006). *Whose freedom? The battle over America's most important idea.* New York: Farrar, Straus, and Giroux.

Lapham, L. (2004). *Gag rule: On the suppression of dissent and the stifling of democracy.* New York: The Penguin Press.

Lather, P. (2004, November). This IS your father's paradigm: Government intrusion and the case of qualitative research in education. *Qualitative Inquiry, 10:1,* pp. 15-34.

Lewis, A. (2007, December 20). [Review of the book *The nine: Inside the secret world of the Supreme Court.*] The Court: How 'so few have so quickly changed so much.' *The New York Review of Books, LIV: 20,* pp. 58-61.

Liebman, M., and Paulston, R. G. (1994). Social cartography: A new methodology for comparative studies. *Compare, 24:3,* pp. 233-245.

Lincoln, Y. S., and Cannella, G. S. (2004), Qualitative research, power, and the radical right. *Qualitative Inquiry, 10:2,* pp. 175-201.

Lind, M. (1995). *The next American nation: The new nationalism and the fourth American revolution.* New York: Free Press.

Livingston, D. (2004). Wondering about a future generation: Identity disposition disposal, recycling, and creation in the 21st century. In W. M. Reynolds and J. A. Webber (Eds.), *Expanding curriculum theory: Dis/positions and lines of flight* (pp. 35-45). (W. F. Pinar, Ed., Studies in Curriculum Theory series.) Mahwah, NJ: Lawrence Erlbaum Associates, Publishers.

Longstreet, W. S. (2000). Afterword: The age of pluralism. In J. D. Marshall, J. T. Sears, and W. H. Schubert, *Turning points in curriculum: A contemporary American memoir* (pp. 244-248). Upper Saddle River, NJ: Prentice-Hall, Inc.

Lopez, G. R. (2002, April). From sea to shining sea: Stories, counterstories, and the discourse of patriotism. *Journal of Qualitative Inquiry, 8:2,* pp. 196-198.

Lundgren, U. P. (1983). *Between hope and happening: Text and context in curriculum.* Victoria, Australia: Deakins University.

Lyotard, J-F. (Trans. G. Bennington and B. Massumi) (1984). *The postmodern condition: A report on knowledge*. (W. Godzich and J. Schulte-Sasse, Eds., Theory and History of Literature series, 10) Minneapolis: University of Minnesota Press.

Mailer, N. (2003). *Why are we at war?* New York: Random House.

Mannheim, K. (Trans. L. Wirth and E. Shils) (1936). *Ideology and utopia*. New York: Harcourt, Brace & World, Inc.

Marshall, J. D., Sears, J. T., and Schubert, W. H. (2000). *Turning points in curriculum: A contemporary American memoir*. Upper Saddle River, NJ: Prentice-Hall, Inc.

Matthews, Chris (2001, December 16). American revival. SFGate.com. Retrieved October 27, 2007 from www.sfgate.com/cgi-bin/article.cgi?file=/chronicle/archive/2001/12/16/IN87407.

McLaren, P., and Farahmandpur, R. (2005). Critical revolutionary pedagogy after September 11: A Marxist response. In G. E. Fischman et al., *Critical theories, radical pedagogies, and global conflicts* (pp. 263-292). Lanham, MD: Rowman & Littlefield Publishers, Inc.

McGovern, G. (2002, January 1). The healing in helping the world's poor. *The New York Times*, Op-Ed, p. A23.

Meier, H. (Trans. J. H. Lomax) (1995). *Carl Schmitt and Leo Strauss: The hidden dialogue*. Chicago: The University of Chicago Press.

Micklethwait, J., and Wooldridge, A. (2004). *The right nation: Conservative power in America*. New York: The Penguin Press.

Miller, W. L. (2002, April). A time for butterflies and salmon. *Journal of Qualitative Inquiry*, 8:2, pp. 156-157.

Mouat IV, T. W. (1996). The timely emergence of social cartography. In R. G. Paulston (Ed.), *Social cartography: Mapping ways of seeing social and educational change* (pp. 81-116). New York: Garland.

National Commission on Excellence in Education (1983). *A Nation at Risk: The imperative for educational reform*. Washington, D.C.: U.S. Government Printing Office.

Nicholson-Goodman, J. (1996). A ludic approach to mapping environmental education discourse. In R. G. Paulston (Ed.), *Social cartography: Mapping ways of seeing social and educational change* (pp. 307-326). New York: Garland.

Nicholson-Goodman, J. (2006). Confronting authority and self: Social cartography and curriculum theorizing for uncertain times. In N. B. Garman and M. Piantanida (Eds.), *Authority to imagine: The struggle toward representation in dissertation writing* (pp. 49-63). New York: Peter Lang Publishing, Inc.

Nicholson-Goodman, J. (2007, June). Mapping an autobiography of post-9/11 America: A new paradigm for policy-making—constituencies for a curriculum of possibility. *Journal of the American Association for the Advancement of Curriculum Studies*, 3 [Online]. Retrieved from http://www.ustout.edu/soe/jaaacs/vol3/nicholson.htm.

Nicholson-Goodman, J., and Paulston, R. G. (1996). Mapping/remapping discourse in education policy studies. In R. G. Paulston, M. Liebman, and J. Nicholson-Goodman, *Mapping multiple perspectives: Research reports of the University of Pittsburgh Social Cartography Project, 1993-1996* (pp. 95-130). Occasional Paper Series, Department of Administrative & Policy Studies (APS), School of Education, University of Pittsburgh.

Ninnes, P., and Mehta, S. (Eds.) (2004). *Re-imagining comparative education: Post-foundational ideas and applications for critical times*. New York: RoutledgeFalmer.

Ong, A. (2004), Higher learning: Educational availability and flexible citizenship in global space. In J. A. Banks (Ed.), *Diversity and citizenship education: Global perspectives* (pp. 49-70). San Francisco: Jossey-Bass.

Paulston, R. G. (1993). Mapping discourses in comparative education texts. *Compare*, 23:2, pp. 101-114.

Paulston, R. G. (1995). Mapping knowledge perspectives in studies of educational change. In P. W. Cookson and B. Scheider (Eds.), *Transforming schools: Rhetoric and reality* (p. 137-180). New York: Garland.

Paulston, R. G. (Ed.) (1996). *Social Cartography: Ways of seeing social and educational change*. New York: Garland.

Paulston, R. G. (1997, March). The perspectivist turn in comparative education. Paper presented at the Comparative and International Education Society Annual Meeting, Mexico City, Mexico.

Paulston, R. G. (2005, March). Mapping reality turns in Western thinking and comparative education studies. Paper presented at the 49th Comparative and International Education Society (CIES) Annual Meeting, Stanford University, Palo Alto, CA.

Paulston, R. G., and Liebman, M. (1996). Social cartography: A new metaphor/tool for comparative studies. In R. G. Paulston (Ed.), *Social cartography: Mapping ways of seeing social and educational change* (p. 7-28). New York: Garland.

Paulston, R. G., Liebman, M., and Nicholson-Goodman, J. (1996). *Mapping multiple perspectives: Research reports of the University of Pittsburgh Social Cartography Project, 1993-1996*. Occasional Paper Series, Department of Administrative & Policy Studies (APS), School of Education, University of Pittsburgh.

Phillips, K. (2007). *American theocracy: The peril and politics of radical religion, oil, and borrowed money in the 21st century*. New York: Penguin Books.

Pinar, W. F. (Ed.) (1975). *Curriculum theorizing: The reconceptualists*. Berkeley, CA: McCutcheon Publishing Corporation.

Pinar, W. F. (1994). *Autobiography, politics and sexuality: Essays in curriculum theory, 1972-1992*. New York: Peter Lang Publishing, Inc.

Pinar, W. F. (2000). Foreword. In J. D. Marshall, J. T. Sears, and W. H. Schubert, *Turning points in curriculum: A contemporary American memoir* (pp. v-viii). Upper Saddle River, NJ: Prentice-Hall, Inc.

Pinar, W. F. (2004). *What is curriculum theory?* Mahwah, NJ: Lawrence Erlbaum Associates.

Pinar, W. F. (2006a). *The synoptic text today and other essays: Curriculum development after the reconceptualization*. New York: Peter Lang Publishing, Inc.

Pinar, W. F. (2006b). From chattel to citizenry: The gender of the law in the sexual politics of race. In G. H. Richardson and D. W. Blades (Eds.), *Troubling the canon of citizenship education* (pp. 103-112). New York: Peter Lang Publishing, Inc.

Pinar, W. F., Reynolds, W. M., Slattery, P., and Taubman, P. M. (Eds.) (1995). *Understanding curriculum*. New York: Peter Lang Publishing, Inc.

Popkewitz, T. S., and Brennan, M. (Eds.) (1998). *Foucault's challenge: Discourse, knowledge, and power in education*. New York: Teachers College Press.

Porter, J. (1999). *Reschooling and the global future: Politics, economics and the English experience*. Wallingford, Oxford, U.K.: Symposium Books.

Post responds to Woodward's revelations (2005, November 17). MSNBC.com. Retrieved October 27, 2007 from www.msnbc.msn.com/id/10075158/print/1/displaymode/1098.

Postman, N. (1986). *Amusing ourselves to death: Public discourse in the age of show business*. New York: Penguin Books.

Pratt, L. R. (2000). Academic freedom and the merits of uncertainty. In P. J. Hollingsworth (Ed.), *Unfettered expression: Freedom in American intellectual life* (pp. 99-116). Ann Arbor: The University of Michigan Press.

Project for the New American Century (1997). Statement of principles. Retrieved March 19, 2003 from http://www.newamericancentury.org/statementofprinciples.htm.

Reynolds, W. M. (2004). To touch the clouds standing on top of a Maytag refrigerator: Brand-name postmodernity and a Deleuzian "in-between." In W. M. Reynolds and J. A. Webber (Eds.), *Expanding Curriculum Theory: Dis/positions and lines of flight* (pp. 19-34). (W. F. Pinar, Ed., Studies in Curriculum Theory series.) Mahwah, NJ: Lawrence Erlbaum Associates, Publishers.

Reynolds, W. M., and Webber, J. A. (Eds.) (2004). *Expanding curriculum theory: Dis/positions and lines of flight*. (W. F. Pinar, Ed., Studies in Curriculum Theory series.0 Mahwah, NJ: Lawrence Erlbaum Associates, Publishers.

Rich, F. (2001, October 13). No news is good news. *The New York Times*, Op-Ed, p. A23.

Richardson, G. H., and Blades, D. W. (Eds.) (2006). *Troubling the canon of citizenship education*. New York: Peter Lang Publishing, Inc.

Rieger, J. (2001, September 12). What does retaliation mean in a media war? Retrieved March 19, 2003 from tompaine.com, TP.commentary.

Robertson, R. (1992). *Globalization: Social theory and global culture*. London: Sage.

Safire, W. (2001, November 15). Seizing dictatorial power. *The New York Times*, Op-Ed, p. A21.

Scahill, J. (2007). *Blackwater: The rise of the world's most powerful mercenary army*. New York: Nation Books.

Scheuerman, W. E. (1997). *Between the norm and the exception*. Cambridge, MA: The MIT Press.

Schlesinger, Jr., A. M. (1998). *The disuniting of America: Reflections on a multicultural society*. New York: W. W. Norton & Co.

Schmitt, C. (Trans. G. Schwab) (1996). *The concept of the political*. Chicago: The University of Chicago Press.

Schmitt, C. (Trans. J. Seitzer) (2004). *Legality and legitimacy*. Durham, NC: Duke University Press.

Schmitt, C. (Trans. G. Schwab) (2005). *Political theology: Four chapters on the concept of sovereignty*. Chicago: The University of Chicago Press.

Shenkman, R. (2008). *Just how stupid are we? Facing the truth about the American voter*. New York: Basic Books.

Shor, I. (1986). *Culture wars: School and society in the conservative reformation, 1969-1984*. Boston: Routledge.
Smith, D. G. (2006). Troubles with the sacred canopy: Global citizenship in a season of great untruth. In G. H. Richardson and D. W. Blades (Eds.), *Troubling the Canon of Citizenship Education* (pp. 124-135). New York: Peter Lang Publishing, Inc.

Stevenson, N. (Ed.) (2001). *Culture & Citizenship*. London: Sage Publications Ltd.

Taylor, B. (2001, October 24). Heed not the calls of the consumers-in-chief. Retrieved March 19, 2003 from tompaine.com, TP.commentary.

References

Taylor, M. L. (2005). *Religion, politics, and the Christian Right: Post-9/11 powers and American empire*. Minneapolis, MN: Fortress Press.

Tierney, W. G. (2002, April). A walk in the olive grove. *The Journal of Qualitative Inquiry*, 8:2, pp. 183-185.

Turner, B. S. (2001). Outline of a general theory of cultural citizenship. In N. Stevenson (Ed.), *Culture & citizenship* (pp. 11-32). London: Sage Publications Ltd.

Twitchell, J. B. (2004). *Branded nation: The marketing of Megachurch, College, Inc., and Museumworld*. New York: Simon & Schuster.

United States Department of Justice (2008, July). An investigation of allegations of politicized hiring by Monica Goodling and other staff in the office of the Attorney General. Washington, D.C. Retrieved August 22, 2008 from http://www.usdoj.gov/opr/goodling072408.pdf.

Unleashing the loyal opposition. *The New York Times*, Editorial, April 15, 2002.

Urban, W., and Wagoner, J. (2000). *American education: A history*. Boston: McGraw-Hill.

Usher, R., and Edwards, R. (1994). *Postmodernism and education*. London: Routledge.

Vellenga, T. (2001, October 1). Now, engage the world: Uncovering the value of multilateralism. Retrieved March 19, 2003 from tompaine.com, TP.commentary.

Vinson, K. D., and Ross, E. W. (2003). *Image and education: Teaching in the face of the new disciplinarity* (J. Kincheloe and D. Weil, Eds., extreme teaching, rigorous texts for troubled times series, 7). New York: Peter Lang Publishing, Inc.

Watson, K. (1998). Memories, models, and mapping: the impact of geopolitical changes on comparative studies in education. *Compare*, 28:1, pp. 5-31.

Watson, K. (1999). Comparative educational research: The need for reconceptualisation and fresh insights. *Compare*, 29:3, pp. 233-248.

Weis, L. (2002, April). Thoughts beyond fear. *Qualitative Inquiry*, 8:2, pp. 153-155.

West, C. (2004). *Democracy matters: Winning the fight against imperialism*. New York: Penguin Books.

Westheimer, J., and Kahne, J. (2004). What kind of citizen? The politics of educating for democracy. *American Educational Research Journal*, 41:2, pp. 237-269.

Zinn, H. (2001, September 13). Not vengeance, but compassion. Retrieved March 19, 2003 from tompaine.com, TP.commentary.

Author Index

Ahmed, Z. N., 152
Americans for Victory Over Terrorism (AVOT), 26, 61, 104, 111, 172
Anderson, B., 16, 20, 36, 61, 65, 67, 77-78, 79-86, 89, 196, 201
Anderson, W. T., 67, 155
Appadurai, A., 12, 16, 20, 29, 36, 40, 60, 62, 64, 67, 77-78, 86-91, 98-99, 107, 156, 164, 166, 170, 173, 201, 226
Apple, M., 37, 50, 51
Arendt, H., 6, 13, 38, 220, 231, 234
Banks, J. A.., 226
Barber, B. R., 8, 11, 12, 20, 36, 40, 78, 79, 84, 89, 90, 91, 94-96, 170, 189, 217
Barry, T., 57, 67, 111, 160
Barthes, R., 4, 29, 38, 127, 162
Beck, U., 12-13, 20, 40, 186-189, 197, 225
Berger, P. L., 66
Berman, M., 1, 6, 203
Bhaba, H., 12, 16, 20, 40, 60, 78, 91-94, 156, 173
Blacker, D., 51-53, 99, 221
Block, A. A., 14
Bochner, A. P., 112-113, 116
Bollinger, L. C., 44, 45-47, 51
Books, S., 8
Boston, B. O., 12, 225
Bourdieu, P., 30-31, 34, 39, 221, 229
Boydston, J. A., 7
Brady, I., 140-141, 148
Brennan, T., 161
Brennan, M., 41-43, 97, 221
Bumiller, E., 230
Burleigh, N., 129, 130
Bush, G. W., 4, 17, 26, 61, 104, 109, 162
Campaign for the Civic Mission of Schools, 225
Cannella, G. S., 38
Carroll, K. T., 153

Carson, T. R., 226
Carter, J., 175
Castles, S., 226
Chang, N., 7, 160
Charmaz, K., 28, 126-127, 130
Christina, R., 72
Ciepley, D., 161
Corn, D., 122-124
Coulter, A., 13, 172
Curran, J., 189-190
Dahl, G., 38
Dahlgren, P., 189, 190-192
Danner, M., 27, 119-120, 124
Dean, J., 6
Deleuze, G., 1, 18, 20, 49, 57, 107, 111, 155, 164-165, 170, 230, 231
Denzin, N. K., 107, 142-143, 148
Dewey, J., 7
Dowd, M., 113-114, 116
Edwards, R., 74
Eisner, E. W., 16, 58, 62, 104, 168
Ellis, C., 125, 130
Epstein, E. H., 153
Erkilla, C., 152
Falwell, J., 176
Farahmandpur, R., 7
Faux, J., 132-134, 135-136
Fine, M., 25, 71, 131-132, 135, 195, 234
Fischman, G. E., 153
Flinders, D. J., 1
Ford, R., 114-115, 116
Foucault, M., 31, 51, 70, 84, 230
Freire, P., 2, 214, 221
Garman, N. B., 3, 73, 152
Gergen, K. J., 28, 141-142, 148
Gergen, M., 28, 37, 139-140, 147
Giroux, H. A., 2, 7, 38, 41, 160, 182
Gitlin, T., 60, 192-194

Goodall, Jr., H. L., 143-145, 148
Gore, A., 4, 175
Gostoriaga, J., 152
Gough, N., 3, 20
Greene, M., 1, 2, 13, 17, 19, 20, 21, 31, 62, 69, 87, 154, 163, 215-223, 224, 233
Greenwood, D. J., 117-118, 124
Grumet, M. R., 33, 151, 157, 205, 234
Guattari, F., 1, 20, 49, 57, 107, 111, 155, 164-165, 170, 231
Gutmann, A., 2, 59
Habermas, J., 12, 14, 20, 186, 189-191, 211, 225
Hagler, G. S., 146-147, 149
Halstead, T., 17
Harvey, D., 7, 38, 41, 71
Hedges, C., 176, 220
Helvarg, D., 115-116
Henderson, J. G., 12, 157, 229
Hersh, S. M., 6
Hollingsworth, P. J., 44
Huff, A. S., 159, 167
Hughes, L., 2, 216, 225
Kahne, J., 225-226
Kellner, D., 170
Kemmis, S., 30, 52, 154, 157, 205-215, 229
Kesson, K. R., 12, 157, 229
Kincheloe, J., 16, 63, 103, 104-105, 204
Klein, N., 8, 28, 38
Krugman, P., 120-121, 124
Lakoff, G., 56, 59, 64, 65
Lapham, L., 7, 160
Lather, P., 38
Lewis, A., 4
Liebman, M., 58, 59, 72, 158, 167
Lincoln, Y. S., 38, 107
Lind, M., 17, 86
Livingston, D., 231
Lobe, J., 57, 67, 111, 160
Longstreet, W. S., 31
Lopez, G. R., 1, 127-128, 130
Luckmann, T., 66

Lundgren, U. P., 30, 52, 208, 209
Lyotard, J-F., 19
McLaren, P., 7
McGovern, G., 145-146, 148
Mailer, N., 15, 29, 32, 91, 96, 107
Mannheim, K., 65-66
Marshall, J, 2, 151, 155
Matthews, C., 6
Mehta, S., 154
Micklethwait, J., 4, 6, 14, 17, 67
Miller, J., 33, 229
Miller, W. L., 29, 137-138, 139
Mouat, T. W., 70-71
Nicholson-Goodman, J., 32, 40, 59, 70, 72, 111, 152, 158, 162, 186-187
Ninnes, P., 154
Ong, A., 226
Palermo, J. A., 134-135, 136
Paulston, R. G., 55, 56, 58, 59, 70, 72, 73, 151, 152, 158, 162-163, 167
Phillips, K., 176, 220
Piantanida, M., 73
Pinar, W. F., 3, 14, 15, 16, 17, 18, 21, 27, 29, 32, 33, 37, 39, 49, 57, 58, 59, 103, 104-105, 151, 154, 159, 165, 167, 204, 206, 209, 215, 221, 222, 223-225, 226, 234
Pinar, W., Reynolds, W., Slattery, P., and Taubman, P., 28, 32, 33, 34, 37, 58, 59, 157, 229
Popkewitz, T. S., 41-43, 97, 221
Porter, J., 12, 20, 40, 41, 97, 181-186, 202
Postman, N., 12, 13, 221
Pratt, L. R., 47-50
Project for the New American Century (PNAC), 6, 111
Reynolds, W. M., 2, 18, 19, 20, 40, 113, 153, 155, 204
Rich, F., 118-119, 124, 161
Rieger, J., 121-122, 124
Robertson, P., 176
Robertson, R., 40
Ross, E. W., 12, 13, 61, 202-204
Ryan, M., 115, 116

Safire, W., 120, 124, 175
Scahill, J., 8
Schlesinger, A. M., 16, 67
Schmitt, C., 230, 231, 234
Sears, J. T., 2, 151, 155
Schubert, W. H., 2, 151, 155
Shenkman, R., 57, 234
Shor, I., 16, 67
Smith, D. G., 226
Sparks, C., 189, 190, 192
Steinberg, S. R., 16, 63
Stevenson, N., 55, 64, 68, 194-197
Taylor, B., 134, 136
Taylor, M. L., 176, 220
Thompson, D., 2
Thornton, S. J., 1
Tierney, W. G., 125-126, 130
Toobin, J., 26
Turner, B. S., 61, 197-201
Twitchell, J. B., 21, 96, 203, 232-233
U.S. Department of Justice, 9
Unleashing the Loyal Opposition, 25, 64
Urban, W., 86
Usher, R., 74
Vellenga, T., 146, 149
Vinson, K. D., 12, 13, 61, 202-204
Wagoner, J., 86
Watson, K., 153
Webber, J. A., 2, 18, 19, 20, 40, 113, 153, 155
Weis, L., 136-137, 138
West, C., 3, 7, 20, 155
Westheimer, J., 225-226
Wooldridge, A., 4, 6, 14, 17, 67
Zinn, H., 138, 13

Subject Index

Academic freedom, 44-51, 60, 131, 132, 214, 215
Academics, 36, 38, 44-52, 215
    And public desire for certainty, 45
    Role and responsibilities of, 36, 38, 44-50
Accountability, government, 8, 11, 12, 41 121, 124, 172
    And policy-making climate, 184
Activism, 34, 66, 105-106, 112, 136, 139, 160, 165-167, 171, 173-174
    Anti-dissident, 26, 172
    Collective, 220
Activist(s), Americans as, 59, 98
Agency, 33, 78, 86-87, 131, 155-157, 158, 163, 214, 221
    Mapping as tool for, 131
    Narratives reflecting, 158
Al Qaeda, 5, 67, 97
America,
    As God's instrument, 88
    As regulator of global community, 56
    Repositioning of, in world, 56, 69
    Transformation of, 6
American,
    Exceptionalism, 30, 133
    Ideals, 1, 14, 17, 55-56, 69, 112, 128, 166, 169, 172, 174, 176, 209
    Public trauma, post-9/11, 3-11, 11-14; Implications for education, 14-15
    Tradition, 45, 219, 233
    Voices, 103, 226
Americans for Victory Over Terrorism, 26, 61, 104, 111, 162
Anarchy, 11-14, 79; pluralism and, 91-94; 136; neo-liberalism and 184-186; risk society and, 186-189; 215
Anthrax incidents, 5, 113-114, 119, 142

Aspirations, 17, 33, 65, 88, 106, 135, 160, 176; curriculum and 208-210; 217; currere and, 223-224
    Remembered and revived, 225
Attacks on the homeland, 3-10, 28, 56
Authoritarian, 229-233
    Government, 26, 229-233
    Government, theory of, 21
    Nationalism, 161
    Regime(s), 7, 159, 185
Authority, 30, 88, 92, 106, 131, 165-166, 171, 172, 173
    Cultural, 198
    Faith in, 30
    Governmental, 12
    Public, 192
    Pedagogic/ Representational/ Research, 19
    Pressure from, 27
    Responses to, 165-166
    Science's aura of, 52
    Voice of, 168
Autobiographic terrain, mapping, 151-177
Autobiographical process, 3, 28, 29, 36-37, 99, 167
    Analytical moment, 29
    Progressive moment, 28
    Regressive moment, 28
    Synthetical moment, 32, 36-37
Autobiographical, 71, 108, 157-159, 161, 163-164, 167-168, 169, 170-171, 174, 177, 208-209, 211, 215, 219, 221, 223, 226, 229, 231, 233, 234
    Claims, 163-164
    Disputes, 40
    Narratives, 43; contributions of, 35
    Possibilities, 25-26, 42
    Visions of the nation, 56

Work, 20, 38-40
Autobiographical project, 3, 33, 36, 39-40, 69, 161, 171, 208, 219, 221, 223-224
Autobiography, 1, 3, 6, 15, 16, 17, 18, 20, 21, 27, 29, 32, 33, 34, 35, 36, 37, 38, 40, 41, 42, 52, 96, 103-107
    As 'revolutionary act,' 21, 57, 154, 215, 221, 223
    Political-philosophical, 33
    Of a nation, 3, 78, 79
Bin Laden, Osama, 5, 97
Branded nation, 232
Brand USA, 96
Bush, George W. (see President Bush)
Bush-Cheney administration, 6, 7, 9, 10, 57, 97, 110
    Agendas, 5, 6, 9
    And public opinion, 6
    Competence-in-crisis, 9
    Contra-democratic measures, 11
    Deception(s), 9, 10, 97
    Inaction in face of disaster, 9
    Neo-conservative imperialism of, 7
    Partisan retribution, 9
    Recklessness; ruthlessness, 10
    Scandal(s), 10
    Secrecy of, 6-7
Chaos, 13-14, 78, 106, 117
Censorship, 35, 45, 131
Cheney, Lynne, 4, 48
Citizen(s), 58, 61, 90, 135, 136, 145, 146, 147, 159, 160, 161, 163, 165, 166, 167, 168, 169, 170
    Diligent and concerned, 4
    Engaged, 21
    Naïve, 5
    Without frontiers, 90
Citizenship, 17, 95-96, 170, 171
    Efficacy of, 96
    Foundations of, 17, 34, 105, 106, 165, 170
    Meanings of, disputed 18, 36
Civic,
    Debate, 5, 14, 68, 106, 166, 169, 175

Development, 31
Dialogue, 14, 32
Discord, 25
Engagement, 14, 34, 105, 106, 160, 165, 166, 170, 171
Disengagement, 27
Civic courage, 3, 25, 27, 32, 34, 35, 36, 37, 38, 58, 61, 63-64, 68, 69, 72
    Needed to stand up to triumphal mood of nation, 175
    Needed for civic-cultural dialogue, alternative imaginings, 210
Civic-cultural,
    Climate, 57
    Community, 82
    Construct(s), 78
    Context, 27
    Development, 31
    Identity, 89
    Perspective, 91
    Portrait, 18
    Sense-making, 65
    Skirmishes, 56
    Terrain, 78
    Upheaval, 36, 40, 44
Civic-cultural struggle(s), 2, 4, 32, 33, 34, 57-63, 73, 78, 87, 96
    future shape of, 69
Civic-cultural surround, 12, 26, 37, 38, 40, 42, 59
Civil,
    Liberties, 29
    Society, democratized, 14
    Polity, 31
Collective good, 14, 135, 202
Community, 16, 33, 38, 51, 53, 61, 69, 82, 83, 84, 87, 91, 92, 93, 94, 99, 104, 106, 132, 135, 159, 169, 172, 173, 174, 195, 196, 201, 219, 226, 233, 234
    And school, 213
    Envisaged as project, 92
    Gestalts of, 98, 178
    Interpretive, 33

Subject Index

Of scholarship, 107, 115, 116
Thick, 201
Thin, 201, 202
Virtual, 199
Comparative cartography (see Social cartography)
Comparative education, 18, 70, 152, 153, 154
Congress, 6, 9, 10, 26, 111, 118, 121, 175
    Black Radical, 131
    Hearings, 9
Consensus, 17, 50, 132, 168, 170, 172, 184, 207, 215
    Lack of, 226
    Suffocating, 132
Control, 2, 7, 9, 12, 17, 26, 30, 34, 36, 39, 44, 62, 64, 103, 105, 106, 110, 111, 113, 116, 117, 118, 119, 125, 127, 131, 142, 159, 165, 166, 167, 171, 172, 174, 175, 185, 203, 208, 211, 213, 214, 215, 220, 221, 229
    By media, 171
    Of citizenship, 226
    Of education, 210
    Of knowledge, 198
    Of social action, 212
    Over schools, 184
    Over teachers' work, 184
    Societies, 19
    Techno-economic, 14
    World spinning out of, 79, 91
Conventional wisdom, 16, 68, 129, 130
Corporate, 49, 87, 121, 134, 135
    Elites, 8
    Welfare, 8
Coulter, Ann, 13
Critical moral judgment, 14, 206
Cultural,
    Absorption, 91
    Artifacts, 26
    Codes, 72
    Collisions, 74
    Identification, 78, 94
    Practices, oppressive, 88
    Surround, 47, 79
Cultural division, 4, 14, 94, 109, 110, 120, 169, 212
    Internal division, 60
Culturalism, 88, 98
Culture, 7, 13, 77-99
    Corporatist, 38, 136
    Locality of, 77, 94
    War(s), 11, 16, 31, 40, 60, 118, 161
Cultures of citizenship, 18, 20, 107, 108, 151, 159, 167, 170-174, 221
    And civic-cultural struggle(s), 159
Currere,
    16, 32, 33, 41, 58, 63, 103-104, 165, 223, 224, 225
    Autobiography and currere, 233
Curriculum, 3, 12, 13, 16, 18, 19, 20, 25, 26, 27, 29, 30, 31, 32, 33, 34, 35, 37, 42, 58, 60, 69, 72, 97, 104, 105, 127, 154, 157, 165, 204
    As political text, 34
    As poststructuralist/deconstructed/ postmodern text, 34
    Contours of, 12, 18, 19
    Enunciated, 42
    Metaphorical, 27
    Of our times, 3
    of possibility, 13, 20, 32, 68, 157, 189
    Of schooling, 184
    Of silence, 25, 27, 37
    Of voice, 31, 37, 58
    Theorizing, 60, 71, 159, 165
    Workers, 151
Curriculum
    Code(s), 30, 209-210
    Inquiry, 40, 58, 60, 62, 63, 69, 73, 154, 155, 157, 169
    Autobiography as, 63
    Epistemological, 43
    'Line of flight' for, 18, 20, 40
    Political, 43
    Wisdom, 157
Curriculum Inquiry project, 18, 26, 35, 58-59, 69, 163

And hermeneutic of imagination, 222
Democracy, 2, 3, 4, 7, 11, 12, 13, 14, 17, 18, 84, 88, 91, 95, 97, 98, 106, 107, 108, 109, 116, 128, 132, 139, 144, 147, 157, 164, 171, 181, 182, 187, 188, 189, 191, 193, 195, 197, 198, 199, 200, 202, 205, 207, 214, 225, 226, 229, 232, 233, 234
  Achieved, 30
  Deliberative, 2, 37, 59
  Dependent on culture, 7
  Future of/for, 13, 16, 17, 18, 36, 59
  More, stronger, 12
  Portal for, 20, 223
  Re-envisioning and re-enacting, 12
  Under threat, 94
Democratic
  Aspirations, 3, 20, 26
  Society, 25, 69
  Structures, disintegration of, 26
  Trajectories, anti-democratic, 79
  Vision and imagination, 17, 37
Dialogue, 2, 14, 37, 39, 58, 68,
  Authentic, 97
Diasporic escalation, 89
Difference, 14, 15, 19, 21, 26, 27, 39, 50, 56, 88, 92
  Collapse of support for, 64
  Domains of, 78
  In civic matters, 63
  In struggle for autobiography, 59
Disagreement, moral, 2, 17
Disaster(s), 10, 11
  'Disaster capitalists,' 8
Disciplinarities, terrorizing, 19
Discourse(s), 42
  Critical, imaginative, interpretive, 42
  Of possibility, 61
  Public, political, and academic, 16, 33, 34
  Triumphal/ist/ ism, 3, 5, 28, 29, 30, 32, 36, 38, 52, 64, 72, 78, 96, 107, 109, 133, 160, 162, 167, 171, 172, 173, 174, 176, 210, 220, 230
Disinformation, 5, 10, 11
  Logic of, 18
Disorientation, 2
Displacement, 8, 88, 94
  Of the nation, 88
Dissent, dissenters, 5, 25, 26, 56-58, 64
  Right to, stifled, 77
Diversionary strategies, White House, 7
Diversity, 17, 74
Domestic,
  Re-ordering, 3
  Turmoil, 12
Education, 39
  As moral-political activity, 51-53
  As source of hope, 2
  Era of uncertainty, 12, 20, 40-41
  For democracy, 12, 18, 33
  For future citizens, 11
  'Impoverished landscape' of, 3
  Role of, in society, 39
  Hope for, 1
  Socio-political, 14
  Space of, 2, 6
  'The nightmare that is the present,' 3
Educational experience, 18,
  Public educative experience(s), 55, 57, 69
Emancipatory/emancipation, 16, 62
Epistemological,
  Choices, 30
  Foundations for citizenship, 34
  Limits, 92
  Narrative, 30
  Positions, 30
  Unconscious, 30, 35
Epistemology,
  Of resentment, 30-32, 38, 40
  Positivist, 30
Excavating/excavation, of knowledge, 17, 37, 40, 70-71
Failure,
  Of democracy, 57

Subject Index

Of imagination, 43
Of leadership, 8
Of public itself, 38, 56, 68
Of public sphere, 7, 38, 56
Fascism, 38
    Proto-fascism, 38
Fear, 1, 2, 11, 14, 25, 27, 28, 32, 40, 58, 68, 69
    Crisis of, 60
'Fifty-fifty nation,' 4, 17
Flight 93, 4, 28
Freedom and Culture, 7
"Get Right or Get Left Behind," 4
Global,
    Consciousness, 39, 40
    Context, 12, 39
    Elites, 8
    Environment as 'totalizing,' 12
    Exchange, 41
    Media, 20, 87-94
    Migration, 20, 87-99
    Security forces, privatized, 8
    Village, as mediated construct, 90
Globalization, 12, 74, 79, 86
Government, American
    Corporatist, 28
    Executive branch of, 6, 26
    Fraud and failure, 6, 9, 11, 56
    Legitimate function of, 8
    Indifference, 9
    Ineptitude, 9
    Secrecy, 56
Grumet's sense of currere, 33
Hardball, MSNBC's, 6
Hegemonic unilateralism, 7
Hegemony/hegemonic, 2, 45, 53
Hermeneutic circle, 73
Hermeneutic of imagination, 72
Higher education and corporate power, 49-50
    Utilitarianism, 50
Hope, 1, 2, 3, 4, 19, 20, 29
Hopefulness, 1, 29
Hostility/hostilities, 17, 25

Human,
    Community, 93
    Interaction, certainty in, 50
    Psyche, 45
    And communal responsibility, 3
    Rights, 11
    Suffering, 10-11, 91
    Understanding, limits of, 35, 36
Hurricane Katrina, 8
Hussein, Saddam, 10
Ideology, political, 9
Ideological, 1, 3, 5, 38, 48, 65-66, 80
    Discrimination, 9
    Power, 3
    View, 32
Illumination, 35, 53, 62
Illustration, 35, 53
Image(s), 74, 86, 90, 98-99
    As curriculum, 29
    Power of, 12
    Reshaping schooling, 12
Imagination/imaginative, 2, 3, 46, 68, 77-99
    As global cultural practice, 62, 78
    Momentary demise of, in America, 2
    Moral, 79
    Praxis, 19, 40, 63, 87, 97
    Sympathetic, 46
    Terrorizing practice of, 19
    Unleashing of, globally, 78
Imagining(s), 6, 30, 96, 97
'In-between,' the, 2, 93
Information Age, 14, 122, 181
Iraq, invasion of, 26
    Iraqis, plight of, 10-11
Knowledge,
    Act of producing, 26
    And learning undermined, 14
    Archaeology of, 70
    As social practice, 42
    Contested terrain of, as dispersion, 70
    Creation, 17
    Discursive domain, 70

Educational change, 72
  Limitations of, 44
  Of world, 2
  Nodes, 25, 26, 36, 39, 40, 41, 42, 43
  Past and present, 2
  Privileging certain kinds of, 30
  Self-, 2, 17
  Study of, 43
  Venues, 26
Knowledge production, 36, 43, 44-50,
  Complexities of, 26, 27
  Limitations of, 29-32, 48-53
Knowledge work, 25, 27, 28, 36, 38, 39,
    43, 44-50, 74
  As non-innocent practice, 51-53
  Crises in, 50
  In 'age of extremes,' 50
  Long-standing traditions, 50
Knowledge/power nexus, relations, 31, 44,
    48-53, 71
  Language(s), changed, 30, 56, 64
Leadership, 5, 30, 37, 64
Legitimacy, 17, 44, 81-82
Libby, 'Scooter,' 10
Loss, 2, 28
Mapping (see Social Cartography)
Master code(s), 55-56, 64, 68
Meaninglessness, 28, 55, 64
Media, 5, 9, 13, 60, 64, 82-86, 90
  And other contextual literacies, 86
  As cultural products, 82
  As knowledge nodes, 80
  Global electronic, 36, 61, 86
  Juxtaposition of stories, 13
  Legitimizing role, 9
  Mainstream, 25, 26, 28, 62
  News-talk shows, 13
  Offensives, 9
  Print-capitalism, 80
  Radio talk-show hosts, 25
  Representations, 56, 79
  'Right-wing,' 25, 62
  State-centric, 5, 25
  'Talking heads,' 5

Moral disagreement, 2, 3
Moral fabric, 2, 87, 233
Multiculturalist cause, 92-94
'Mushroom cloud' threat, 10
Narrative(s), 1, 2, 16, 20, 58, 88, 91
  And print culture, 84
  Autobiographical, 43
  Hegemonic, 60
  Normalized, 3
  Of fear, 2
  Of hope, 2
  Of identity, 85
  Of loss, 2
  Of possibility, 2
  Of progress and reconciliation, 43
  Post-9/11 American, 20
  Psycho-social, 61
  Triumphal-nationalistic, 3
Nation, 3, 7, 9, 15, 17, 58, 61, 73,
  And print culture, 77-86
  And global electronic media, 77
  And global migration, 77
  As metaphor, 93-94
  Anthropological framing of, 77-99
  Attacks on, 27
  Autobiography of, 18
  Awakening of, 27
  'Branded,' 21
  Divided, 14
  Epistemological views of, 26
  Imagined community, 16, 36, 61, 67,
    77-99
  Limits of, 62, 86, 91, 99
  Place in the world, 12, 17, 96
  Sense of ourselves as, 37
  Terroristic threats against, 40
  Toll of the war on, 11
Nation-state(s), 12, 77-99
  Altered place of, 78
  Failure to accommodate difference,
    88
  Pushed toward irrelevancy, 79
  Symbol-ordering boundaries of, 12,
    36, 77-99

Subject Index

National
    Autobiographical propensities, 38
    Consciousness, 84-85
    Identity, 5, 11, 15, 16, 20, 21, 58, 87, 96
    Identity crisis, 15, 16, 25, 29, 32
    Literature, 82-86
    Psyche, 15, 32, 80
National identity, 5, 11, 15, 16, 20, 21, 58, 87
    Identity branding, 28
Nationalism, 5, 20, 32, 77-99
    As new form of consciousness, 86
    Coercive, 32, 64, 72, 87
    Hyper-, 32, 72
    Limits of, 78
'Nation-ness,' 16, 77-99
Neo-conservative
    Agenda, 5, 41
    Worldview, 7
    Foreign policy, 7
    Posture, 56
Neo-liberal
    Agenda, 5, 41
    Domestic restructuring, 7
    Imperialism, 7
    Posture, 56
New American wilderness, 1, 2, 4, 6, 8, 11, 18, 20, 26, 27, 42, 56
    Space of disorientation, 1
New Orleans, devastation of, 8
New Right, 4, 56-57
    As movement, 67
    As new brand for nation, 5
    Use of the term, 67-68
New world (dis-) order, 5
New York City, 28
Nomad/nomadic
    Positioning, 19
Normalcy, return to, 11, 13
Normalization, 13
Oneness, 5, 27
Ontological choices, 39
Orthodoxy, 36, 50, 57, 72, 96

New patriotisms, 88
Pentagon, 4, 5
Perspective(s), 50
    Alternative, 19
    Nascent, 18
    Of choice, 13
President G. W. Bush, 10, 109, 110, 111, 113, 120, 122, 129, 134, 142, 146, 236
    Dividing world into friend and foe, 113
Police state, de facto, 9
Political-cultural-economic *coup*, 6, 11
Political, 3-9, 11-14, 16, 19, 26-27, 31-34, 36, 38, 40, 43, 45-46, 50-51, 53, 57-58, 61, 65, 66-67, 71, 80-81, 87-89, 91-93, 98, 104, 111, 114, 117, 119, 121, 124, 131, 132, 136, 143-144, 145, 155, 157, 159, 161, 170, 181-204
    Change, 12, 40, 181, 186
    Ideology, 9, 185
    Power, 58, 71, 80, 187
    -Philosophical approach, 33
    Struggle, 4, 33, 65-66, 71, 212
    System, 88, 189
Politics, 13, 30, 38, 40, 47, 48, 50, 60, 65, 88, 90-91, 133, 136, 161, 183, 187-188, 191-193, 200-201, 215, 223, 226, 229, 232-233
    Identity, 60, 88, 99, 161
    Of memory, 90-91
    Of science, 30
    *Non-*politics, *sub-*politics in risk society, 187-189
Possibility, possibilities, 1, 2, 12, 18, 37, 40, 87, 90
    Alternative, 17, 32, 88
    Autobiographical, 25, 26, 37
    Of pluralist democracy, 31
    Range of, 30, 43
Post-9/11,
    America, 6, 8, 14, 17, 18, 20, 96
    American identity, 28, 59, 64

Post-colonial/post-colonialism, 40, 41, 60, 93, 153
Post-democracy/post-democratic, 14, 38, 58, 98
Postmodern, 67, 72, 92, 151-157
    Sensibilities, 34, 74
Post-national/post-nationalism, 12, 16, 20, 36, 40, 41, 67, 77-99
    'Communities of sentiment,' 36, 170, 201
    Space, post-national 12, 20
Power, 182-183, 187-188, 192, 194-195, 198-199, 200, 202, 203, 205, 208, 212, 214, 216, 220
    Abuse(s) of power, 5, 9, 64
    Enunciations of, 29, 4
    -Knowledge-change relations, 42
    Ideological, 3
    Of cognitive structures, 66
    Rhetorical, 30
    Study of, 52
    Techno-economic, 5
Power's microphysics, 52
Privatization/privatized, 8, 133, 186
Project for the New American Century (PNAC), 6
Propaganda, 10, 17
Psycho-analytic framework, 15, 16
Psycho-social,
    Disintegration, 15
    Shock, 11
    Slippage/slide, 3, 205
Public,
    Anxiety, 6, 11, 12, 32
    Consciousness, 7, 62
    Desire for belief, certainty, order, 30, 36, 60
    Dialogue, 25, 68, 139, 205
    Distrust, 4, 10, 14, 125, 130,
    Indifference, 9, 12, 91, 171, 186, 221
    Intellectuals, 14, 25, 51
    Mind, 14, 18, 43
    'Mis-educated,' 14, 39
    Opinion, 6, 8
    Will, 20, 39
Public sanction, 26, 116, 124, 159, 166, 171-172, 175, 220, 234
    Of orthodoxy, 171
Public sphere(s), 7, 9, 13, 14, 20, 25, 27, 33, 38, 39, 60-61, 62, 87, 89, 92, 97-98, 106-107, 119, 129, 145, 156, 162-163, 164, 166, 167, 174, 181-204
    Commodification of, 60
    Diasporic, 77-99
    Electronic, 61, 189-190,194, 197, 199-202, 203-204
    Erosion of, 13, 36, 60, 201, 219
    Manipulation of, 13, 60-61, 124
Public trust/distrust, 4, 5, 10, 12, 14, 110, 125, 130, 166-167, 234
Qualitative-interpretive inquiry, 62, 73-74
Radical
    Agendas, 3-10
    Revolution, 3-10, 57
Reason, 17, 34, 45, 50, 105, 106, 107, 126-127, 130, 147, 159, 165-166, 169, 172, 173, 175-176, 196, 215, 220
    As framework for citizenship, 169
'Release from arrest,' 17, 165, 204
Remembering/forgetting, 16, 84-86
Representation, 4, 17, 60, 64
Research,
    And theoretical modesty, 52-53
Resentment, epistemology of, 30-32
Resistance, 2, 5, 28, 39, 72
Responses to governance, 17, 151-177
Rhetoric, 25-30, 55-57, 61, 63, 64-65, 67, 68, 114, 119, 160-161, 182, 192, 220, 231
    As mediator of 'Truth,' 5
    Manipulative, 3, 56
    Prevailing public, 57, 63-64
'Right,' 4, 5, 13, 15, 25, 56-57, 61-62, 63, 67-68, 88, 109-112, 118, 161-162, 169, 171, 182-183, 220, 233
    As new brand for nation, 5
    'Christian Right,' 88, 109

Subject Index

Risk, 11, 12-13, 18, 20, 40, 41, 181, 186-189, 197, 229
    Anxiety in, 13
    As catastrophic society, 12, 186
    Disempowerment , 13
    And drastic change, 12
    'Exceptional condition' in, 12
    Loss of social thinking, 12
    Paradigm, state-mediated, 18, 20, 40?
    Politics in, 13
    Production and distribution of, 12
    Systemic transformation, 13
    Techno-economic powers, 12
Schooling, 33, 39, 41-42, 61-62, 97-98, 181-186
    As public project, 12, 14
    Diminished role for, 12, 41, 97
    For social change, 12
Security, 11, 68, 97
    Forces, privatized and global, 8
    Measures, 14, 28
    State, 40
September 11,
    Events of, 3, 4, 9, 15, 16, 17, 27, 29, 32, 33, 44, 55
    Clarification of meaning, 63
Shock, 4, 8, 10, 28
    Wave(s), 4, 6, 11, 15, 16
Silence, 25, 27-29, 30, 38, 39, 58-60, 68
Silencing, 21, 27-29, 38, 43, 50
Social action, 36, 39, 44
    And educational change, 70
Social cartography, 18, 20, 37, 53, 55-63, 69-73
    Aesthetic sensibilities, and, 62
    And autobiography, 59-63, 151-177
    And discursive knowledge production, 69-75
    As cognitive art, 58, 72, 74
    As curriculum inquiry, 55-59
    As qualitative, interpretive inquiry, 62, 73
    Mapping as metaphorical device, 56
    The imaginary of spatiality, 72

Social epistemology, 42-43
Social imaginaries, 29, 31, 42-43, 61, 63, 64-65, 67, 79, 87, 129, 163-164, 213, 221-222
    As fuel for action, 87
    'Communities of sentiment, 67, 87
    Plurality of imagined worlds, 87
    Use of the term, 64-65
Social imagination, 20, 29, 36, 39-40, 43-44, 57, 67, 68, 78, 80, 87, 97
    As spur to alternative visions, 57
    Autobiography and, 39-40
Spatial/spatiality
    Concern for public space, 199
    Imaginary of, 71-72
    Impact of electronic public sphere on democracy, 199
    Perspectives, 151
    Relations in knowledge work, 203
    Sensibility, 154
    Surround, socio-cultural, 40; geopolitical, 40
    Worlds, possible, 71
Spectacle, 4, 10, 27, 171, 182, 192-193, 201-204
    2000 election as, 4
    As stolen, 4
    Machiavellian maneuvering, 4, 38
    Outing of CIA operative, 10
    Supreme Court *pronuncio*, 4, 26
    -Surveillance paradigm, 61
State, one-party system, 9, 64, 160, 175
State of the Union Address, 17, 26
Techno-culture thesis, 20, 181-204
Television, as delivery system, 27, 28
Terrain, disputatious, 18, 74
Terror/terrorism, 98
    Of other imaginings, 78
    Threats of, manufactured, 11
    Acts of, real 11
    Effects of, 26
Third Reich, 21
Totalitarian/totalitarianism, 7, 38, 210, 225, 230-234

Transformation of public sphere, 20, 90-91, 181-204
Transformation of subjectivities, 87-99
Triumphal narrative, 30, 72, 78, 96
    Bravado, 38
Truth, 45
    For all the people, 17
    Mediator of, 5
Tyranny, inadvertent, 95
Uncertainty, 11, 14, 18, 48
Unity, 5, 25, 30, 56, 109-110, 117, 124, 127, 144, 159-163, 234
    Unified stance, 28, 37
    Unity-as-defense, 5, 25
University, 41, 98
    Administrators, 25
    As global communicator, 41
    As knowledge node, 27
    As mediator of knowledge, 41
    As social space, 44-53, 60
    Ethics of, 51
    In collision with public, 50
Utopia(s)/utopic space, 1-2, 65-66, 21
Value(s) deconstructed, 13, 56
Vice-President Cheney, 8
Vice-President Gore, 25, 64, 175
Virtual democracy, 36, 181-204
'What-can-be,' a sense of, 19, 20
'Wide awakeness,' 17, 216, 218
'Wild capitalism,' 8, 79, 91
'Wild terrorism,' 79, 91
Within, within-beyond, 1, 11, 27, 40, 42, 78
World Trade Center, 4, 5
World war, 1, 7, 65
Writing, 4, 7, 29, 38, 53

Complicated Conversation

A BOOK SERIES OF CURRICULUM STUDIES

This series employs research completed in various disciplines to construct textbooks that will enable public school teachers to reoccupy a vacated public domain—not simply as "consumers" of knowledge, but as active participants in a "complicated conversation" that they themselves will lead. In drawing promiscuously but critically from various academic disciplines and from popular culture, this series will attempt to create a conceptual montage for the teacher who understands that positionality as aspiring to reconstruct a "public" space. *Complicated Conversation* works to resuscitate the progressive project—an educational project in which self-realization and democratization are inevitably intertwined; its task as the new century begins is nothing less than the intellectual formation of a public sphere in education.

The series editor is:

>Dr. William F. Pinar
>Department of Curriculum Studies
>2125 Main Mall
>Faculty of Education
>University of British Columbia
>Vancouver, British Columbia V6T 1Z4
>CANADA

To order other books in this series, please contact our Customer Service Department:

>(800) 770-LANG (within the U.S.)
>(212) 647-7706 (outside the U.S.)
>(212) 647-7707 FAX

Or browse online by series:

>www.peterlang.com